60 Shades of Green

Musings on Sustainability

Dr Prasad Modak

Copyright © Dr Prasad Modak

301/302, Third Floor, Godrej La Vista,
MB Raut Road, Shivaji Park, Dadar,
Mumbai 400028 Maharashtra, India
+91-9820126074
prasad.modak@emcentre.com

Copyedited by Divya Narain
Copyediting assistance by Sonal Alvares
Book and Jacket Design by Kedar Prabhavalkar, Studio Inspira
Illustrations by Manish Rangnekar
Author's photo by Harshad Parashare

First published in India in 2016
Typeset in Palatino Linotype and Amatic SC by Shrutee Arts, Mumbai, India
Printed at Sundaram Art Printing Press, Mumbai, India

ISBN : 9781539379430

About The Author

Dr Prasad Modak holds BTech (Civil Eng) & MTech (Environmental Science and Engg) from the Indian Institute of Technology (IIT) Bombay, and Doctorate in Environmental Engg from Asian Institute of Technology, Bangkok, Thailand. He joined the Centre for Environmental Science and Engineering at IIT Bombay as a faculty member in 1984. He left IIT Bombay in 1995 to set up Environmental Management Centre. In 2012, he established Ekonnect Knowledge Foundation – a Section-8 not-for-profit company. He also serves as Dean, IL&FS Academy for Applied Development (IAAD) and functions as Chief Sustainability Officer at IL&FS Ltd. He is currently, Adjunct Professor at the Centre for Technology Alternatives in Rural Areas at IIT, Bombay.

Dr Modak has worked with almost all key UN, multi-lateral and bi-lateral developmental institutions in the world. Prominent amongst these are UNEP Geneva, Paris and Osaka offices; UNDP and UNDESA, New York, UNIDO, Vienna; DFID, London; GIZ and CDG, Germany; Asian Productivity Organization (APO), Tokyo; SIDA; Embassy of the Netherlands, New Delhi; FAO; the World Bank; IFC; Asian Development Bank and the New Development Bank, China.

Apart from the Government of India and various State Governments, Dr Modak has advised the Governments of Bangladesh, Egypt, Indonesia, Mauritius, Thailand and Vietnam. Recently he was invited to join the India Resources Panel (for secondary material flows) by the Ministry of Environment & Forests and Climate Change, Government of India.

Dr Modak has published books with the UN University on EIA (translations in Chinese, Japanese), Tokyo; Oxford University Press; UNEP, Paris on Textile Industry and Environment and Centre for Environmental Education in India on Waste Minimization. He served as Hon. Editor of the Journal of Indian Water Works from 1998 to 2004. He coordinated the chapter on Waste Management and Recycling in UNEP's Green Economy Report; contributed a chapter on Waste and Resource Management in UNEP/ISWA's Global Waste Management Outlook and assisted UNCRD to establish IPLA - International Partnership for Expanding Waste Management Services of Local Authorities.

Dr Modak has received the Distinguished Alumni Award of AITAA in 2010 for Significant Contribution to International Affairs. He was elected to the Board Certified Member at the American Association of Environmental Engineers in recognition of his work in research & practice.

Music, Education, Travel and Environmental Movements are some of his passions in life.

TABLE OF CONTENTS

Foreword

This collection of thoughts or *60 Shades of Green,* is my attempt to raise important environmental concerns specific to India.

I started penning down these thoughts in the form of a blog since July 2014. Over the last 24 months I have posted more than 120 mostly, every Sunday morning. This book has a select set of 60 articles in celebration of my completing 60 years.

The articles on the blog have been well received. Today there are more than a 1300 followers. Several of these followers and friends suggested that I publish a compilation of these articles. This positive feedback encouraged me to publish this book.

In my life, I have been fortunate enough to become a Professor, practice as a Consultant and establish an organization as an Entrepreneur. Furthermore, my proximity to the Government, International Development Financing Institutions and Corporates, has given me unique exposure and experience. Indeed, these multiple roles have helped me acquire a holistic perspective on environmental management and put sustainability into practice. My extensive travel across continents has added yet another dimension of professional and personal experience that I really cherish.

In all the articles, I use humor and satire to discuss various issues on environment through stories. 'My Professor Friend' is a character I have created, essentially to provide another point of view. I simply adore this character and often wish that he was real!

Most of the 'stories' I tell are not real ... but created from my experiences and suitably crafted for the purpose of sharing. It greatly amuses me however, to receive emails asking "is this story really true?" or "is this really my point of view?"

Sometimes I cite names of people, only to weave in a feel of 'authenticity'. No offence is intended to anyone. And I do hope that the readers understand this perspective. The messages of the stories are the key takeaways. But these messages are often hidden.

One of the characteristics of the articles is that while narrating these stories, knowledge is embedded in an implicit manner. Sometimes references are cited for further reading. Many of the articles in this book could therefore be of educational value to students as well as to teachers. The book could potentially be used as a supplement to a course on Environmental Management & Sustainability. Some of the articles could be used to open up group discussions or formulate assignments.

The second collection titled "Blue, Green and Everything in Between" of 50 articles will soon be released as a companian.

Visit https://prasadmodakblog.wordpress.com/ and stay tuned.

THE GREY
POLLUTION

01
Upstream vs. Downstream

Resource extraction across the world is getting more and more intensive. Material flows (both of virgin and used materials) are getting skewed.

Some of the important factors responsible for the shift are market globalization, presence of perverse subsidies (i.e. unrealistic resource pricing) and unevenness in environmental governance.

These changes have a major significance for the economy and more so for the very resource security of this planet. There is no doubt that we need to think of waste and resources at the same time as it is followed in a circular economy.

One of the most effective UPSTREAM strategies to address this increasing threat to resources is to REDUCE consumption and redesign the products we make and the services we offer.

The first strategy requires change in the behavioural patterns or the way we live. Given the rising rate of urbanization, the increasingly prosperous middle class (especially in Asia) and the promotion of consumerism through media, it is extremely difficult to expect this change will ever happen! If you say no to a product because you feel there is no need, someone will simply dump the product on you (as a free trial or as a friendly gift) to trap you or enslave you!!

The second UPSTREAM strategy of REDESIGN requires innovation, risk appetite and top management commitment - and this cannot be achieved overnight.

Here, companies need to exhibit *out-of-the-box thinking* to find ways to reduce material and energy intensity and increase recycled content in their products. Products need to be redesigned to reduce/eliminate hazardous substances, increase recyclability (and improve safety during recycling) and make remanufacturing possible with most of the components getting reused.

Here, we are essentially talking about smart manufacturing in the true sense. All this should lead to reduction in the wastes we produce and reduce consumption of our limited resources.

Due to increasing consumption and years of inefficiencies in manufacturing practices, however, waste volumes across the world have been on a steep rise. This has led to a sunrise in the global waste management industry. This industry is thriving on the DOWNSTREAM strategies of waste RECYCLING & REUSE – extracting metals, bio-solids, Refuse or Solid Derived Fuels, bio-gas, syngas, heat, electricity, engineered materials etc. from and reversing material flows and thereby reducing the consumption of virgin resources. The waste industry today supports significant employment – both in formal and informal sectors. Millions of poor people in the world's largest cities earn their livelihood because waste is around.

Therefore the waste industry wants more waste to be produced– so that it can grow and survive. REDUCE at UPSTREAM can affect the DOWNSTREAM opportunities of REUSE and RECYCING.

I remember the CEO of a waste-to-energy plant who used to hate bans on plastics as they would reduce the calorific value of waste. A Common Effluent Treatment Plant (CETP) company I know, discouraged members of the CETP to reduce the effluent volumes by specifying in the contract a guarantee for effluent supply. So has been the case in many Public Private Partnership contracts (PPP) for managing Municipal Solid Waste wherein waste supply guarantee is an essential precondition. 'Don't you ever REDUCE waste', the PPP partner warns.

There are many such examples of conflicting interests between UPSTREAM and DOWNSTREAM resource and waste management. There is no doubt, it defeats sustainability.

I like the picture below that shows priority among REDUCE, REUSE and RECYCLE.

So REDUCE should always be the first priority, followed by REUSE and RECYCLING.

Note that the players in the REDUCE and REUSE & RECYCLE space are generally different. In REDUCE, top management, product designers and consumers play a dominant role whereas in REUSE & RECYCLE, waste pickers, community and waste processing specialists have a greater interest.

What we need is an integrated approach. Bringing these stakeholders together to ensure an integrated waste & resource thinking is very

important. We don't see that happening. Very rarely do product designers and waste processors talk. Products when redesigned cleverly can not only REDUCE material and energy intensity or eliminate hazardous substances but also increase potential REUSE and provide more opportunities for RECYCLING. A systems thinking is necessary. And we need examples that show possibilities and benefits of such integration.

I would love to conduct workshops to bring these stakeholders together and explore how to resolve the apparent conflicts between UPSTREAM and DOWNSTREAM. These workshops will perhaps help in better communication between the stakeholders and lead to more partnerships and motivational examples to share. Let UPSTREAM meet DOWNSTREAM.

02

Indoor air is considered safe by many. When outdoors, we encounter pollution from vehicles and industries and these emissions worry us. No wonder, the statistics reported on air quality are generally on outdoor air or ambient air. Standards for ambient air quality have been set in countries around the world and so also in India.

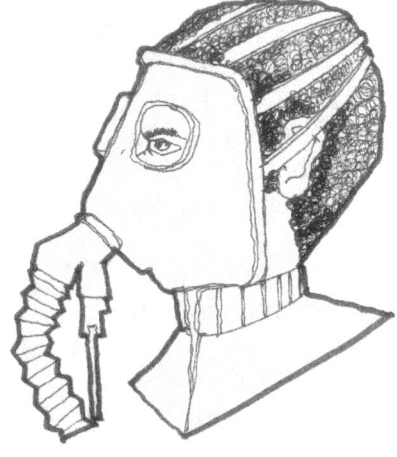

In some cities in India, ambient air quality is displayed on panels that are connected to real time automatic air quality monitoring stations. These displays provide us information on the air we breathe when outside – albeit in approximation. I say 'approximation' because ambient air quality is monitored only at a monitoring station and one station does not represent the area-wide ambient air quality. Further, we are subjected to pedestrian exposure when we walk on the streets - and that's different from the ambient air quality.

Talking about exposure, we tend to believe that staying indoors shields us from outdoor air pollution. We feel safe in enclosed spaces like offices, homes, malls and theatres, air conditioned cars, buses and railway coaches. Unfortunately, the situation is to the contrary. Indoor Air Quality (IAQ) can be just as bad as or even worse than ambient or outdoor air quality.

There are a number of reasons why IAQ can be of concern. Emissions emanate from cooking, cigarette smoking, burning of scented sticks (agarbattis) and mosquito repellent coils, paint on the wall, seals from furniture, coatings from fabrics and carpets – releasing complex pollutants. The pollutants released include Particulates, Formaldehyde (HCHO), Radon, Tolune, Ammonia, Benzene, 2-furaldehyde, Benzyl alcohol, Monocyclic monoterpenes, Dichloromethane, Ethylhexyl phthalate, just to name a few. Most of these "micro-pollutants" are carcinogenic and difficult as well as expensive to monitor. Many times, naturally ventilated buildings are designed poorly and buildings with forced ventilation or enclosed with air conditioners, do not maintain adequate ventilation or cycles of air exchange. As a result, the micro-pollutants that are released indoors get accumulated – sometimes overshooting the acceptable values.

Acceptable IAQ is defined by the American Society of Heating, Refrigeration and Air Conditioning Engineers (ASHRAE) in ANSI/ASHRAE standard 62.1 as: "Air in which there are no known contaminants at harmful concentrations and with which a substantial majority (usually 80%) of the people exposed do not express dissatisfaction"

Traditionally, IAQ has been associated with Sick Building Syndrome (SBS). The World Health Organization (WHO) compiled common reported symptoms into what was defined as SBS. These symptoms included: eye, nose, and throat irritation; sensation of dry mucous membranes; dry, itching, and red skin; headaches and mental fatigue; high frequency of airway infections and cough; hoarseness and wheezing; nausea and dizziness; and unspecific hypersensitivity. Most of us are facing these problems today and frequently so. We have to keep visiting doctors and chemists.

India does not have IAQ standards. Research on IAQ in India has also been limited. Spot studies in 2005 showed high values of CO_2 in auditoriums in Vadodara crossing three times the IAQ standard. I shudder to think what air we must be breathing when travelling in overnight AC buses or coaches on the train. Inside slum shanties where ventilation is poor and fuel such as wood and cow dung is used, the pollution levels have been found to be very high, leading to severe respiratory ailments, especially in women and children.

China set standards for IAQ as early as 1976. Korea has

IAQ standards even for metro buses! IAQ standards in Japan and Germany cover most of the micro-pollutants listed above. It is a pity that in India we haven't taken IAQ seriously.

But is just setting of IAQ standards going to be enough. How can we enforce such standards?

The approach will have to be multi-pronged, focusing on prevention and control. We will need to bring key stakeholders such as architects, paint manufacturers, furniture makers, HVAC manufacturers, green building rating agencies, medical professionals etc. together. A combination of control, reduction (modification) with standards/guidelines may work. See Figure on the right.

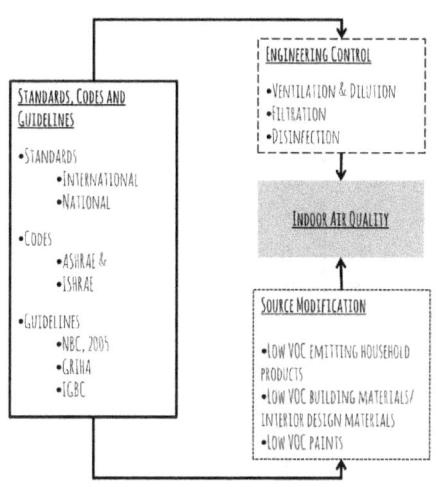

STANDARDS, CODES AND GUIDELINES

- STANDARDS
  - INTERNATIONAL
  - NATIONAL
- CODES
  - ASHRAE &
  - ISHRAE
- GUIDELINES
  - NBC, 2005
  - GRIHA
  - IGBC

ENGINEERING CONTROL
- VENTILATION & DILUTION
- FILTRATION
- DISINFECTION

INDOOR AIR QUALITY

SOURCE MODIFICATION
- LOW VOC EMITTING HOUSEHOLD PRODUCTS
- LOW VOC BUILDING MATERIALS/ INTERIOR DESIGN MATERIALS
- LOW VOC PAINTS

I had organized stakeholder workshops on IAQ in Mumbai and Delhi a few years ago and tried lobbying for IAQ standards and a multi-pronged approach. I, in fact, developed a Roadmap for IAQ in India and presented it in these workshops. There was significant support and interest to follow up but we couldn't succeed much.

There is a need to form a National Association on Indoor Air Quality in India and take on this issue with the Ministry of Environment & Forests on a collective basis. Till then, maybe it's a good idea to wear oxygen masks, whenever indoors! It's our choice to make – oxygen masks or the Sick Building Syndrome.

03

I wanted to refill petrol in my car so I drove to my usual petrol pump located at Turner road in Bandra. The lane to the petrol pump was choked and it was after more than 15 minutes of 'car crawl' that I finally managed to reach the pump. When I asked Abdul, my usual pump mechanic, he pointed me to a billboard that red – **"Buy 40 liters of petrol and get 2 Portable Oxygen Cylinders Free"**. Apparently this "hot deal" was the reason for the rush. "Oxygen cylinders for what?", I asked and the guy ahead of me in the queue said "to save you from air pollution" in a matter-of-fact tone. I didn't quite like the idea of marketing emissions (i.e. petrol) with oxygen!

I was visualizing the city of Mumbai looking like a planet with no atmosphere and people carrying oxygen cylinders like astronauts. I was simply horrified at the thought.

"Are we exaggerating this issue of air pollution in Indian cities?" I called on my Professor friend in anguish. "Given the contaminated food we eat and the polluted water we drink, air pollution that we breathe in should not be a big deal. We know how to survive or otherwise. We better worry about the high incidence of lifestyle disorders like diabetes. We should offer sugar-free candies at the petrol pumps instead of oxygen cylinders. These candies should be sponsored with the CSR budgets of Parley or Cadbury"

My Professor friend was busy taking a close look at one of the N-95 masks that was produced by a Chinese company for marketing in Mumbai. This company was planning to manufacture some 1 million masks a month for Mumbai, to start with. The mask carried a certification "Proven Effective in Beijing". The Professor turned to me and said, "Look at these masks – they filter almost all the $PM_{2.5}$ matter in the air and cost only Rs. 5! Next time you go the shopping mall, you will be asked – do you want to buy a carry bag or a mask?"

"Wearing masks will help in many ways – he said. It will reduce the incidence of H1N1 and the future H2N2 series. And since it will be difficult to know who is behind the mask – masks will reduce the incidents of eve teasing by ogling men at bus stops – That could be an immense social benefit – something not easily understood and appreciated"

"But what about disposal of the 1 million used masks" I ventured to argue with the Professor. We will need to dedicate a special landfill site for getting rid of used masks. Besides the city will look like a place infested by dacoits like in the movie 'Sholay'. The Professor was in no mood to listen.

"We have to think out of the box for reducing air pollution first" he said. The 100 smart cities program of the Prime Minister is hoping to achieve,

for instance, optimization of traffic signals based on real-time measurement of air pollution. When the air quality index at a traffic junction goes high, you will be asked to change your route and will be guided accordingly to reach your destination"

I was wondering how hard it will then be to drive from my office in Nariman point to home on Carter road, if such an intelligent air pollution sensitive system was put in place. I would perhaps be 'circling' the whole town for over two hours to help reduce air pollution at a traffic signal but emitting an extra ton of air pollutants in the process. Not such a smart an idea I thought.

Professor had more ideas to share. "I have recommended to the Secretary, Transport to introduce a rule whereby vehicles ending with odd number plates will be allowed on the road for Mondays, Wednesdays and Fridays and those with even number plates on Tuesdays, Thursdays and Saturdays. Sundays will be for cars with number plates

ending in zero. This will greatly reduce the road traffic and hence the air emissions. Public transport will be encouraged"

"People will use fake number plates, Professor and have duplicate plate numbers" I said with a smirk.

Professor ignored my pessimistic view.

"Display boards will be set up at all major traffic junctions in the city to make people aware of the average air quality they breathe. Mobile apps will be developed so that you can browse the air quality trends and also get some forecasts. If the forecast shows that high levels of air pollution are expected, then the public may decide to stay indoors." I wasn't much in the favor of this option as people would stay home watching TV shows giving an excuse of outdoor air pollution.

The Professor then moved the focus to emission monitoring and control. "Directions will be given to industries to monitor emissions from stack online. The emission data will be pooled through the server of the Pollution Control Board. Initially we will measure the Particulate Matter (PM) and provide a star rating. Industry with PM emissions well below the prescribed standard for

instance will get a 5-star rating"

Impressive Professor – I said.

"Hold on – the big game is much more than just emission monitoring and rating". Professor said this with a mysterious smile.

The star ratings will be displayed real time at the Bombay Stock Exchange (BSE). This will greatly influence the psyche of the stock traders. More stocks will be bought of companies with 5-star ratings and companies with one star rating will simply be dumped – independent of their financial performance.

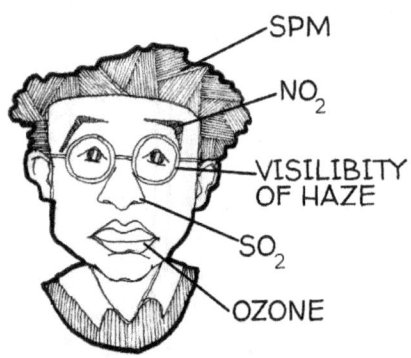

(I started visualizing that air pollution sensitive and committed stock trader of BSE)

"I am conducting a series of training programs for stock traders in Gujarati (PMO likes that) to explain air pollution, its seriousness, stock traders' responsibility and the environmental and economic implications. You should give a couple of lectures in my course, my friend"

I was even more impressed even though my Gujarati was no good …

"The Indian insurance industry has already initiated discussions on refixing premiums based on an Air Quality Index (AQI). Lower is the AQI (implying higher level of air pollution), higher will be the premium," Professor explained. That's another economic implication.

But why don't you think more radically, Professor? All this discussion is happening because we are perhaps monitoring and reporting air quality from wrong locations in the cities. Many of the stations that are operated are next to streets under direct influence of traffic emissions and not reflecting the ambient levels where the prescribed standards are strictly applicable. City of Pune for instance was declared as highly polluted because the reporting was done from a kerbside monitoring station and ambient air quality standards were compared! The air quality levels 'improved', the moment the station was shifted.

"Oh – for a change you are talking sense," The Professor said taking a deep puff from his cigar. He looked outside the window at a grey sky. "Let me come up with a national site audit program right away for resiting of monitoring stations to be done on an immediate basis. Relocating stations at correct and representative places will indeed lead to lower level of air pollution and the problem will be solved bang at the source!!"

I left Professor's office with the N-95 mask that the Chinese company had left behind on his desk.

The Union Minister of Environment & Forests in India announced a national Air Quality Index (AQI). The AQI will reflect eight major pollutants that impact respiratory health. AQI will be reported first in cities with populations exceeding one million and in the next five years it will be gradually mandated for the rest of the country. Details on the proposed AQI can be found at URL below[1]

Do visit www.aqicn.org. This website is supported by a team located in Beijing. Much of the data on this website

---

1   See http://www.indiaenvironmentportal.org.in/files/file/Air%20Quality%20Index.pdf

is driven by the real-time data monitored at the US consulates.

You may like to visit US Embassy's website in New Delhi[2] to see real time AQ reporting in some of the Indian cities. US Embassies report AQI as per US Environmental Protection Agency (EPA). The Indian Meteorological Department (IMD) in Delhi displays AQ using IMD's own AQI that is different from that of the U.S. EPA as well as from the proposed national AQI. The State Pollution Control Boards provide data in raw format (concentrations) and currently do not follow any AQI. I guess over the next six months, the reporting will happen through the proposed national AQI. The US Consulates should then ideally report results in Indian AQI to avoid confusion. The same should be done by the IMD in Delhi.

Speaking about consulates, in India, a number of countries have now issued guidelines for their diplomats on how they can protect themselves from air pollution. Countries like the US, Germany and Japan have reduced the tenure of their diplomats in Delhi from three years to two years. Further, concerned over high pollution levels in the capital, European Union has directed its diplomats here to install air purifiers in their offices and residences soon.

Greenpeace provides very telling infographics on the effects of PM2.5 and how to use N95 masks[3]. A joint study by the universities of Chicago, Yale and Harvard found that half of India's population may be losing up to three years' lifespan because of poor air quality.

Beijing has put in place a time-bound action plan with a health advisory and a four-level alarm system which includes closing of schools, factories and cutting down the number of cars on the roads depending on pollution levels[4]. Indian metros such as Delhi or Mumbai have no such plan.

---

2   See http://newdelhi.usembassy.gov/airqualitydata.html

3   See http://www.greenpeace.org/eastasia/campaigns/air-pollution/problems/coal-hard-truth-airpollution/

4   See http://www.rtcc.org/2015/03/16/toxic-delhi-earths-most-polluted-city-has-no-plan-to-cutemissions/

04

WHY TREAT WATER IN THE CITY AT ALL? WHY NOT LIVE WITH THE WATER PURIFIERS AT HOME?

I opened the Morning Newspaper and on Page 3 read the news that Neha Malini, a famous Bollywood actor – had publicly announced that she would no longer endorse Zero Water Purifier . In an exclusive interview Neha said that she felt endorsing water purifiers for homes is not correct – safe drinking water should be supplied by the municipal corporations in the first place and there should be no need to treat water further at home. She thought that the life cycle impact of a water purifier was worrisome. The newspaper reporter ended the column saying that by turning down the offer from Zero Water Purifiers, Neha sacrificed INR 5 million per year in revenues just based on this principle! And I was impressed.

Wondering what led to this transformation, I called my Professor friend on his mobile phone. He sounded busy but after some pleasantries, when I asked him about Neha Malini's stand, he said "Oh, this was expected. It's all due to the session I did last week with Bollywood actors – it was a discourse on products they should NOT endorse as brand ambassadors. And I gave the example of water purifiers and a dose on Life Cycle Assessment. Neha was present during the session. Even Shah Mukh, who was around, is now convinced and will stop campaigning for Safe Water Purifier LLP that he has been supporting for years. See the next Sunday edition of the newspaper for his interview expressing his views". This was simply stunning.

I met the Professor at our usual café. We ordered coffee with slices of fresh almond cakes. Dipping a slice in my coffee, I asked "Why are you so against home water purifiers Professor?"

Most of the water purifiers in the market today offer 3-stage or 4-stage or even 5-stage water treatment that consist of a filter, activated carbon, membranes for reverse osmosis (RO) and ultraviolet (UV) radiation chamber. The average capacity of the water purifier is 7 to 9 litres and the purifier typically weighs around 10 to 15 Kg. In most purifiers today Acrylonitrile Butadiene Styrene (ABS) is used. Nearly 50% of the weight of the purifier consists of ABS. The RO membranes and activated carbon are required to be replaced once in a year. Assuming you use the water purifier for 4 to 5 years, you will have these replacements done at least 3 times and in this process, waste-activated carbon and exhausted RO membranes get rejected as wastes. At the end of 4 to 5 years, the entire assembly of water purifier needs to be disposed. All these waste streams and components reach the city landfill as these wastes/materials are NOT collected as part of the Extended Producer Responsibility (EPR) by the manufacturer of the water purifier. There are other issues as well. While the ABS is strong and lightweight material, it is almost impossible to recycle ABS and further it does not biodegrade. Most purifiers are generally not designed for disassembly, take backs and recycling"

Now look at the energy consumption perspective. Operation of the UV chamber in the water purifier requires electrical consumption of close to 10 W. So assuming half a million water purifiers are operating at homes and offices in Greater Mumbai for 1 hour a day, a capacity of 15 MW of power generation is needed at the City's Thermal Power Plant! This would also mean increased GHG emissions.

This life cycle perspective of water purifiers was new to me. The Professor continued his argument

Don't you think that it's important that the municipal corporation understands this implication of water purifiers and makes every effort to provide safe drinking water from our taps? In the United States for instance, the Consumer Confidence Rule requires public water suppliers that serve the same people year round (community water systems) to provide consumer confidence reports (CCR) to their customers. The CCR summarizes information regarding sources used (i.e., rivers, lakes, reservoirs, or aquifers) any detected contaminants, compliance and educational information. The reports are due to the customers by July 1st of each year. CCRs are available on the web for those interested.

If we have such a system mandated in India, I don't know how many municipal corporations will have the courage to issue such certificates. In the US and EU, since most of the water supplies are operated by private organizations, CCRs can be imposed. For the water purifier makers, the market lies in the developing world, where there is poor or no assurance on the quality of water supply."

I knew that the water purifier industry in India was booming. This industry is expected to grow at the rate of 24% over the next 4 years touching a market of INR 60,000 million! More the cases on the supply of foul water or outbreak of water borne diseases, better is the market for this industry.

The Professor had to rush. While settling the bill he said in a hush hush voice "The other day I was at the city water treatment plant and the supervisor said that the supplies of alum and chlorine to the plant were getting erratic. This was a concern for him. However, in a lighter vein, he said that in any case everyone has a water purifier at home, so a little downgrading of water quality occasionally should not really matter"

A wild thought then came to my mind - can we not do away with the central water treatment systems in Indian cities? If the confidence in the water quality of our supplies is anyway low then all of us could continue to use the Zero and Safe Water purifiers. This will not unnecessarily "duplicate" the efforts and save huge amounts of materials (alum, lime, chlorine) and energy.

I thought that Neha Malini and Shah Mukh should then reconsider and take up once again the endorsements of water purifiers! And the Professor should perhaps conduct another session with Bollywood but now with the new perspective. But what about the life cycle costs of the water purifiers? Unless the purifier makers become more responsible in the design or practice take-back, it may not be a good idea to promote water purifiers at home.

Visit US EPA's website[5] for an interesting read on CCR

Students – You may like to conduct a Life Cycle Analysis of a Home Water Purifier.

---

5   See http://water.epa.gov/lawsregs/rulesregs/sdwa/ccr/index.cfm

05

MAKE WASTE SEGREGATION A HABIT AND NOT AN OBLIGATION

Segregation of waste at source is important. It's an effort that pays everybody and solves half the city's problem of waste management. Waste segregation costs nothing and takes hardly any extra time. It's a matter of understanding and more about responsible behavior.

When you segregate waste into two basic streams like organic (degradable) and inorganic (non-biodegradable), the waste generated is better understood and consequently recycled and reused with higher potential for recovery. Waste pickers typically use inorganic waste and segregate waste further into paper, metal, plastic and then sell them to earn a livelihood. These waste streams get collated through the informal 'eco-system' of waste bankers and waste traders who become 'material suppliers' to the formal manufacturing sector. As a result, you see products being made out of recycled plastic, metals getting reused

for product-making and waste paper getting mashed into pulp to make recycled paper.

The organic waste component is often converted into compost and/or methane gas using Mechanical Biological Treatment (MBT). Compost can replace demand for chemical fertilizers and biogas can be used as source of energy. As a result, much of the waste gets utilized as a resource – benefitting waste pickers, waste traders, small and medium industries, citizens and the local municipal authority.

16

Waste, if not segregated, can pose risks and constraints on the choice of operation of waste processing technologies. Plastic in waste if incinerated could lead to release of dioxins that are toxic. Household hazardous waste if not segregated (e.g. spent batteries) can result in compost that is contaminated.

Proper segregation of waste thus leads to a "circular economy" creating green jobs, reducing consumption of virgin resources and promoting investments and innovations. Furthermore as waste transportation reduces, emissions reduce; life of the landfill increases and risk to the ecosystem goes down. Segregated waste reduces health and safety related risks to waste pickers and to the ecosystems around the waste treatment and disposal sites.

It is intriguing however that despite these benefits, waste segregation does not happen much at the source. Most of us understand the importance of waste segregation but still do not practice. **So where is the problem? Is it an issue of attitude or do we simply not care!**

Today, the percentage of waste segregation in Asian cities is rather low. It hovers between 30% and 60%. Segregation at source is however much higher in Japan, EU and Northern America, where it ranges between 60% and 90%. Some cities have progressed on waste segregation by raising awareness, offering incentives and by imposing penalties or through enforcement. Providing business links, facilitating micro-finance, providing waste sorting infrastructure and setting up better institutional arrangements through establishment of Public Private Partnerships (PPP) have been the other strategies.

Cities like Singapore and Hong Kong where availability of land is an issue, waste sorting centers or Material Recovery Facilities (MRFs) have become integral to building design. Generally, for sorting, basements of building are used. Chintan, an active NGO in India has come up with planning norms for locating waste sorting centers in cities based on surveys carried out in New Delhi. Local authorities are encouraged to provide sorting sites on this basis, in order to promote segregation. The National Solid Waste Management Department (JPSPN) in Malaysia is distributing for free 120 L Mobile Garbage Bins (MGB) with two compartments to be installed in the premises of households in Kuala Lumpur. These MGBs are compatible with the new Refuse Collection Vehicles (RCVs) and hence less waste is expected to reach the landfill.

Tamil Nadu State in India is attempting various incentives to increase the extent of segregation. In the city of Coimbatore financial incentives are given to the wards that perform better on segregation of waste at source. So the ward officers and communities work together to improve upon segregation. In the city of Salem in Tamil Nadu, one pencil is given for 1 kg of plastic waste and a notebook if 10 kg of plastic waste is segregated. The community in turn sells plastic at INR 2.50/ kg to the market. Jars are kept outside city temples where worshipers are encouraged to bring used glass bottles. Glass then sold at INR 0.5/kg and the monies collected are used to whitewash the temples. So here the strategy is to tap into the religious sentiments6 of the people!

Waste segregation is best promoted by involving communities and self-help groups. In Mumbai, more than 400 self-help groups operate as Advanced Locality Management (ALM). Every housing society that registers with ALM contributes Rs 1/day to promote waste segregation at source. Today most metro cities in India have such citizen groups and are supported by local municipal authorities.

Levying fines has been a strategy 'enforcing' waste segregation. City Government of San Fernando in the Philippines has imposed penalties for individuals who fail to segregate under its program **"HandaKa Na Ba San Fernando? Now Na! Mag-Segregate Na!"** (Are you ready, San Fernando? Now is the time! Do segregation now!) Fernandinos are asked to segregate their garbage or pay P500 to P1000 if waste comes from a residential source. Business establishments found violating the law are fined P2000 to P50007.

In order to 'localize' the benefits of waste segregation, technology is brought in for the rescue. Companies that are famous for molded water tanks are now producing

---

6 See http://www.slideshare.net/cloverorganicpvtltd/waste-mgt-ideas-and-models

7 See http://www.sunstar.com.ph/pampanga/local-news/2011/05/07/city-fine-people-failing-segregate-solid-waste-154136

quick-install biogas plants. Vegetable waste goes into a fermented segment in these units and, with the help of microbes, starts producing methane that can be piped to a stove in the kitchen. The sludge that remains at the end of the process is applied to plants as fertilizer. A version of this technology that uses waste vegetables and sugar won an Ashden award for the NGO ARTI in Pune, in India a few years ago. These emerging technology options will certainly provide an incentive towards waste segregation at the source.

So, it is rather worthwhile if you take a few minutes of your time, to put the 'waste' in your household and premises 'in order!' Waste segregation pays, benefits all and makes our cities sustainable and livable. **Waste segregation should become our habit rather than an obligation?**

(This article is a modified version of the original piece contributed to Green Prospects Asia)

Do refer to the resources below on waste recycling business

Report prepared by IGES Japan for Asian Development Bank[8]. We did the India chapter.

Report on Waste Recycling Seminar held in Mumbai that was part of the IGES project[9]

---

8   See Final_report_recycling_business_FINAL-July28 2014
9   See Ekonnect Seminar_Proceeding_Waste Recycling_210612

06

CAV CAV AND SWATCH BHARAT ABHIYAN

My Professor friend just returned from a training program on learning Cav – the Crow Language. The idea was to understand conversations by the Crows. It was a two weeks intensive course that was conducted by the NACIT (Native American Crow Indian Tribe – also called the Apsáalooke). NACIT has now migrated to Canada, just south of Lake Winnipeg. This Tribe understands the cav language of the Crows and knows how to teach Cav.

Teaching Cav to my Professor Friend was one of the major objectives of Indo-Canadian

cooperation on Science & Technology (S&T). This was perhaps as important an event as signing of the deal on the sale of Uranium for India's nuclear plants. But very few knew about this – as the item was not listed in the bi-lateral S&T cooperation agenda, being a top secret. Only the Prime Minister (PM) and my Professor friend were involved.

Let me give you some background. PM Modi launched "Swatch Bharat Abhiyan" in India a few months ago. Since its launch, a number of initiatives were undertaken with several top personalities appointed as the 'ambassadors'. This campaign was officially launched on 2 October 2014 at Rajghat in New Delhi, where Prime Minister Narendra Modi himself cleaned the road. Swatch Bharat Abhiyan (SBA) is today India's biggest ever cleanliness drive. SBA is not only a sanitation programme but includes solid waste management and waste water management.

PM has directly linked the implementation of SBA with the economic health of the nation. This mission, according to him, can contribute to the GDP growth, provide a source of employment and reduce health costs, thereby furthering economic growth to reach a target of 8%.

Cleanliness is also connected to tourism and it is time that India's top 50 tourist destinations display highest standard of hygiene and cleanliness so as to change the global perception. SBA can bring in more tourists, thereby increasing revenue although there will be reduction in those tourists who visit India to experience the filth as a novelty.

Monitoring the progress of SBA was therefore crucial for India's economy. Although all conventional and routinely followed information gathering approaches were used (e.g. tapping of the telephones), the Ministries of Home Affairs and Information & Broadcasting were unable to report the progress to the PM on a comprehensive and reliable basis. The PM therefore consulted my Professor friend.

Professor came up with a brilliant and unconventional idea. He proposed that we mingle with the crows and understand their perception on the Swatch Bharat Abhiyan. For crows, SBA would matter as they are so intimately con-nected to the state of 'uncleanliness'. Certainly, crows must be discussing the impact of SBA on their lifestyles and livelihoods. Therefore we must learn the cav language of the crows.

Given the serious implications of Swatch Bharat Abhiyan on India's economy, as outlined by the PM himself, Professor volunteered to learn the cav language. Hence the training by NACIT was taken up on top priority.

On returning from Canada, Professor went straight to one of the largest waste dumps in Dharavi in Mumbai. As usual, he took me along to take photos and notes. There was a National Convention on Swatch Bharat Abhiyan going on as organized by the MCC (Mumbai Chapter of Crows) – not to be confused with the Mumbai Cricket Club.

Around 200 prominent crows were attending the Convention. Many crows had flown from long distances. In few minutes, Professor told me that there were different dilects of cav spoken such as

Tamil cav, Bengali cav, Punjabi cav etc. He was therefore paying close attention to the speeches and conversations. He was translating all the cav spoken into English so that I could take down notes

The President Crow was giving an opening address.

"The Swatch Bharat Abhiyan by PM Modi is something of great concern. We all should be worried. If this campaign actually works, then we and all our future generations will be in grave trouble. There will be a huge issue of food security i.e. food shortage. We must all work together to ensure that the Swatch Bharat Abhiyan fails. Lack of cleanliness is the foundation of sustainable development of crows and we must strive towards the same. Please share your ideas and strategies".

The President Crow ended his speech.

There was silence except the "gur gur" sound coming from the old aged crows who were the past presidents. Then a young crow who represented the Crow Youth Wing spoke "Sir, you are right. I am coming in from the city of Warangal. In this city, a cleanup drive was carried out by the people in just one week. This was a spirited movement. As bulk of the waste was eliminated or diverted, the campaign led to starvation of some 1000 crows. These crows have fled to nearby cities. See the Warangal success story video.[10] Apparently, the Warangal experiment has inspired other cities such as Coimbatore and Vizag. That will lead to more such impacts.

A crow who represented the Political Relations Subcommittee said that all crows of the second generation should consider migrating to non-BJP ruled States. By default, being in opposition, these States will not follow up the SBA seriously, pocket the grants while the filth continues to remain or grow. The President opined that this was an important suggestion and

10 See http://timesofindia.indiatimes.com/tv/news/hindi/Satyamev-Jayate-2-highlights-the-importance-ofwaste-management/photostory/32154207.cms

should be kept in mind.

There were many crows living at dump sites or landfills. They had another concern. According to them, the citizens have taken waste segregation and composting rather seriously. Many such plants are being operated in cities on a decentralized basis – some of them are community-driven and some operated through partnerships with the private sector. Therefore not much organic refuse has been reaching city landfills. It became a matter of real concern when it affected adequate supply of food. A number of case studies presented by crows living in landfills, offering heart-rending statistics on the issues of starving and malnutrition.

Then came some complaints from the female crows, in a lighter vein. They shared how they now miss the whole fun of perching on the open-container vehicles, sampling the waste food and impressing the male crows sitting on the street lamp posts. After the launch of SBA, most city corporations have started covering of the container vehicles. Female crows have ceased to perch on the containers and the male

crows miss the whole thrill of eve-teasing. "This is leading to social fragmentation – an impact to note", a crow who normally sits at the gate of Tata Institute of Social Sciences said in a serious cav.

A crow who used to regularly sit on the window of the office of the Dean of Indira Gandhi Institute of Development & Research (IGIDR) in Mumbai came up with calculations on how consumption of waste by crows is saving urban India around INR 4000 million in waste management. He made a strong case that the Ministry of Urban Development set up a Crow Welfare Fund of INR 4000 million recognizing the contribution by crows. (See a very interesting article that makes such estimates. This article gives a statistic that urban crows in India consume 3,150 tons of organic waste/day or 11,50,000 tons/year[11])

In the international session, there was a huge commotion when a Crow from Singapore presented a slide that showed how Government of Singapore had started killing crows as they didn't need them any more due to high levels of

---

11   See http://birdsofindia-ssen.blogspot.in/2011/08/in-praise-of-crows.html

cleanliness. The President wondered whether such genocide may happen in India if the SBA really succeeds. Again there was a silence.

The Convention ended with the vote of thanks. While we returned to our car, the Professor overheard the conversation between two prominent crows who had not spoken at the Convention. The first crow said "I am still not worried. In India, abhiyans are often launched, glamorized and later forgotten. Investments get made but projects are not implemented properly. Much of the budget is spent in financing NGOs and not in carrying out actual awareness campaigns. Waste is shown to have reached the designated locations but the waste is mostly dumped on the way or the containers are loaded with construction and demolition waste. This SBA will not be an exception. However, we need to track the progress of SBA on a regular basis. Let us form a core crow team and after some training, let them sit on windows of the offices of Chief Secretaries of some of the key filthy States. They should be present when meetings on SBA happen. Generally I know these meetings will only review the past minutes of the meeting, with not much action reported

on the ground and simply push the agenda for the next meeting". When Professor translated this cav for me, I wasn't sure whether I should record this conversation as a part of the brief to the PM. And the Professor agreed not to report to the PM.

A week later, I received a call from Secretary, Urban Development of the Government of Maharashtra to attend a meeting on Swatch Bharat Abhiyan. I told the Secretary's PA that the meeting should be held in an A/C conference room (where the A/C actually works) and no windows should be open.

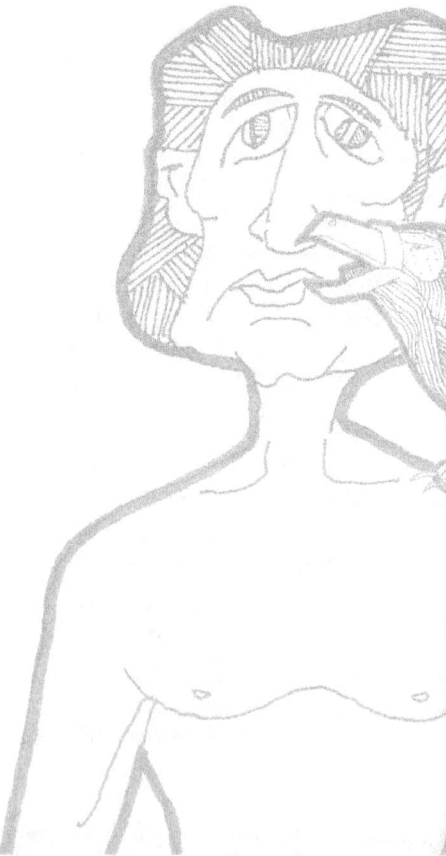

GREY ON GREEN

Environmental Impacts

07

IMPACT ASSESSMENT OF ENVIRONMENTAL IMPACT ASSESSMENT

One of the reasons why the Ministry of Environment & Forests (MoEF) introduced the Notification on Environmental Impact Assessment (EIA) in 1994 was perhaps to create new business avenues for environmental consultants to monitor laboratories and related assignments. In fact, as per the Notification, EIA reports were required for projects listed in a Schedule based on certain thresholds (the logic of which is not known even today) and the project proponents looked for agencies that could help them get Environmental Clearance (EC) at the least cost and in the shortest possible time.

The consulting fraternity in India responded to this need and mastered the art easily, using technology from Microsoft – i.e. MS Word (with control C and control V being the main tools). During the EC process, committees were created at the State and Central levels, and members of such committees got an opportunity to showcase their expertise and ask questions so that the EC process resembled a long tunnel – the journey being in "darkness". When Public Hearing was included in the EC process, it opened another Pandora's Box – creating a role for environmental activists.

Some truly believed, and naively so, that the 'impact of EIA' in India had been a positive one and ensured that major developmental projects included environmental and social considerations to reduce risks and add a value. If one were to ask project proponents

26

and consultants today, they would be able to quote very few instances or case studies wherein real benefits of EIA had been realized. Getting an EC 'somehow' has been the main driver in most cases.

EIA in India has not yet seen the maturity that the country deserves. In many cases EC has been a political process and not that of scientific inquiry. ECs are issued on project basis – i.e. isolated – and not on cumulative or regional considerations. Who cares for the carrying capacity? Tools like Strategic Environmental Assessment that are legislated in many countries are not even discussed. Integration of Climate Change (CC) in the EC process of large projects is not even thought about yet. Now that MoEF has a new name with CC added to it, consideration to Climate Change should be given in the EIA process. Am I being too optimistic here?

So since 1994, more than 2 decades now, has EIA benefited India in helping improve our projects (concept, scale, design, siting and technologies) and protect/ conserve our environment? Has EIA provided better alternatives? It's time that we do an impact assessment of EIA in India.

For Students – You may like to visit websites of State Environmental Appraisal Committees and analyze the statistics on EC, time taken for clearance, conditions stated and cumulative impacts that are not considered. Visit http://www.greenclearancewatch.org/ in particular.

27

08

Modelling of Environmental Impacts – A Ritual? Or Reality?

Mathematical modelling of environmental impacts has often been an important part of Impact Assessment. Modelling of air emissions, noise, thermal discharges, wastewater releases on the shore and through outfalls have been some of the common applications.

Mathematical models are used to simulate emissions, meteorology, and hydrology/hydraulics and arrive at ambient concentrations to compare with applicable standards under various scenarios. These results are then used to make decisions on stack heights, outfall length, noise barriers and design of green belts, level of control or pre-treatment of emissions needed, sulphur content in the coal etc. **There are significant implications of model-based decisions on the costs.**

Results of simulation depend on the model being used. In air quality modelling, for instance, results of Industrial Source Complex (ISC) model and that of AERMOD can differ by an order of magnitude! Hence, which model is used for impact assessment becomes a very important question. There have been instances in India wherein a Flue Gas Desulphurization (FGD) unit has been slapped on a Coastal Thermal Power Plant based on results of a basic Gaussian Plume Model (GPM) that did not factor-in coastal conditions (i.e. sea breeze and fumigation). Underneath the façade of science – there can be the elegance of ignorance!

In countries such as the United States, Australia and EU, certain models are recognized as 'regulatory' models and these models are recommended for impact assessment. Importantly, this list of models is regularly updated. You may like to refer to the website of US EPA for recommended air quality models[12]. The Ministry of Environment and Forests (MoEF) in India has listed a number of models for impact predictions. See: http://envfor.nic.in/divisions/iass/eia/Annex5.htm. This list of models however is dated (e.g. it lists ISC-2 as one of the recommended air quality models, when today AERMOD is recommended in the United States even in place of the ISC-3). Further, no guidance is provided on the use of these models. The last publication on Guidance on Air Quality Models was brought out in 1997-1998 by the Central Pollution Control Board (CPCB).

No research studies have been commissioned by the MoEF to test the accuracy of these mathematical models under Indian conditions and using Indian data. Have we ever conducted verification studies on model predictions?

Modelling is hardly taught at universities, so most Indian 'modelers' use modelling software as a black box. Plug data in and spew the results!

Against this background, how accurate the results of modelling are, is another important question. Indeed, the results of models in most cases are quite different from the observations. Reasons are several, including data inaccuracy in quantifying emissions (especially non-points and fugitives), inability to mimic complex meteorology/hydraulic conditions and reactions. The differences can lead to incorrect decisions and inappropriate communication.

I would like to draw your attention here to a very interesting observation made in Hong Kong[13]. This observation pertains to the importance of model accuracy or confidence and communication of modelling results regarding air quality. I am reproducing two interesting paragraphs from this note that are worth pondering over.

---

12 See: http://www.epa.gov/airquality/modeling.html
13 See: http://www.legco.gov.hk/yr12-13/english/panels/ea/ea_anlp/papers/ea_anlp0628cb1-1393-2-e.pdf

Air Quality in Hongkong

We welcome the Subcommittee's review of "Air Pollution Modelling in Hong Kong". Hong Kong's air quality is a topic of great public concern. The lack of progress in improving air quality has led many to question the effectiveness of our air quality management system. Most people understand that air quality modelling is important for our air quality management system because of its role in air quality impact assessment. However, not many people understand the details of air quality modelling as modelling is relatively technical and complicated. Hence, most people prefer to treat it as a black box. **People don't like black boxes, particularly when our air quality management system does not seem to be working. Therefore, there have been growing concerns about of the accuracy and application of air quality models in Hong Kong........**

So, we have a peculiar situation: for the past 15 years, the air quality models used in the EIAs are projecting compliance with the AQOs, while observations by EPD showed continual noncompliance for Hong Kong. **This apparent contradiction is an important reason why many are skeptical about the EIA process in general, and lost trust in the air quality models in particular.**

In India, we include modelling more as a ritual in the EIA reports. We use outdated models and our model application quality is poor. Results of modelling, especially the limitations of the model, are not communicated effectively to the stakeholders and to the public. Model verification and validation studies are seldom carried out. If used on a mature basis, modelling indeed has a value – but we haven't learnt the art and science of modelling in this perspective

We need to ask MoEF/ CPCB to update the list of recommended math models, provide guidance on their use and interpretation, and sponsor model verification studies. Let us also work together to offer hands-on training programmes on application of some commonly used models. Let us not make modelling a ritual.

For Students – Research on how a model reaches a state of a 'regulatory model' for impact assessment. Take a case study of ISC-2, ISC-3 and AERMOD in US EPA. Understand how models are field-verified and what is involved in Prediction Audits of a model.

For more serious research in this arena, I would recommend you to see an excellent article **by Matthew Cashmore**[14] **'The role of science in environmental impact assessment: process and procedure versus purpose in the development of theory'** as a start. The list of references in this article is very comprehensive and very helpful for a beginner.

---

14 See http://faculty.mu.edu.sa/public/uploads/1338109315.1011EIA-8.pdf

09

DATA, INFORMATION AND KNOWLEDGE IN ENVIRONMENTAL IMPACT ASSESSMENT

In Environmental Impact Assessment (EIA), we take decisions on the project, the preferred alternative and the required environmental management measures.

To improve our understanding and take appropriate decisions, transforming data into information and into knowledge is required.

It is often hard, however, to differenciate between data, information and knowledge (DIK). Sometimes these terms are used interchangeably.

EIAs are often weak because they rely mostly on data, less so, on information and least of all on available knowledge. Most EIA report contains only data. I would attribute this to the lack of proper training.

What is data? Data is a fact that is not significant on its own, as it does not relate to other data. Data is essentially a raw entity. It simply exists and has no significance beyond its existence. Data can exist in any form, usable or unusable. It does not have any meaning in itself.

Data may answer a very basic *what* question e.g. what are the concentration levels of air pollutants in an urban area? As an answer, we provide values of SO_2, NO_x, and RSPM at 10 locations over 5 years.

What is information? Information is data that is *related* and is therefore to be viewed in a certain context. Information is processed or transformed data that relates to *who, what, where* and *when*, providing a foundation to the overall *understanding*. Information is data that is useful.

A comparison of air pollutant concentrations with air quality standards leads to *information* on violations. Air Quality Index developed on the basis of data on concentrations of air pollutants is another example. Air Quality Index provides information on the overall status on air quality.

While information may become the input for making or evaluating decisions, the level of understanding may limit the completeness and correctness of the decision. To improve the understanding further, we require knowledge.

What is knowledge? Knowledge is the application of information. Knowledge addresses *how* and *why*, in addition to *who, what, where* and *when*. Knowledge often contains a set of instructions and know-how. Knowledge links all the relevant information together along with *experience* to help us take a better decision. Knowledge is often expert resident and tacit. It needs to be captured. When done so, it forms an asset for the organization.

Application of knowledge is critical to EIA as the assessment requires information from multi-disciplinary sources and responses of diverse stakeholders.

Let us revisit the case of urban air quality impact assessment. Here we need data on air pollutant concentrations. This data needs to be processed to draw information on the extent of violations. Information on the percentage of time the violation occurs, magnitudes of these violations, and the extent to which violations have been contiguous in time needs be processed for each pollutant. This information improves the understanding on the status of air quality and possible air quality related impacts. See the Table below as a dummy illustration for Mumbai, India.

To assess the impact on health of people due to such violations, we need to process information on all the pollutants (to address the cumulative effect), assemble more pieces of information such as age, sex, exposure (indoor, travel & work patterns) of the people, coupled with research and field studies as evidence. This exercise is essentially taken up to understand the *pattern* and

Pollutant	% Violations over 1 year	Magnitude of Violations (Maximum)	Contiguous Period of Violations
SO2	20	150% exceedance on July 12 at Andheri	3 days between May 10 to 12 at Bandra
NO$_x$	10	200% exceedance On February 15 in Bhandup	2 days between April 5 and 6 in Dadar
RSPM	40	350% exceedance on November 1In Mulund	9 days between Oct. 28 to Nov. 6 in Sion

apply this knowledge to take decisions.

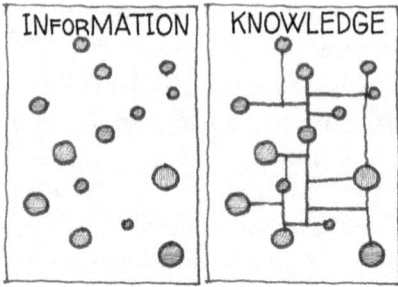

Knowledge represents a pattern that connects and generally provides a high level of predictability as to what is described or what will happen next. For example, we can come up with knowledge to speculate what could happen to the health of people over the next 10 years as result of deteriorating air quality in the city. We also need here a pool of experts who could share their experience on health impact assessment, especially the damage in economic terms, with supporting data and information. This may require holding of a specialized knowledge workshop. If in this workshop, gaps in the knowledge get identified, then these gaps would need to be addressed through directed research. EIA reports should therefore not simply state the impact and its significance, but the certainty of assessment based on DIK. EIAs should provide leads to the research required.

Therefore to assess the significance of impacts for coming up with appropriate management measures, we need a structured approach to DIK. What is required is a careful planning of the data elements, data processing logic/algorithms with tools, followed by application of knowledge. The figure below shows such a desirable progression.

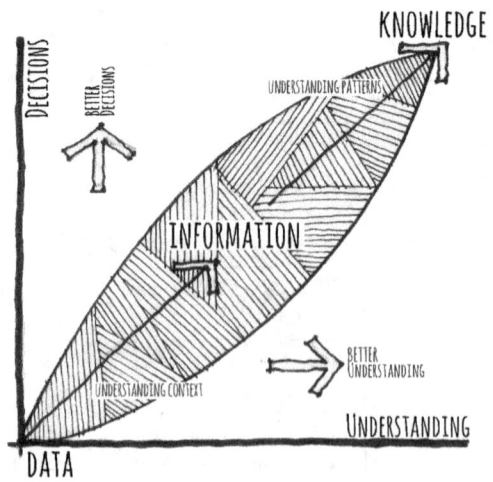

In most EIAs unfortunately, data is either incomplete, irrelevant or outdated. Processing of data to draw meaningful information is seldom done – sometimes due to lack of training and tools. Further, weak information structuring and lack of appropriate expert input leads to poor application of knowledge. Quality of EIA thus suffers. The decisions taken are often 'foggy' and 'inappropriate'. See the Figure below.

We need good examples to show how proper planning and processing of DIK helps improve the quality of EIA. These examples can serve as guides for the purpose of training and EIA review. Do we have such examples? I will be very interested to know. I would be most grateful if the readers to this blog are willing to share.

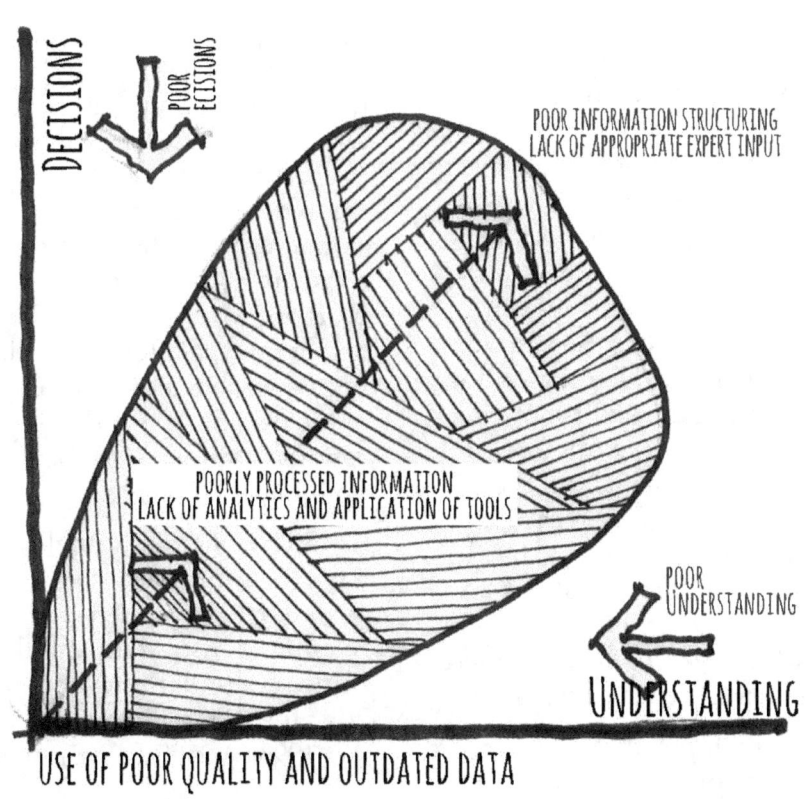

USE OF POOR QUALITY AND OUTDATED DATA

10

Utmost Good Faith

The TSR Subramanian Committee in India came up with several radical recommendations to improve India's environmental governance

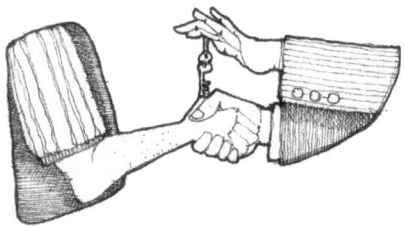

The new concept of 'utmost good faith' has been proposed through a new legislation, Environmental Laws (Management) Act (ELMA). ELMA would oblige an applicant to disclose everything about a proposed project. The disclosure will need to include a project's potential to pollute and its proposed solution – in short, everything that is relevant for making a decision on granting or refusing the environmental clearance applied for. The project proponent, and the experts who support the case, will be required by this law to certify that *'the facts stated are true and that no information that would be relevant to the clearance has been concealed or suppressed'*.

If at any time after the application is received - even after the project has been implemented and is in operation – it is discovered that the proponent had, in fact, concealed some vital information or had given wrong information or that the certificates issued by the experts suffer from similar defects, then severe consequences will follow under ELMA. They include heavy fine, penalties including imprisonment and revocation of the clearance, – and in serious cases arrest of the polluter.

'Utmost Good Faith' shall have the same meaning as understood in the law relating to Insurance; and the principles underlying Section 20 of the Marine Insurance Act 1993 (Act 11of 1963) shall apply.

The court room was packed. The judge called the court to order. The case involved breach of Utmost Good Faith by the Agyani Group. Newly-enacted ELMA was triggered. An environmental NGO called Facts and only Truth (FoT) had filed the petition.

I took my seat. I was keen to attend the case as my good Professor friend was leading the Technical Counsel on behalf of the giant Agyani Group. This was the first ELMA case in the country.

Agyani's thermal power plant was discharging hot water into the sea. This had led to migration of the fish that the local fishermen were dependent upon. FoT found that at a distance of 12 km to the south (where the currents were heading) breeding of turtles was also affected. These turtles were a rare species.

Agyani had underplayed information on the impact of thermal discharge and indicated the impact to be minor and adverse but reversible. The EIA report was then prepared by my Professor friend.

Data from FoT (supported by direct measurements as well as satellite data) showed that Agyani's discharge was carrying temperatures of around 4^0C more than the mean sea temperature with its present 25% of operations running. The EIA report had stated that the temperature of the discharge will not cross 7^0C, as per the requirement of the Ministry.

FoT argued that when 100% of the plant will be operational, the temperature of the discharge will certainly be more than the 7^0C threshold. The EIA report should have addressed such possibilities clearly and come up with a robust environmental management plan. Information on the turtle breeding ground was also suppressed, with no consideration being given to the thermal discharge.

The charge was that of non-disclosure. The FoT had demanded that the environmental clearance to the Power Plant must be revoked, corrective action be taken or the plant be shut down.

In response to the petition, my Professor friend rose from his Chair. He said 'Non-disclosure

can be classified into three types – *Innocent*, *Negligent* and *Deliberate*. The case of Agyani (not because the name suggests so) was that of 'innocent non-disclosure' and hence they should not be punished harshly under ELMA.

First of all, the baseline data collected in the EIA report showed an existing decline in the fish population over past 5 years. This trend was thus present much before Agyani's operations. How can then Agyani be blamed for the continued decline in the population of fish, especially when the thermal discharge from Agyani was only 4^0C higher as against the threshold of 7^0C?

"The EIA study was scoped, as per Ministry's guidelines, to a 10-Km radius. Obviously, the EIA followed this guideline and did not look into anything beyond the 10-Km radius – and thus missed looking at the turtle breeding ground that was at a distance of 12

Km– something that was not intentional!"

Professor then submitted to the Court statistical data on the fish population over past 10 years that indeed showed fall in population prior to Agyani' s discharge. The computations were done using Mann-Kendall (M-K) test using MATLAB. He also spoke about literature demonstrating thermal resistance of the coastal fish and that the 7^0C elevation was of concern only if temperature was high continuously for over 30 days.

"When occasions of 7^0C happen only for a week; the fish of the kind we have are not that severely affected. This is an ongoing research however and one should wait till definitive conclusions can be drawn." He said flashing some of the recent articles from the Journal of Marine Ecosystems.

"Regarding the turtles issue – we are sponsoring a research project being carried out by marine ecologists and marine hydrographers at the Institute of Marine Sciences. This three-year study will tell us about possible impact of our discharges. We will submit to the Honorable Court this independent assessment report in 2018 so that a view could be taken"

"What about the chemical composition of the discharge," I asked the Professor when we were exiting the swamp Court corridor. The Professor, while joyous of his victory in stalling the ELMA case for a few more years, said "I knew you will ask me such kind of questions – in fact, a representative of FoT also asked the same question."

Taking a deep puff from his favorite cigar, he said "I told the Judge that in the cooling water we use chemicals that have been certified by the Global Association of Green Chemicals based in Atlanta, USA. We simply trust them for their competencies and reputation. The chemicals they certify must indeed be safe. We are unable to disclose the chemical composition as it is proprietary and we have signed a Non-Disclosure Agreement to this effect – I

thus pleaded for innocence and it worked! "

I took a taxi home with Ultimate Good Faith in my Professor friend.

Making use of the concept of Ultimate Good Faith for 'speedy Environmental Clearance' is a recommendation that we should actively debate. To me, it violates the precautionary principle, simply passes the buck and questions the very sustainability of development. Its application will do more harm to our environment, resource security and the economy – than otherwise!

Facts in the environmental domain are difficult to establish and will always remain a challenge.

You may like to read

Utmost faith in corporations? You must be kidding me![15]

Panel on changing green laws puts 'utmost good faith' in industry. Is that good enough?[16]

---

15 See http://www.greenpeace.org/international/en/news/Blogs/makingwaves/utmost-faith-incorporations-you-must-be-kidd/blog/51569/

16 See http://scroll.in/article/695328/Panel-on-changing-green-laws-puts-'utmost-good-faith'-in-industry.-Isthat-good-enough

11

How to get Speedy Environmental Clearance?

Making a presentation at the Environmental Clearance (EC) Committee is often an ordeal. A lot depends on the moods and whims of the committee members. The fate of the project i.e. Go or No Go depends on the presentation made by the consultant hired by the Project Proponent.

A considerable time is spent on the preparation of the presentation. Often rehearsals are made and advice is sought from the past Committee members. The consultant brings along a dozen team members representing various domains of expertise ranging from air pollution to economics, biodiversity, gender and social inclusion. An expert is also brought along, who represents 'nobody or nothing' i.e. understands or knows only the project politics. This expert watches and does not generally speak and follows up after the meeting. Despite such heavy preparations, many of the outcomes of the meeting are

unpredictable. Getting an EC is just a probability.

I was told that some Project Proponents go to temples, pray and make promises to the Gods with a hope that the *Mortal Gods* of the EC Committees are kind enough to accord the EC. A temple next to the Ministry of Environment and Forests and Climate Change (MoEFCC) has a special counter called *Tatkal EC*. Those interested, pay a donation of Rs 100,000 to help get the EC on priority. If you pay Rs 500,000 then prayers are made in a more elevated manner, requesting the Gods that EC be issued with least conditions. Cheques/drafts and credit cards are accepted and official receipts are issued. It is a transparent process.

 Behind the building where EC Committee meets, there is a small lane where good-luck charms are sold. Legend has it that a project proponent wore a stone of *Guru* (Jupiter) and the most vocal member of the Committee suddenly developed a sore throat and could not ask a single question! Getting the EC was then a cake walk.

There are also *Swamis* who bless the project proponent for the success of EC. They conduct a ritual that includes chanting of mantras for "SRK" (Not Shah Rukh Khan but the planets *Shani-Rahu & Ketu*).  You need however a prior appointment. These *Swamis* charge a success fee of 0.001% of the project cost and the money is to be paid in cash. Advance payment is required and a refund is provided in case EC is not granted.

There are mixed opinions on which strategy is more effective, i.e. temple offerings, wearing of stones or following the Swamis. A PhD student at IIT is doing a research project focussed on this by conducting interviews and applying some psycho-spiritual models that are based on game theory.

I thought of discussing this interesting facet of EC in India with my Professor friend. As usual he was busy. "All these strategies to obtain EC are rubbish. You need a scientific approach and proper training. Come to the Little Theatre at Lodhi Road at 6 pm in the evening to witness how I address this challenge". I had always liked to eat the mini samosas sold in the foyer of the Little Theatre, so I carried six samosas for me and the Professor in a paper bag and entered the Theatre.

Professor was right on the stage wearing the gown of the 'Play Director'. He was in action and didn't notice me coming in. On the stage, there was a long table with 6 people sitting with grim faces, representing the Environmental Clearance Committee. In the front (like a *darbar*) there were 11 people (poor souls) who represented the Project Proponent. There was an LCD projector in the middle. Some slides were being projected by the Project consultant. This guy had a trembling voice, and his posture was very apologetic. The project was about the construction of a township for 40000 people on a hill.

One of the committee members who was wearing thick spectacles spoke. "All this is fine, but have you carried out *climate proofing* of the township? I was hoping to see the application of SimChimp software to estimate floods that may happen in 2040. It is important to know whether your stormwater system has factoredin such extreme events that may happen in the future. You should see my recent publication in *Current Science* stressing the importance of climate proofing in EIA".

Before, the project consultant could answer, a member from the College of Architecture intervened, "The entire project proposal has missed the point on sustainability. Your township must be zero energy, zero waste and zero water. You have to come up with a plan that ensures the township does not draw a drop of water from outside, recovers all the waste and requires no additional source of energy. The project should become a model to others. I would like my students to get involved in this project to reshape/ redesign".

Then a man wearing a sling bag and a Gandhi *topi* spoke in a deep voice "Have you considered what will happen to the tribals on the hill? I don't believe the number of people you have quoted as displaced is true. You are simply providing wrong data. All the project-affected people need to be compensated for and provided employment. There should also be benefit-sharing out of your profits. This was the latest recommendation from the World Bank during the meeting in Washington DC that I attended. My NGO will be very interested to work as a monitoring and evaluation agency."

The members spoke one after another and the project consultant was doing his best to defend the project – sometimes requesting members of his expert team to chip in. Heated discussion ensued, with the committee members becoming abrasive. One member suggested that given the sensitivity of the project location, the project proponent should carry out a one-year baseline study with remotely-sensed imageries at 0.5 meter resolution. Another member wanted an amphibian survey – "we would like to have this data for research purpose," he said. "This may not be relevant but there are no publications on this topic and it will be good to know."

At this point the project proponent lost his temper.

"Cut! Cut!" My Professor friend stopped the conversation. "You cannot lose your temper Sir! Have patience and be philosophical"

The mock drill was over. The stage was now 'converted' into a classroom. The EC committee members, who were the 'actors' before, took 'ordinary seats'. The professor trained the project proponent and his consultant on how to make PowerPoint slides, explaining minute details such as slide template, font color and size and then how to speak, where to pause and how to speak blatant lies with an innocent face, where to bow down even if the question asked was stupid or irrelevant, where to praise the review committee member and where to make tall promises etc. This session was also theatrical as the Professor enacted a few sessions himself. This made the training very real and effective.

As we came out of the Little Theatre, the Professor said, "Such training helps. The success rate is really high and almost all the project proponents who have gone through my training have received speedy Environmental Clearances. All are happy".

"You must publicize this training programme Professor – it's an important national service that you are offering," I said as I finished the leftover samosa. "Oh, I will never do that," said the professor. "I don't want this to become a business or a profession. I am sure the NABET of Quality Control Association of India will then come up with another category of accreditation called 'EIA Theatre Directors'. Theatre personalities like Naseeruddin Shah, Paresh Rawal, Alyque Padamsee, with very little environmental training, will then take over and conventional EIA consultants will have little role to play in getting the Environmental Clearance."

12

It's clear that the world needs development banks both to scale up the level of investment and to give developing countries better representation in the world of development finance. Yet these new banks need to play another role: championing sustainability as they usher in more development. Will this really happen?

The Asian Infrastructure Investment Bank (AIIB) was proposed by China in 2013 and was launched at a ceremony in Beijing in October 2014. AIIB was to be fully established by the end of 2015.

AIIB is considered by some as a rival to the IMF, the World Bank and the Asian Development Bank (ADB), which are regarded as dominated by developed countries like the United States. The United Nations has dubbed the launch of AIIB as 'scaling up financing for sustainable development' for the concern of Global Economic Governance.

As of April 15, 2015, almost all Asian countries and most major countries outside Asia had joined the AIIB, except the US, Japan (which dominated the ADB) and Canada. China is a major contributor to AIIB followed by India and Russia.

It was late in the night in Mumbai. There were sixty people in the banquet room of the legendary Taj Mahal Hotel having a buffet dinner. Out of the sixty, fifty seven were Ministers of the member countries who represented the newly-formed Asian Investment Infrastructure Bank (AIIB)

The meeting was chaired by the two Premiers – of course, of China and of India. (China holds nearly 29% of the stake in AIIB and India enjoys around 9%)

The sixtieth person in the room was my Professor Friend who had recently assumed the position of the Advisor to AIIB

44

on Environment and Social Safeguards (ESS). He was sitting next the two Premiers.

I was also around, but was not officially included in the list for obvious reasons. I was asked to be disguised as a waiter and serve a blend of Chinese and Indian (means Gujarati) food. Fortunately, the members of the AIIB were cooperative and tolerant of such a terrible cuisine combination.

Strict instructions were issued to ensure that there was no American presence inside and outside of the Taj property. All American tourists in the Taj Mahal hotel were evacuated and sent to hotels in Kabul at discounted rates. This was because Americans were not supporting AIIB and, in particular, the World Bank Group had considered AIIB as a threat.

To sabotage AIIB, I was told, the World Bank had instigated a host of international NGOs to ask AIIB questions on their Environmental and Social safeguards. A special capacity-building program for NGOs was launched to this effect, under the Technical Assistance of some Trust Funds. I was told that these funds generally dump money and don't look at the outcomes.

In an interview to the Wall Street Journal, the President of the World Bank had said that AIIB will be diluting the ESS while funding trillions of dollars of infrastructure projects. This will cause unevenness across development financing institutions of the World and pose risks to the very sustainability of the planet. He sounded concerned.

The management of AIIB strongly disagreed with the President's statement.

My Professor friend had completed a research investigation and had found that it was in fact the World Bank (WB) that was systematically diluting the ESS over the past two decades. The new draft ESS of the World Bank was a glaring example of how one can make a clever blend of dilution and complexity a maze of ambiguous procedures and of passing the buck when it came to the accountability.

A Chinese version of the Professor's report was intentionally leaked. This led to a fierce global discussion and arguments on AIIB vs. WB safeguards. Several people undertook lessons in Mandarin just to read and understand Professor's findings and participate in the debates. The percent of population 'able to read and speak Chinese' was in fact expected to increase over the next three months. I was really impressed with Chinese Premier's strategy. I suggested to my Professor friend that India should also leak this report in the national language Gujarati, Oops! Hindi.

While the dinner was getting served at the round tables, the Premiers opened the meeting. The Chinese Premier introduced the purpose of the meeting and Indian Premier welcomed the members of AIIB. Discussion on AIIB's environmental and social safeguards was the focus. My Professor friend presented his investigative report on what's happening on ESS across institutions like the WB, Asian Development Bank, European Investment Bank, JICA, and KfW etc. It appeared that most of these institutions were (happily) following the WB ESS. WB was the 'big daddy'.

The first question came from the representative from Russia while he was having Chinese soup with a dash of *Methi*. "How do we handle Environmental activist organizations? We want to do what we want to do. But then how do we ensure that these activist organizations remain quiet?"

The Indian Premiere smiled and said "Look, it's easy. First put all the environmental activist organizations under the scanner of Ministry of Home Affairs. Get their books of accounts checked by the Enforcement Directorate. More than 80% of such organizations would have flouted the rules under Foreign Exchange Regulations Act (FERA) one way or other. Issue notices and freeze their accounts/funds transfer. Once done, no activist organization will raise a voice against what AIIB will do. We have already done this in India and this step has removed all the barriers to the investment flows in India's infrastructure sector. There is now a queue of international investors. There are no public protests anymore! In fact the other day, leaders of Indian media approached me in despair that there were no more stories to tell about people protesting infrastructure projects even if the projects posed risks to our natural reserves. Media is now asking me for alternate news bytes. I am helping them by exposing some of our own scams and scandals! But that's another story".

The member from Russia got convinced.

"How about the process of public consultation and conducting of analyses of alternatives etc." The member from Brazil said while sampling *Undhiyo*. I served another portion of *Undhiyo* to the Member to show my appreciation for the pointed question he asked. I also placed a glass of Lassi on his table because I knew he did not know the impact of the spice in *Undhiyo*.

My Professor friend interjected: "AIIB will mostly support refinancing of the projects. In refinancing, most of the water has already flown under the bridge. The project is already halfway so most of the steps of ESS cannot be executed. There is no public consultation to be done nor are project alternatives to be explored and evaluated. We will still say that public consultation and alternatives are hallmarks of AIIB's Environmental and Social Safeguards – but when situations are beyond control and when the interest of the development of the country is to be looked at, we will abide by what is proposed and getting implemented. For the sake of completeness, however, we will conduct an Environmental and Social Due Diligence (ESDD) and if gaps are found we will provide Technical Assistance (TA) to address them and will encourage the borrower to

comply"

Wow! I was impressed. This was a great example of avoidance and passing the buck.

"And remember", the member from Netherlands said, "Let us all continue to focus more on project preparation (i.e. application of ESS to create documentation) and less on the supervision (i.e. implementation of ESS). We should follow the World Bank here. The WB and most of the development financing institutions spend 70% of the resources in getting project approvals and use 30% or even less sometimes, to check whether ESS is actually implemented in letter and spirit. I like this style as it shows the rigor at the superficial level, provides green jobs to all the (brown) environmental and social consultants and creates employment with hefty pensions to all the Bank staff. We must keep producing smart documents, upload them on our website (anyway hardly anyone reads them) and create records so that we can defend ourselves should anyone question us – of course if at all"

I found this approach really strategic. I decided to add a scoop of chocolate ice cream with Chinese wheatgrass on the gentleman's plate.

The question & answer session continued further and several bright ideas emerged on AIIB's comprehensive ESS. My Professor friend was taking meticulous notes. Meet me tomorrow to write down the minutes, he whispered to me while gobbling a piece of crunchy Chinese chicken rolled in *amsul* sauce.

As the meeting was about to end (and so was the food), the member from Mongolia asked a question.

"How about application of ESS to the Treasury department of AIIB? Will there be any restriction or guidance on where our own Treasury will invest? In order to multiply our own money for infrastructure investments, we will need to put our money in *funds of funds* that will provide at least 20% of returns and AAA rating. I reckon that investing in funds of funds that may, in turn, invest in mines will be good as the mines today are giving great profits. But will mines be in the exclusion list of AIIB's investments?"

"What about the environmental and social mess the mines create – how can AIIB invest in mines?" I was about to ask this question but realizing that I was supposed to be in disguise, simply zipped my mouth.

The Chinese Premiere smiled like Buddha "Oh, no worries, we will apply the principle of exclusion *selectively* to the Treasury department. We will keep the money in the funds of funds and won't go too much downstream to investigate where money will actually be invested. So the *downstream* projects could well be mines. And my friend – don't ask this question again"

He then turned to the Professor "Get me details on where does the Treasury of the World Bank, IFC, KfW etc. invest – which sectors, which fund of funds and markets are their favorites and to what extent do they apply Environmental and Social safeguards for their own investment operations. Let us copy their style *in toto*. We will have to stay consistent. **After all, we have to take care of our own safeguards"**

I would recommend that you visit interesting blog posted at the website of World Resources Institute[17]

You may also like to read the letter to the World Bank by US Senate that is quite telling[18].

17 See http://www.wri.org/blog/2015/04/asia%E2%80%99s-investment-bank-new-chapter-sustainable-development

18 See http://www.inclusivedevelopment.net/wp-content/uploads/2014/12/Senate-World-Bank-Safeguards-Letter-12-15-14.pdf

GREEN GOVERNANCE
Environmental Policy and Regulations

13
CONSENT TO CLOSE

In India, as in most countries, permits are required to establish and operate businesses that have environmental and social sensitivities. The Pollution Control Boards (PCBs) in India require businesses to obtain consents to establish and operate, following a well-laid-down review and permitting process.

These consents prescribe the conditions that are to be met. The conditions generally refer to the mitigation plans, the monitoring and the reporting. Inspections are then carried out by the staff of the PCB to check the compliance. The consent to operate requires to be renewed after a stipulated time period.

The business on account of economic conditions, labor issues, dispute etc. sometimes shut down their operations and exit. There are several approvals required in closing down the business. However, there is no consent required from the PCB.

Many businesses in their exit phase simply spew away pollution and residues causing serious concerns to the safety of workers and neighborhood and the environment. There are instances when sludges and rejects were injected into borewells on the site or buried in the top soils. Barrels and contaminated sacks and such packaging materials are left on the site. In effect, the site is deserted in a contaminated state and it continues to pollute natural resources, causing a liability to the next occupier.

In India, we do not have site assessment as a formal requirement. We do not have regulatory frameworks e.g., standards, to address the issue of contaminated lands. So when serious issues of land and water contamination get reported, the PCBs step in and act suo moto to remedy the site and recover the remediation costs from the polluter. The costs of remediation are often high and implementation takes quite some time. In-country experience on remediation is also low. Besides, identifying the 'culprit' is often difficult and one needs to use advanced techniques of environmental forensics to know whom to blame.

The website www.pollutedplaces.org provides examples of contaminated lands in India and other parts of the world. I am clipping below just one case of Hema Dyechem

Hema Dyechem Private Limited, formerly Hema Chemicals, operated a Chromium Sulphate manufacturing unit in the Gorwa Industrial Estate of Vadodara (a city about 115 kilometres south of Ahmedabad) from 1965 to 2001. Despite the enactment of the Hazardous Waste Rules in 1989, the company disposed off approximately 77,000 tons (estimated by the Gujarat Pollution Control Board or GPCB) of toxic Chromium waste around the unit. The laborers working in the factory were unaware of potential health risks, and used the Chromium-rich sludge to fill up low-lying ditches in the neighborhood. They also mixed the sludge with cement

to construct their houses and spread it across the boundaries of surrounding fields. The abandoned plant site itself covers about 15,000 square feet and is contaminated with chromate salts. The illegal dumping areas may cover as much as seven kilometres of filled trenches along the roads in the vicinity of the factory. Hema's illegal dumping at this site has spurred the largest Public Interest Litigation in Indian history. GPCB has sued the company for INR 170 million.

Instead of responding on a reactive basis it may be worth acting proactively on such issues. One possibility could be to introduce a mechanism of **consent to close** i.e. permission required from the PCB to allow closure of the business. This requirement may be restricted to only those businesses that fall in the red category, above a threshold of manufacturing or investment, or when the business activity is proximal to a sensitive natural resource or population.

Consent to close will require conducting site audits by the PCB or a PCB-accredited agency. Financing institutions and regulatory agencies (e.g. industries department or factories department) may insist on obtaining consent to close from the PCB. This requirement will help avoid dumping of wastes and residues by the industries during operations or prior to closure.

A requirement for consent to close may avoid to a great extent instances of site contamination and subsequent remediation. Perhaps the TSR Subramanian Committee set up by India's Ministry of Environment & Forests & Climate Change for reforms in Environmental Laws in India should consider this proposition.

14
Operations without Certification

Today in India, you cannot operate a boiler without a certified operator, but you can operate a wastewater treatment plant without such a certification requirement. Our regulators, the Pollution Control Boards (PCBs), do not think that it is critical to insist that operators running the wastewater treatment plants have the necessary training.

Programs for training and certification for operation of wastewater treatment plants have matured over the decades in countries such as Germany (i.e. the German Association for Water, Wastewater and Waste or DWA) and United States of America (i.e. the Water Environment Federation). In these countries, certification of operators of wastewater treatment plants is a full-fledged industry and a career for young professionals.

I do not know how many wastewater treatment plants are 'registered' or are under the scanner of PCBs in India. I don't recall any recent work done on such an inventorization on a national scale. But as a guesstimate, the number could well be close to a 100,000. And if we assume an average of 4 operators at each treatment plant, then we are talking about training and employment of 400,000 to 500,000 young professionals!!

Employment however is not the objective here. The idea is to improve compliance and professional management of the 'treatment plant' to make it worth its investment. Performance evaluations of Sewage Treatment Plans (STPs) and Common Effluent Treatment Plants (CETPs) in India have clearly concluded that sloppy operation of treatment works and absence of professional training are the principal reasons for non-compliance and not as much the faults with technology or design. Following are some of the findings of such evaluations:

- **Out of the 152 STPs, 30 STPs non-operational and performance of 28 STPs not satisfactory.** (CPCB, 2013)

- In 2005, the Central Pollution Control Board studied the performance of **78 CETPs** operating throughout the country. **Only 20 (i.e. 25.6%) complied** with the prescribed limits for general parameters pH, BOD, COD and TSS but 15 of these were not able to comply with the prescribed limit for TDS.

Who should take the lead in designing and conducting training programs for treatment plant operators? How do we make certification a requirement? These are important questions to answer.

I have been lobbying for the above steps for past 2 decades and have attempted models through PCBs, roping Industrial Training Institutions (ITIs) in India. One of the major constraints that were found was absence of trainers and involvement of industry associations.

To address these concerns, I recently launched a Training of Trainers programme with the support of DWA and GIZ, Maharashtra Pollution Control Board and CETP Company of the Thane Belapur Industries Association (TBIA). We just completed a 2-day training program for Trainers, who were Senior Chemists and Supervisors of the ETPs/CETPs in the TBIA. Another six-module training programme will be conducted for the operators, on the same lines in January 2015. The content of this training programme was developed based on a Training Needs Assessment workshop that was conducted with industries, equipment suppliers, regulators and academia. The idea is to offer these modules twice a week in the evenings over six weeks with practical sessions at ETPs/CETPs. A neighborhood concept will be used for networking, keeping CETPs as the nuclei.

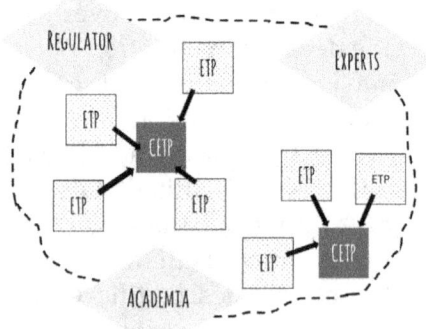

Training and certification of the treatment of operators can help bridge the gap between 'theory' and 'practice'. Today, the design guidelines in India are not based on the actual performance of the wastewater treatment plants. Again, the field data is generally limited to the final discharge point i.e. end of the pipe – and not collated and analyzed to assess the performance of individual treatment units e.g. a clarifier. For instance, we do not have design graphs that are built on actual field performance data between say overflow rate or weir loading rate to the removal of Suspended Solids and BOD. Hopefully, once a system of operator certification is introduced, we could build such a 'culture' and identify treatment plants wherein such data could be pooled. These plants, called 'research plants' could be interfaced with academia where students and faculty could work to develop design and performance equations - something really required for improving our understanding of the process and practice. Importantly, such data over national scale will lead to building benchmarks – e.g. on energy consumption– and provide guidance for optimization of costs and improving the performance.

So the advantage in introducing training and certification of operators could be multi-fold:

- **Better** compliance
- **New job** opportunities
- **Savings** in costs
- **Knowledge** creation
- Building new **partnerships**

So let us work together to achieve these objectives. I would urge you to take this as a mission at the national level.

15

Compliance with environmental standards is expected to be 100% and on 24×7 basis in most countries including India. This means that if you draw a sample at any time, the concentrations of the specified pollutant must be within the set limits or standards. If not, it becomes a case of violation or non-compliance that the regulator can act upon. Even one single default becomes a case of non-compliance.

This situation is applicable for both emission/effluents as well as for ambient environmental standards. Given this expectation, can any polluter be truly compliant? And when ambient environmental standard gets violated, how do we find the 'culprit'? And do we act in case of such a violation, against the regulator or against the regional agency responsible?

But I wonder how realistic it is to ask for 100% and 24×7 compliance in the first place. We all know that emissions and effluent streams are to be released after required treatment. The design of treatment and disposal systems is to be done such that compliance can be ensured. The treatment systems however receive variable quantities and sometimes unpredictable characteristics of 'inputs'. Even given this variability (often beyond the control of the treatment system designer and operator), 'outputs' are expected to meet

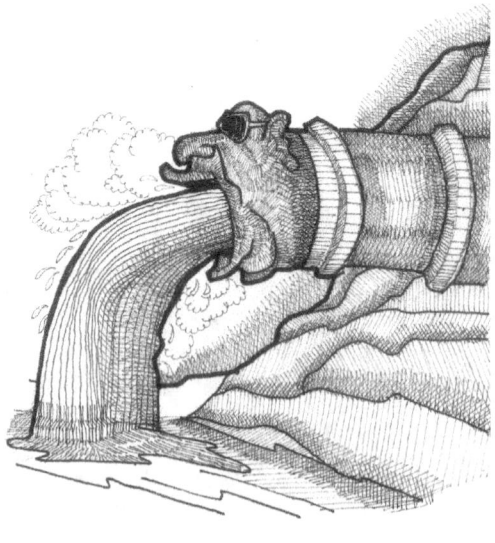

the standard, 100% of the time. Is this reasonable? And isn't this asking for too much?

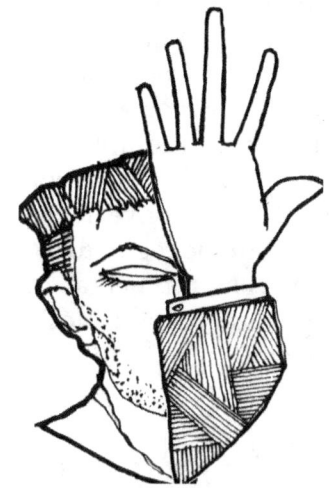

On most occasions, the regulators (e.g. Pollution Control Boards in India), use their discretion based on how frequently the emission/effluent concentrations cross the limits? To what extent is the violation? Which are the parameters and how critical are they in positing risks or causing damage to humans and ecosystems? Occasional and marginal 'defaulters' are then let go with warning and fines. This can be a subjective process. Most polluters follow this first option of negotiation with the regulator and pay fines especially when the violations or non-compliances come to light.

The second option is to 'overdesign' the treatment and disposal systems with a 'factor of safety' to handle the input variability. Most industrial effluents today are subjected to flow and load balancing and equalization tanks get added to the 'process train'. In some cases, additional treatment processes are introduced or the treatment units are oversized. This strategy of ensuring compliance however requires more capital investments.

The third option is to reduce variability of inputs at the source itself by introducing process controls and practising effluent segregation. This option is perhaps most effective and goes well in combination with option 2 stated above.

The fourth option is to frame compliance with the standard in a statistical manner. Here, we accept the fact that 24×7 compliance on 100% basis is just not possible.

For ambient air quality in India, compliance for 98% of the time is acceptable with the annual average standard[19]. To calculate the annual average, the number of samples specified is 104 i.e. two samples drawn every week **over 24 hours**. The additional condition is that

---

19 See: http://cpcb.nic.in/National_Ambient_Air_Quality_Standards.php

while 2% of samples may be non-compliant, violation of the standard cannot happen on more than two consecutive occasions.

I like this definition of compliance as it recognizes the fact that 24×7 and 100% compliance for ambient air quality is not possible. It then goes on to accept 98% compliance, defines the sample size and stipulates that more than two consecutive violations will not be acceptable in the non-compliance zone of 2%.

Unfortunately, what has been proposed for ambient air quality in India, the same has not been 'translated' to air emissions from stacks or to effluents from industries. We do not state, for example, that an effluent treatment plant at an industry will report at least 156 samples in a year (i.e. thrice a week), with samples collected on a **composite basis**. Out of the 156 samples, at least 95% of the samples must be compliant. Out of the 5% of the violations, non-compliant samples should not be consecutive or over two successive occasions.

Indeed, we need to bring such anomalies to the notice of the regulators and also the judiciaries. We have to be realistic, scientific and practical. Let us not overstate the requirements of environmental compliance. While we may pursue Options 2 and 3 stated above, let us lobby with the regulators to refine environmental compliance in a statistical framework.

You may like to the read report on Environmental Compliance and Enforcement in India: Rapid Assessment.[20]

For students – Take up a research project to review statistical or probabilistic standards – whether these are in vogue and in which countries do they exist and what has been the practical experience. Cover ambient as well as emission/effluent standards. See paper **"Some Historical Statistics Related to Future Standards"** by **Paul M. Berthouex**[21], as a source of inspiration.

20 See http://www.oecd.org/environment/outreach/37838061.pdf
21 See http://cedb.asce.org/cgi/WWWdisplay.cgi?21665

16

Most Pollution Control Boards in India are now insisting that industries meet the directive on Zero Liquid Discharge (ZLD). So is the judiciary.

The idea of ZLD is to not let polluting liquids be discharged into the environment.

ZLD is directed to industries in locations where there is no receiving water body for evacuating the effluents or the receiving water bodies are already severely polluted. We ask for ZLD here as we don't want to burden these water bodies anymore!

ZLD implies that effluents are 'contained' within the plant itself and intake of freshwater for production is minimal or near zero. Hence ZLD is often imposed on industries at locations where there is poor water availability or the neighborhood is a water-stressed area. In most cases, ZLD leads to 90-92% water recovery, which reduces input water required by industrial processes by as much as 80%.

Sometimes, ZLD is directed as a part of River Action Plans. For example, under the Clean Ganga Action Plan, industries located in the critical stretches of the river have been asked to be ZLD compliant. All effluents must be recycled to 100%. But is this the right solution? We need to ask.

Normally one would expect that for a ZLD compliant industry, no liquid discharge will emanate from its premises. So if you walked around the compound wall of the industry or viewed the industry on Google Earth then you should not ideally see any drain flowing out except the storm water drainage which cannot be intercepted. Essentially, the sewage and effluent generated at the industrial plot cannot be released if the industry wants to be ZLD compliant. Can this be achieved by deep and secured injection of effluents underground? Some industries do that. Should this be permitted?

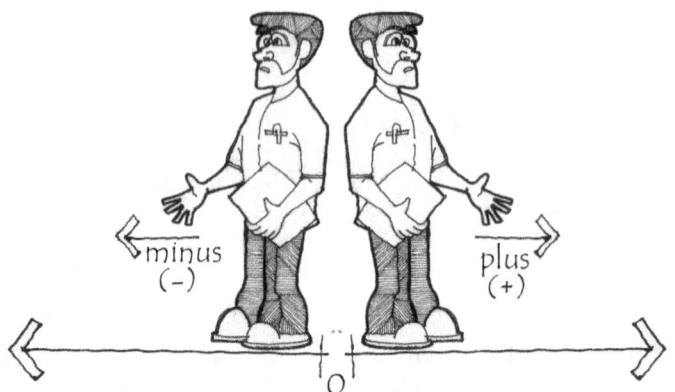

Unfortunately, there is no operational definition of what is meant by ZLD. If you know one, I will be keen to know.

I have been asking some of the industries in Gujarat about their experience with implementing ZLD systems. Most of them say that ZLD systems were very expensive to invest in and operate. Accordingly to Sustainability Outlook[22], a ZLD plant operating at 5 Million Liters per day will incur between INR 500-600 million (USD 4-5mn) in CAPEX and spend INR 15,000-25,000 (USD 250-400) as OPEX per day. Thus, the treated and recycled water costs will work out to approximately INR 200/kl, while the cost of water extraction from the ground or from the municipality would be between INR 30-60 per kiloliter. Consequently you will often see compromises being made in the material specs of the ZLD units to save capital costs. This results in problems of early corrosion, lower life of membranes etc. leading to poor performance, non-compliance and high operating costs. For ZLD, short cuts on cutting costs don't seem to work.

The technologies commonly used in ZLD systems such as Reverse Osmosis (RO) and Multiple Effect Evaporators (MEE) are the main energy guzzlers. If we accounted for the consumption of fossil fuels and air emissions arising from pumping, heating and combustion, then on a 3600 evaluation, the ZLD solutions may not be environmentally sound and in fact could lead to high carbon footprints. Further, we cannot forget the challenge of the management

22　See http://www.sustainabilityoutlook.in/content/zero-liquid-discharge-treating-effluents-resource-streammight-be-way-forward-481407

of residues (salt and sludges) – costs of residue management (destruction/transport) for a ZLD plant are exorbitantly high!

In this case, it will be interesting to carry out material and energy balance calculations for the ZLD plants. Such evaluations, I am sure must, have been done by industries internally but there is a need for these assessments to be conducted in the style of environmental accounting following a life cycle framework.

These independent assessments should ideally be sponsored by the Pollution Control Boards with outcomes discussed with industries in workshops. Indeed, there is a need to demystify the 'good and ugly' part of the ZLD solutions[23].

Whether ZLD is applicable and relevant for Small and Medium Enterprises (SMEs) is a question. While on individual basis, ZLD for an SME may be almost impossible to achieve, but on a collective basis, SMEs could achieve ZLD. ZLD at the Common Effluent Treatment Plants (CETPs) of Tirupur in Tamil Nadu is an example where effluents are recycled from the CETP back to the member SMEs.

To develop an economical ZLD solution, key strategies are– segregation, chemical/material substitution, process optimization/change for reduction in effluent loads, followed by selective reuse, recycling and recovery operations. It's the 'systems approach' that is needed. If implemented in the right spirit and rigor, an imposition of ZLD could trigger cleaner production opportunities for the industry resulting into profitability and proactive compliance. In all of the above, the choice of technology (in process in particular) and economics (especially on chemical and water recovery) plays an important role.

Innovations are possible through ZLD. But then these possibilities are not commonly observed and reported across industries for the purpose of guidance and inspiration. ZLD is often limited as an add-on or a 'tertiary' treatment unit. This perception must change as 'end of pipe' driven ZLD systems are often seen as

---

23 You may want to read the article by Rajakumari, S.P. / Kanmani, S. titled Environmental life cycle assessment of zero liquid discharge treatment technologies for textile industries, Tirupur – A case study in Journal of Scientific and Industrial Research; 67, 6; 461-467

economically unviable over the long run. Unfortunately, most ZLD solution providers focus on the end of pipe approach and so does the industry. Process optimization and process changes followed by recovery & recycling should be the focus of ZLD systems.

Many a times, we see that the economics of ZLD is not favorable because of the use of certain 'dirty' processes and chemicals (salts) and because of the 'scale' on which the industry operates. If ZLD is imposed on such industries then the industries would rather shut down instead of attempting implementation of ZLD. When backed by the judiciary, such closures do happen. Some argue that in this process, we achieve the goal of 'ecological modernization' to benefit the environment over the long term with the negative of loss of jobs to the workers! So there is something to gain (positive) and something to lose (negative)

Should a central financing scheme be put in place for implementation of ZLD plants is therefore a question to ponder over. And should such a scheme have components of grants and subsidized loans, especially for SMEs? But will this not go against the 'polluter pays' principle?

We badly need a national workshop on ZLD to get all key stakeholders involved. We do see conferences where the focus is ZLD technologies but the policy, economics and the total cost (environmental) accounting perspective are rarely discussed. We need to know whether in achieving the 'zero' in the ZLD, we are creating something negative or positive for the industry, environment and the society.

minus
(−)

17

Change the Lens
and the Climate will Change

World leaders are meeting this week in Paris (COP21) to discuss and agree on collective actions to be taken to combat Climate Change. I don't know whether the 10^0C weather in Paris is going to be conducive to the discussions on the 2^0C plus issue, especially to the warm and warming country like India

The UN Environment Programme (UNEP) published a report showing that global emissions levels should not exceed 48 gigatonnes (GT) of carbon dioxide equivalent by 2025, and 42 GT by 2030 to avoid crossing the change of 2^0C on average above pre-industrial temperatures. The 2^0C threshold is regarded by scientists as the limit of safety, beyond which the ravages of climate change – such as droughts, floods, heat waves and sea level rise – are likely to become catastrophic and irreversible.

Think about rise in our body temperature by 2^0C – isn't it enough to feel feverish? So for the planet earth a 2^0C rise is like an influenza hit by viral infection that may not be easy to handle through conventional medications such as a *Crocin* or *Metacin*. Perhaps even antibiotics may not work!

One of the medicines to combat the 'Planet Carbon Fever' is taking pledges, known as Intended Nationally Determined Contributions (INDCs). INDCs are likely to lead to emissions of 53 to 58 GT of carbon dioxide equivalent in 2025, and between 54 and 59 GT in 2030. The task in Paris will be

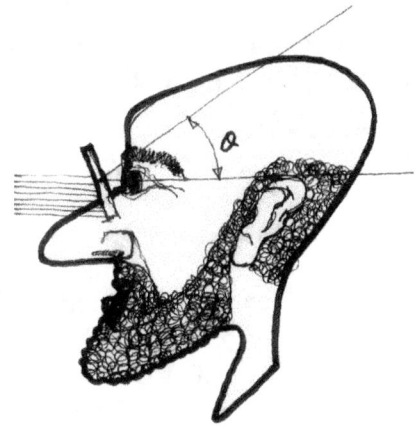

to convert these INDCs into harder commitments. Idea is to get the 2030 projected aggregate to 50 billion tonnes or lower, and then set the world on a trajectory to net zero carbon emissions by 2100.

Afforestation has been one of the commonly expressed commitments across the INDCs. The Intergovernmental Panel on Climate Change (IPCC) estimates that sequestration through afforestation would require up to twice the landmass of Africa to stay below 2^0C. That is just not possible. We therefore need multiple interventions. The National Governments will have to go much further in their pledges to limit future carbon dioxide emissions.

But the root, we all know, is overconsumption and that is more about a self-pledge and not about INDC.

I wonder how much will the carbon footprint be of the Paris COP21 itself. I am sure someone not attending the meeting is calculating!

I don't particularly like the term INDC as it is difficult to pronounce. It is even more difficult to remember its expansion. And the terms 'intended' and 'determined' are complex to comprehend and communicate to a lay person

Clearly, the INDCs will require regular re-appraisals, probably every five years, to know the progress. This would be a new departure, as the history of UN-brokered deals on climate change to date has been a stop-start process, with major conferences – such as Kyoto in 1997 and Copenhagen in 2009. The GHG accounting business will certainly flourish if not the actions.

You should carefully read India's submission of INDC. It's a 38-page report that outlines projects, programs and policy measures that India intends to im-plement along with climate-related financing. While all key aspects such as renewable energy, energy efficiency, green infrastructure, sustainable mobility, smart cities and climate finance are detailed, the section on pollution abatement is rather poor and not stated in context. It appears a bit out-of-place showing the weakness of Environment Ministry as against other Ministries, especially the Ministry of Power. You will also see that most actions proposed are 'obvious' or already committed or initiated in the country, independent of the call on climate change. The drivers for these actions are economic, taking into account the status of national and world resources, addressing poor infrastructure (transport, energy and infrastructure in cities) and political priorities. Our climate change related commitments are thus essentially like old wine in new bottle! INDCs of other countries also follow the same pattern. But that's not necessarily a bad thing assuming that a 'laundry list' of interventions will now get integrated and will be operated in a mission mode.

We must not forget that business has been and will be influencing the national governments during the negotiations. Nexus between energy, socio-economic development and climate change is rather complex and business is bound to play a rather slippery and changing role. One does see therefore that most of the intentions expressed by business are cosmetic commitments. The oil industry for instance is emphasizing that natural gas – fracked or otherwise – is the future of clean energy, despite evidence showing that methane leakage during the extraction process can cause more damage to the atmosphere than coal. ExxonMobil has put an internal price on carbon,

between $60 and $80 a tonne but they're still investing in the use of fossil fuels. Response from multinational business houses is going to be like a chameleon changing colors, given the unevenness in the INDC and the skewed geopolitical context. I agree that I sound rather skeptical here.

The business implications of climate change have reached the level of grass-root farmers. The Global Alliance for Climate Smart Agriculture in Paris for instance is supposed to help small farmers adapt to climate change while reducing emissions. The Alliance has defined 'climate smart agriculture' to add a new green tint to business as usual, promoting the same practices that have led to deforestation, land grabs, biodiversity loss and soaring emissions. The Alliance seems to be hijacked however, by synthetic fertilizer companies like Yara and Monsanto. More than 350 civil society groups are calling on COP21 to reject the concept and the Alliance, labelling it 'green-washed false solutions'.

So the COP21 in Paris is not just a discussion between the political leaders of governments but a complex maze of hidden forces triggered by the business of the powerful, mighty NGOs and researchers/academicians who often provide conflicting information.

There is a lot for the business to win and lose due to actions on climate change. The renewable energy sector will particularly be on the rise and pressure on fossil fuel based energy generation is expected to increase closer to 2030. Investors are showing their preferences too, especially towards renewable energy.

Innovation to address climate change is a hope. Here we will see emergence of special funds and long-term partnerships being struck between the academia and the industry in the form of business models. In India we have more than 40 research parks today but none of these parks are looking at producing low-carbon materials, goods/products and services, with combating Climate Change as the umbrella theme. We will certainly need to work on capitalizing innovation while meeting the emission reduction targets. Make in India is therefore very relevant and critical.

I spoke to my Professor friend about my concerns and observations and asked him whether he was attending the COP21 on behalf of the Government of India. He said

indeed he is but this time he has a major role to play as he has been appointed by the UNFCC. I was excited to know more, so we met at our usual coffee shop.

"First of all, on the logistics front," said the Professor. "All COP21 participants will be

staying at hotels with lowest carbon footprints. These hotels have been identified through the application of a comprehensive software application provided by the World Resources Institute followed by site visits conducted by KPMG. To prepare for the event, all staff at these hotels are given an orientation program on Climate Change by Winrock International so that they can understand and converse with the participants in the 'carbon language'. The hotel menus have been decarbonized (low-carb diet essentially) by experts from the FAO. All participants will use public transport. Taxi drivers have been instructed not to take any participants to the conference venue. The idea is to lower the carbon footprint of the event to the extent possible. These are all my ideas," the Professor paused to light his cigar.

"Oh, you are really looking at the details," I said.

There are many such details that I have worked on as regards the venue, but I would rather tell you about the major step that we have taken. It's a secret that will guarantee success in the negotiations – of course all in the interest of this planet.

The Professor was now speaking in a serious tone. So I asked for a second round of coffee.

"One of the major reasons for conflicts and arguments at such meetings is the lack of common vision. Further some leaders are either short-sighted and remain so – causing an obstacle to the long-term thinking and understanding of climate change. Some leaders have a blurred vision and some have color blindness so what they often see is not real! Their suggestions and arguments remain irrelevant.

To correct this situation, we have opened a state-of-the-art eye clinic at the COP21 venue right at the registration counter. Services of the clinic are free and those who use these services will get a free pass to some of the best cabarets in Paris such as Lido, Crazy Horse etc. This is an added attraction.

(I started imagining Lido full of climate-sensitive people attending the second show.)

The Professor continued:

"In the clinic, we will examine the eyes of every participant, see his/her nationality and INDC and provide or change the lenses to correct his/her vision. Visions of all participants with myopia (shortsightedness) will be corrected with appropriate lenses. Participants who wear trifocals or bifocals will be given a progressive lens. Progressive lenses have a smooth progression of power, enabling the wearer to see at intermediate distances as well as near and far. We expect that after changing the lens the participants will take progressive steps towards implementation of their INDCs. Essentially, these participants will take a balanced position for 2030, 2050 and 2100 scenarios and not just focus on 2030.

For business honchos, we will be offering photochromic lenses that automatically darken when exposed to sunlight, eliminating the need for separate sunglasses. Using these lenses, the business tycoons will be able to manage their transition to different geographies, while meeting their personal or business pursuits.

I suspect most influential NGOs are color blind so I will be providing them Enchroma Red-Green lenses.

For economies in transition, I have proposed polarized lenses with anti-reflective coating or blue light protection that reduces glare reflected off surfaces, making images appear sharper and clearer. Participants from transitional economies often suffer from a blurred vision due to astigmatism.

For troubled economies, I have recommended polycarbonate lenses that are resilient and impact-resistant. These leaders need such a lens as they are really on a roller coaster of internal conflicts and wars that are unnecessary.

Then there will be an eye surgery unit that will fix problems of Presbyopia (age-related long sight), Cataracts and Glaucoma. Again no charges will be levied and the vision will be restored or corrected.

This is wonderful Professor. I said "by changing the lens and restoring the vision of the participants to what it should be, you will certainly influence the outcome of COP21."

"Keep this a secret," the Professor extinguished his cigar and said.

"Well, so far so good. I wanted however, your advice. What lenses should I recommend for Prime Minister Narendra Modi and Environment Minister Prakash Javadekar?"

I decided to settle the bill as perhaps this was an easier option than answering the question.

18
ODD VS EVEN

You would not believe that the numbers we use or are assigned to – in many ways, control our lives.

For instance, when I bought my car last year with a number plate DL 8453 little did I know its implications. According to the recently adopted odd-even number policy, I could now drive in Delhi only on Mondays, Wednesdays and Fridays. For me Tuesdays, Thursdays and Saturdays will not be the days to drive as my license number plate ends with in odd number. Only even numbered vehicles will be allowed to ply on Tuesdays, Thursdays and Saturdays. This policy of alternateday driving will be effective from January 01, 2016 in Delhi. A new year of behavior change, will begin.

[As soon as I learnt about this policy, I decided to change my number plate to 'even'. Saturday is a holiday for me and I would like to drive and take my family out, shop in the city malls or visit friends. I am sure most of us would like to do so. I spoke to my agent about finding a way out with the RTO. The agent said that there is quite a rush and I will have to be in a queue for the next six months. For new cars, getting an even numbered license plate will now be at the premium]

The city's vehicular population, which causes choking air pollution and traffic jams, includes about 2.7 million cars. The new odd-even policy will apply to a large bulk of nearly nine million vehicles registered in Delhi, which adds about 1,500 new vehicles to its roads every day. Last year, the World Health Organization (WHO) named the Indian capital as the world's most polluted, with 12 other Indian cities ranking among the worst 20.

In November and early December, Delhi's air quality slumps to alarming levels, with concentration of $PM_{2.5}$ (very fine particles that get lodged inside the lungs and cause the most damage), soaring to 12 times above WHO's safety levels of 25 micrograms per cubic meter.

The city gets a blanket of grey thick smog that lingers till the morning and evening hours. While there is no reliable data on respiratory diseases, most doctors in the capital report a sharp spike in pollution-related illness during the winter months.

The policy of alternate-day driving is called 'road rationing'. There are many variants of road rationing possible. Road rationing could be for all the days or only for one or two days a week or only during peak traffic hours of the day. Further, road rationing may be applicable for the whole country, a city or for a zone in the city.

Road space rationing based on license numbers has been implemented in cities such as Athens (1982), Santiago, Chile (1986 and extended 2001), México City (1989), Metro Manila (1995), São Paulo (1997), Bogotá, Colombia (1998), La Paz, Bolivia (2003), San José, Costa Rica, (2005) countrywide in Honduras (2008), and Quito, Ecuador (2010). More recent implementations in Costa Rica and Honduras had the

objective of reducing oil consumption, due to the high impact the import was having on their economies. Issue of air pollution was not the driver.

The Paris Story

On March 17, 2014, a partial driving restriction was imposed in Paris and its inner suburbs based on license plate numbers. The measure was issued by the city government in order to mitigate a peak in air pollution, caused by Particulate Matter (PM_{10}) attributable to vehicle emissions. Cars with even-numbered license plates and commercial vehicles over 3.5 tons were banned from entering the city from 5:30 a.m. till midnight. Electric and hybrid cars, natural gas-powered vehicles and carpools with three or more passengers were exempted.

Another peak in air pollution affected Paris and Northern France in mid-March 2015. The Mayor of Paris, Anne Hidalgo, requested the central government to implement a driving restriction to mitigate the problem. The pollution index in Paris was at 93 micrograms per cubic meter (mcg/m^3) on Friday 20, 2015, due to increased amounts of pollutant PM_{10}. The accepted limit for PM_{10} was set at 50 mcg/m^3, and the safe limit or alert threshold was set at 80 mcg/m^3 As the pollution episode continued on Saturday, 21 according to Airparif measurements, the central government imposed a driving restriction on Monday, 23 affecting cars with even-numbered license plates and commercial vehicles over 3.5 tons. As in the 2014 episode, complementary measures were implemented including reduced speed limits in the city, free public transportation, free residential parking, and free short-term use for subscribers of bike and carsharing services. The restriction was implemented in Paris and the 22 towns located in the administrative region of Île-de-France.

In Beijing

On July 20, 2008, Beijing implemented temporary road space rationing based on plate numbers in order to significantly improve air quality in the city during the 2008 Summer Olympics. Enforcement was carried out through an automated traffic surveillance network. The rationing was in effect for two months, between July 20 to September 20, as the Olympics were followed by the Paralympics from September 6 until 17. The restrictions on car use were implemented on alternate days depending on the plates ending in odd or even numbers. This measure was expected to take 45% of the 3.3 million car fleet off the streets. In addition, 300,000 heavy polluting vehicles were

banned from July 1, and the measure also prohibited access to most vehicles coming from outside Beijing. Authorities decided to compensate car owners for the inconvenience by exempting them from payment of vehicle taxes for three months. A pilot test was conducted in August 2007 for four days, restricting driving for a third of Beijing's fleet - some 1.3 million vehicles. A 40% daily reduction of vehicle emissions was reported. A previous test carried out in November 2006 during the Sino-African Summit showed reductions of 40% in NOx auto emissions.

In the Delhi case, the odd and even number based driving will not apply to ambulances and other vehicles used for essentials and maintenance of law and order. (Perhaps, these vehicles should be issued number plates ending with zero). Exemptions will not be made for VIP vehicles. Perhaps, VIPs will be permitted to have two vehicles

– one with odd and other with even number plate.

The odd-even policy in Delhi is expected to hit carpooling communities as now they will have to ensure that the pool includes both odd-number and even-number plate holders so that the transportation continues to happen. So there will have to be new conversations. There seems to be no special policy for exempting the carpooling community as done in Paris

Those car owners who hire drivers will probably cut down their salaries to half as driving will happen now only for 3 days in a week. This will lead to loss in the income of the city's driver community and protests will be expected. Some believe that this will lead to driver sharing models – i.e. a driver will work for one odd number plate owner and one even number plate owner. In the process, there will be savings at the owners end. Private taxi operators like Uber and Ola will look at the odd-even policy perhaps as an opportunity. But many feel that this policy will encourage people to own two vehicles – one with odd and one with even number plate. This will be good news for the car makers and not-so-good for the housing societies where car parking is already an issue. It has also been suggested that Delhi makes the use of the Metro free. This will greatly reduce vehicles on the road and the resulting air emissions. The health damage reduced i.e. savings to the citizens will be much more than the loss to the Metro in this process! It will be an interesting exercise for the environmental economists. Indeed, the odd-even policy will lead to a major socio-economic impact that will need to be carefully studied.

I got a call from my Professor friend who is advising the Delhi Government on such matters

"What is your house number?" he asked

When I told him, it is A-7, Munirka – he said "Well Prasad – be prepared now for the next move. The odd-even number policy will soon be expanded to schedule water supply to the flat or a house. Odd-numbered houses will receive water only on Mondays, Wednesdays and Fridays and those with even numbers will get water only on Tuesdays, Thursdays and Saturdays. If you are looking forward to take a tub bath on Saturday morning for example, then better change your house or house number to even – right now! The idea of water rationing on this basis is devised to help meet the ever-increasing water demand of the city".

I told the Professor that in most cities in India water is supplied on alternate days anyways, irrespective of the odd-even policy. But the Professor was in no mood to listen.

I however realized the seriousness of being the 'odd' person out. So I thought of checking 'all my numbers' that define my assets and existence. I decided that I change to 'even' numbers on a mission mode. You never know when the Kejriwal Government will come up with rules such as "You cannot dial out on Mondays, Wednesdays and Fridays from mobile phones that end in an odd number, or you cannot transact credit cards ending in an odd number on Mondays, Wednesdays and Fridays!!" On checking out, I found that in most of the times I was at 'odds'. That was worrisome.

While fervently checking the status of my numbers, a thought came to my mind – Mondays to Saturdays is fine as a split based on odd-even

counts – but what happens to the Sunday? Who can drive and who cannot? And no one is talking about that!

I called up the Professor. He said "Good question – ask Chief Minister Kejriwal"

Visit India Today's website[24] to read more on Delhi's efforts to curb air pollution.

24 See http://indiatoday.intoday.in/story/odd-even-number-vehicles-to-ply-in-delhi-on-alternate-days/1/538688.html

19

The other day, I went across to see Member Secretary of the Maharashtra State Pollution Control Board (SPCB) in Mumbai. The Board entrance looked different. The Board now carried a new title 'The Supreme Pollution Control Board of Maharashtra'. I was surprised to see the change.

When I saw the Member Secretary, he said that such a change has been done all across the country. All SPCBs are now SPCBs with 'S' as Supreme.

I knew my Professor friend must have had a contribution in this change. After all, he is the Secret Advisor (SA) to Minister Prakash Javadekar. I called him up and we went to our usual coffee shop.

"Prasad," the Professor said. "You have to realize that today environmental governance in this country is driven more by the Judiciary and less by institutions like the Pollution Control Boards (PCBs). There have been

serious lapses regarding timely and comprehensive monitoring and enforcement at the end of PCBs. This has caused significant environmental damage and with no environmental justice done especially to those affected. The polluters, which include not just industries but also municipalities, are not behaving responsibly. So those affected are moving to courts and filing petitions, demanding justice. The courts seem to be responding faster than the PCBs. They are not just giving directions but the special courts like the National Green Tribunal (NGT) are pulling up the PCBs for lax performance"

I said "So we seem to have two parallel 'regulators' so to say. One regulator like PCB who is supposed to act – but does not seem to be doing so; and the second i.e. judiciary who is not supposed to be the regulator, acts."

"Precisely the reason", the Professor lighted his cigar. "I therefore advised the Minister to appoint retired judges and lawyers as Chairmen and Member Secretaries of the PCBs and change the name. This will reduce the load on the Judiciary as these retired judges will probably behave as if they are still acting! "

The role of the Indian Supreme Court may be explained quoting the views of Professor S.P. Sathe and Professor Upendra Baxi, two leading academics who have extensively written on the role of judiciary in India. Professor Sathe has analyzed the transformation of the Indian Supreme Court 'from a positivist court into an activist

court'. Professor Upendra Baxi, who has often supported judicial activism in India, has also said that the 'Supreme Court of India' has become the 'Supreme Court for Indians'. Many observers of the Indian Supreme Court including Professor Sathe and Baxi have rightly opined that the Indian Supreme Court is one of the strongest courts of the world. (Taken from Principles of International Environmental Law and Judicial Response in India, Shailendra Kumar Gupta, Sr. Lecturer, Faculty of Law, B.H.U., Varanasi, India[25])

"It's not just the change in the name - I have also introduced key changes in the organization," the Professor continued. All PCB staff will now wear a 'lawyer-like dress' to bring in a courtroom like atmosphere. The industry representatives when visiting the 'S'PCB office will now shudder to see a lawyer-like environmental scientist or engineer and the gravity and seriousness of the situation will register itself. All PCB staff will be

25 See http://www.bhu.ac.in/lawfaculty/blj2006-072008-09/BLJ_2007/11_Dr.%20S.K.%20
Gupta%20-Artical%20on%20Int '1%20Envt'1%20_Law_Corrected_on.doc

trained on environmental law and speak in a 'complex' language like lawyers do and use phrases like 'notwithstanding, not limited to' etc… "Do you know that most technical staff of the PCBs are not trained adequately in environmental law which they are expected to implement!"

"That's quite shocking, Professor," I said. "But what about the retired judges? How will they handle environmental matters, especially the technical details?"

"Oh, I have already thought of this. For the Member Secretary (MS) there will be a Technical Secretary (TS) on of the same lines as the NGT. The NGT has Expert Members who provide technical support. For the 'S' PCBs, TS will be the expert and will discharge in a similar function."

"But still, I have asked the MS and Chairmen to undergo a basic course on Environmental Management," the Professor continued. "These retired judges will be exposed to new and balanced management strategies apart from the usual directions such as closure, phase outs and compensations that they are accustomed to give. This training course will also cover understanding of

the basic technical terms i.e. BOD is *Biochemical Oxygen Demand* and not *Board of Directors* etc."

"Surely you are joking Professor. Everyone in the country today knows what BOD is, thanks to the widely-known failure of the Ganga Action Plan," I said. The Professor did not like my comment.

But your point on compensation brings me to a question that often remains unanswered, I continued.

"How does one decide on arriving at the fines or economic evaluation of the damage caused due to unchecked pollution? And how does one apportion the compensation when multiple polluters are involved? Do you see a need for MoEFCC or CPCB to establish a national framework to assess the damage (i.e. cost of inaction)? Often damage assessment is carried out on an ad-hoc basis or based on shakey assumptions and the results are not realistic or consistent. Further, the basis of calculations is often not shared with stakeholders to ensure agreement as well as transparency"

"The important point is," the Professor said lighting his second cigar. "Scientific

damage assessment is very important and relevant to our case, as in India we tend to let the damage happen first and then approach the Judiciary for environmental justice. Preventive approaches are only talked about in seminars and rarely practiced. I am therefore thinking of adding a position of Environmental Economist at the 'S'PCBs."

"You are very thoughtful professor," I said. "Why don't you create such a position at the NGT itself?"

Hmmm said the Professor.

"Please add a position of Social Scientist too," I pleaded. "What is environment without a social dimension?"

"On the NGT," I added, "I just came across an interesting statistic on the performance of NGT in India. See the paper *National Green Tribunal and Environmental Justice in India* by Swapan Kumar Patra and V Krishna[26]. This paper presents analyses of data from the NGT website. It reports that number of cases judged by NGT have increased from 37 (May-December 2011) to 97 (July-December, 2013) totaling 318 judgments. Out of these, 50% of the judgments came from 4 States alone – Tamil Nadu, Assam, Maharashtra and Karnataka. States with development projects on hydropower and minerals strangely are in the middle. A large number of judgments have been given related to Coastal Regulatory Zone (CRZ)."

"Interesting statistics," the Professor said. "We should use such studies to produce a 'Heat Map' for India. The FDI in these states may get influenced if such statistics are revealed on a quarterly basis. Who would like to get into a 'hot potato' situation? Simply avoid these four states."

"You are right Professor," "I think we should ask the new 'S'PCBs to report not just the consents filed or approved, but also the *consents rejected*. This number is surely going to increase with this 'S' transformation. It will further warm up the heat map you are contemplating," I said in closing, while settling the bill.

The Professor smiled.

26 See http://www.niscair.res.in/jinfo/ijms/ijms-forthcoming-articles/IJMS-PR-April%20 2015/MS%202615%20Edited.pdf

I would highly recommend the paper by Mahajan Niyati, Graduate School of Social Sciences, Waseda University, Tokyo, JAPAN captioned *Judicial Activism for Environment Protection in India.* Available online at: www. isca.in. I have quoted the observations he made in his abstract below:

"The Supreme Court and High Court have worked from case to case for making environment as a fundamental right and then extending its meaning to right for compensation, clean water and air. The closure of limestone quarries in UP, halting of polluting tanneries along the Ganges river, the introduction of the principle of Absolute Liability for hazardous firms are some of the landmark decisions. In response to the court's order different rules and policy changes have been developed such as CNG Policy in Delhi, Municipal Solid Waste (Management and Handling) Rules and Karnataka Municipal (Amendment) Act. However, the effectiveness of judicial activism in bringing about the social transformation is questionable. Although, the judiciary is able to form some strong foundation for environmental protection, but the developments brought about by judicial activism have been proven insufficient to bring satisfactory outcomes."

20
Left vs. Right?

Environmental enforcement of industrial clusters in India is a daunting task for regulators. The clusters consist of micro-small-medium enterprises (MSMEs) who do not have adequate technical capacity, capital and space to install individual pollution control plants. Consequently, common solutions are sought where a pollution control plant for the entire cluster is established and operated. Industries collect effluents and send them for treatment and disposal to this common plant after some pre-treatment.

The concept of Common Effluent Treatment Plants (CETPs) for industrial clusters emerged in early 1977. Professor Nilay Choudhuri, the then Chairman of Central Pollution Control Board (CPCB) produced a landmark publication 'Industrial Estate Planning' after a consultative workshop. I still have a copy of the workshop proceedings. This publication is a must-read.

A scheme to finance CETPs was launched under the Central Loan Scheme. Later, between 1991-1999, the Scheme was supported by the World Bank under the credits lines – Industrial Pollution Control and Industrial Pollution Prevention & Control. Today, nearly 200 CETPs operate in India. These CETPs are owned by companies formed by the member MSMEs who employ or contract operational staff and collect effluent charges based on a formula.

Independent assessments have shown that on an overall basis, the performance of CETPs has not been satisfactory.

The reasons have been several – lack of interest or commitment, technical difficulties in treating complex and variable effluents, unreasonable effluent standards (such as Total Dissolved Solids – (TDS) etc. This has led to public interest litigations and subsequent intervention by the judiciary. In the last two decades, cases of en *masse* closures have taken place under court directives especially in the states of Gujarat and Tamil Nadu. Negligence on environmental matters has thus led to significant economic (business) and social impacts (employment).

I met the Chief Secretary (CS) of one the troubled states where industrial clusters, CETP and judicial intervention had become a serious political issue. We were having dinner. The CS said that it is important that the Chief Minister (CM) of the State is briefed in a 360^0 perspective to get a 'balanced' view on what should be done to address this problem. He asked me if I could give a presentation to the CM on my own assessment of one of the prominent industrial clusters. I generally avoid meeting with politicians but couldn't resist the CS's invite as the CM of the state was known to be one of the sharpest state rulers.

The CS asked me to come one day early, as he wanted to review my slides. When we met in a hotel, he seemed a bit worried. "Dr. Modak, I am not really sure how the tone of your presentation should be. I have been informed that the CM may be having a stake in one of the prominent industrial units in the cluster. So going too hard on the industries may not work and the CM may not like this approach. On the other hand, we have been also informed that the CM wants to show firmness and decisiveness towards environmental matters. *En masse* closure of industries was one way to demonstrate this intent".

"What do you expect from me then?" I asked. I was not comfortable with this complex situation.

I suggest you make two sets of presentations – the CS said. One set will 'defend' the industries and come up with recommendations that will provide them some time, some concessions and technical guidance to reach the desired level of compliance. The second presentation set will present a case that is 'hopeless' and recommend strict punitive actions and even a mass closure if required.

You should start your

presentation using the second set first. I will watch how the CM is reacting. If I see the CM perturbed then I will pass you a chit suggesting you need to switch the presentation. But you will have to do this rather smoothly.

I thought this was going to be challenging but it looked like there was no other option. I wished I was a theater actor.

In those days, we did not use PowerPoint projections. I had a stack of plastic foils or transparencies. I reviewed my slides, added more and split the presentation into two – giving two different points of view. This needed late-night work with a strong South Indian coffee. By 2 am, I had two stacks of slides – one comforting the industries while recognizing that non-compliance was a serious matter (stack A) and the other recommending strong punitive action to show the might of the state (stack B). I decided to put the slide deck B on the 'left' slide of the overhead projector (OHP) and deck A on the 'right'.

When I reached the office of the CM in the morning, the CS was waiting for me. He had organized a trolley with an OHP. "Where your two slide are stacks?" he asked in anguish. "The CM is very busy today and as soon as the red light outside the door turns green, we will enter the room with this trolley and immediately start the presentation. The CM hates wasting time on preliminaries. The Finance and Environment Secretaries are already inside discussing other matters.

I was tense.

As soon as the red light turned green, we rushed inside. I was introduced. The CM spoke to me in Tamil (the State language). I being a *Marathi*, did not understand a single bit of what was said. When he realized that I don't speak or understand Tamil, the CM asked the CS why someone from State of Maharashtra was called to advice. Wasn't there a competent expert available in our state? This conversation took place in Tamil.

I was told later that the CM was really upset and had told the CS to simply pack me off and stop the presentation. "Next time the gentleman should come here to present in Tamil (i.e. he should learn Tamil) or else get me someone else from the State," the CM scorned. The CS had somehow managed the situation by pleading my case and saying that now that I was there ….

In the bargain, my presentation time was reduced

from 20 minutes to 15 minutes!

I had set up the two slide packs A and B on the left and right of the OHP. The presentation began from the 'left'. I was going hard on the industries, the non-compliance, environmental, health and economic damage etc. I showed some statistics and maps. The CS was watching CM's face. I could sense some level of discomfort on his already-agitated face.

And as expected, a small chit came to me from the CS after 5 minutes indicating the need for the switch. I paused and picked up the

transparency from the 'right' side of the OHP now. I said "The situation is grim – however enforcement alone is not going to work. Closing of the industries is not the solution. You need to support and catalyze ecological modernization of the MSMEs"

I picked up the next "right" transparency. I spoke about carrot and stick approaches, market instruments and experiences from other countries.

We need to set up demonstration projects using cleaner technologies where we reduce pollution loads at the source itself rather than following conventional end-of-the-pipe approach. If TDS is the issue, then the solution is not to rely only on the Reverse Osmosis (RO) plants or Multiple Effect Evaporators (MEE). These solutions are both capital and energy intensive. Substitution or minimization of use of salt in the manufacturing processes itself, along with recovery, could be the way out. **"What we need is a strategic approach that blends compliance with competitiveness"**

My last punchline seemed to have pleased the CM. I saw that increasing attention was given to my later slides. The presentation ended exactly in 15 minutes. The CM looked happy and so did the CS.

As we left the room, the Personal Secretary (PS) to the CM came rushing to me. "Good presentation, Sir. Thank you. Only one request from the CM. The CM wants copies of both the slide decks – the one on the left as well as on the right."

My mouth turned dry. I looked at the PS and CS helplessly.

While handing over both the decks to the PS, I realized why this person was the CM of the State and indeed deserved to be! No details were missed despite my attempt at a smooth transition.

I asked the CS to book me on the next flight out of the State. (The other option was to learn Tamil in Mumbai in one of the *Idli* lanes of Matunga)

But fundamentally, left vs. right was the issue. And the issue still remains.

I very much cherish this experience.

21

MORE THAN 2%

I was researching India's recent enactment on Corporate Social Responsibility (CSR). I found that there were mixed views. Some opined that the very concept of CSR is controversial as it is fundamentally an aspirational exercise, and it is very difficult to legislate aspirations. Some however believed that making CSR mandatory was a good step to ensure that business behaved responsibly, contributed to the interest of society and complemented the government's efforts by channeling part of its profits.

India is taking pride in the fact that it is the first country in the world to have made CSR mandatory. The question to ask is why other countries have not done so? There must be good reasons. In fact, India is actually not the first country mandating CSR. Attempts have been made in Indonesia, as early as in 2007, and not been so effective because of ambiguities, poor guidance and involvement of overlapping agencies. (See Manager's Perspective on Corporate Social Responsibility: A Case in Indonesia, Kartika Dewi Sri Susilowati, World Journal of Social Sciences, Vol. 4. No. 1. March 2014 Issue. Pp. 207 – 223[27])

The new Companies Act of India requires companies above a certain size to ensure that they spend at least 2 percent of annual profits on CSR activities. (Why 2%? Perhaps, the Ministry of Corporate Affairs wanted to follow the magic figure of Income Tax surcharge levied on the rich income bracket of India) Some precedence!

In many ways, this 2% imposition is kind of a 'cheeky' way to increase corporate tax. The corporate tax rate in India is 32.45 percent—already one of the

---

27 See http://www.wjsspapers.com/static/documents/March/2014/16.%20Kartika.pdf

highest, compared to the global average of 24%. The Income Tax Act does not yet allow CSR spending as a deduction from profit.

Estimates have been made regarding how the CSR requirement will translate into spending. Around INR 270 billion per year are estimated to be spent as CSR by India Inc. Just to compare – the annual budget of the Ministry of Environment is close to 17 billion and the budget for Ministry of Social Justice and Empowerment is INR 70 billion. So, the estimated CSR spend is a whopping three times more than the combined budgets of the two relevant Ministries. It is expected that India Inc. will deploy their organizational and managerial capacity to play a significant role in activities where government has failed to deliver. That is the hope.

Of course, it is not easy to spend the money as projects that qualify for CSR are often difficult to identify. Further, companies are required to engage not-for-profit agencies (NGOs) that are competent – a combination that is often not easy to find! The NGO community in India is indeed not yet ready to help companies deliver

CSR projects in the required time and quality. That is a constraint.

The Indian Institute of Corporate Affairs (IICA) has launched training and capacity building activities with support from several reputed training institutions in the country. According to Dr. Bhaskar Chatterjee, Director General of IICA, some 30,000 professionals need to be trained. By July, IICA was able to train only 200. Clearly these efforts need to be substantially scaled up and a market needs to be created. The course fees of the training courses are high.

The CSR mandate under India's Company's act is rather project-oriented, more an accounting and reporting exercise than a strategic approach.

It is also averse to linking CSR with the creation of shareholder value. Many activities that companies undertake are both profitable and good for society. Companies undertake these activities regardless of the law, since they are profitable activities. According to Dr. Chatterjee[28] however, "CSR must have an altruistic motive and not end up making profits

---

28 See http://www.indiacsr.in/en/report-on-what-qualifies-as-csr-and-what-does-not/

for the company"

Would making a profitable investment in an energy-efficient operation qualify as 'ensuring environmental sustainability,' even if the firm made that investment on purely financial grounds? What about working with social enterprises where innovations, replications, up-scaling are good possibilities for creating entrepreneurship, employment and investment flows? The law however says a company can undertake its CSR activities only through a registered trust, a registered society or a non-profit (section 8) firm and not through social enterprises.

Given its narrow interpretation and 'play', I wonder to what extent the CSR mandate is going to improve environmental and social sustainability and help demonstrate sustainability-related interventions for the attention of the government.

Companies would mainly use CSR as a brand-building exercise, appeasing local communities around their factories or project operations. If CSR is under the brand function, then the emphasis will be on how prominently the company's logo is displayed at the location of the activity. I won't be surprised if the CSR budgets are used to satisfy the politicians, by launching initiatives in their constituencies. Every politician has an NGO and the easiest way to support them is to hand over a grant to their NGOs. There is a risk therefore that the new law would promote green washing and act as a vehicle for illegitimate transfer of funds.

I have had many occasions to speak at 'sustainability conclaves and summits' of some of the top Indian corporates. My experience has been thoroughly disappointing. The so-called sustainability cells of these companies are staffed with people who are not adequately trained or experienced in the domain and are generally 'irrelevant'. If the top companies do not have the vision and capacity, then is it too optimistic to expect results of change on the ground?

The Schedule 7 under the Company's Act provides broad-brush guidance on CSR and most companies go where they can shine in the media, establish a brand or go by the feel-good proposals of their employees. Amongst the 10 items, only item (IV) suggests 'ensuring environmental sustainability'. The guidance is rather biased towards social (health, water, sanitation) infrastructure. Typical 'investment chunks' of projects therefore include construction of check dams, water treatment plants and toilets. I worry how these assets will be managed, especially with the use or handover phase requiring commitment and ownership from the communities. The need to ensure proper institutional arrangements for project sustainability has been a weak link in the CSR Act and guidance, and the main emphasis seems to be on spending or projectization.

Companies are following several sustainability-related initiatives. In fact, sometimes it's like a maze for communicating sustainability to the internal and external stakeholders and even to the top management. There is too much of a 'vocabulary' used. CSR is just one of the vehicles.

A corporate needs to take a holistic view, develop strategies and practice a code of conduct. One needs to consider employees, neighborhoods (especially the youth), customers, suppliers, investors, regulators, media and academic and R&D institutions. There is a need to envelop the CSR engagements, investments and operations in the code of sustainability. Strategies such as greening of supply chains, extended producer responsibility and practices such as sustainability reporting must be woven. The focus should be on building skills and promotion of innovations that can foster sustainability. The figure below shows such a depiction.

Indeed, we have to think and practice sustainability beyond the 2%. Limiting to '2% thinking' is not going to be enough!

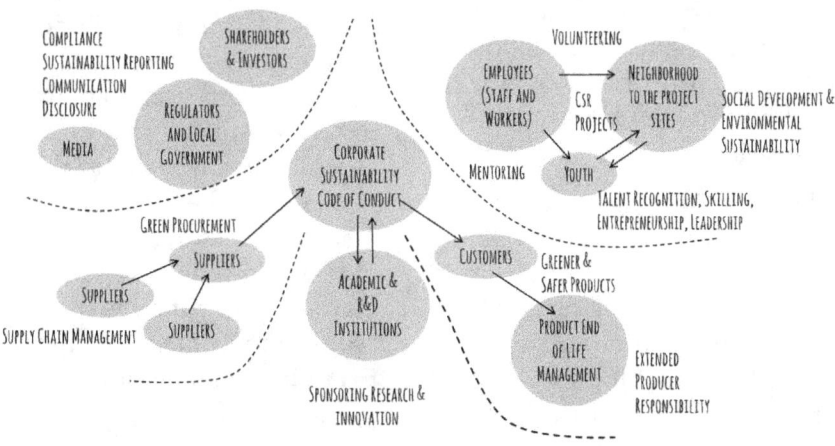

22

WHY MONITOR ENVIRONMENTAL QUALITY? WHY NOT GENERATE RANDOM NUMBERS?

My Professor friend was recently honored by the Ministry of Environment & Forests for his contributions towards saving expenditures on environmental monitoring incurred by the Pollution Control Boards (PCBs), industries and Urban Local Bodies (ULBs). The Professor was in the news, on TV and the print media. The exact details of his precise contributions were not known – but there was praise for his ingenuity, especially about the tool that he developed using 'random numbers' and a practical approach that he followed. The government was expecting to save millions. I was therefore very keen to meet him to learn about this innovation.

When I went to his office, the Professor was on the phone, busy as usual. "No, I am fully booked" he was saying. "Talk to me again next month and we will fix a slot for speaking a month later". He turned to me while slamming the phone

down and said, "too many requests to speak my friend. Everybody wants to know about my random number algorithm on environmental monitoring!" His table was littered with notes (with numbers and some graphs scribbled on them) and with couple of cups of tea with used tea bags in them. Clearly he had had a number of visitors that morning.

I requested the Professor to explain his innovation and apologized at the outset as he must have done it many times since morning! The Professor however didn't mind. "No problems, Prasad, 1 will do this for you. I know you well and you will, I am sure, explain my contributions to others as well – perhaps better than me". He winked. He then walked across to a white board in his room, cleaned it up and started explaining his theory of random numbers as applied to environmental monitoring.

His basic argument was as

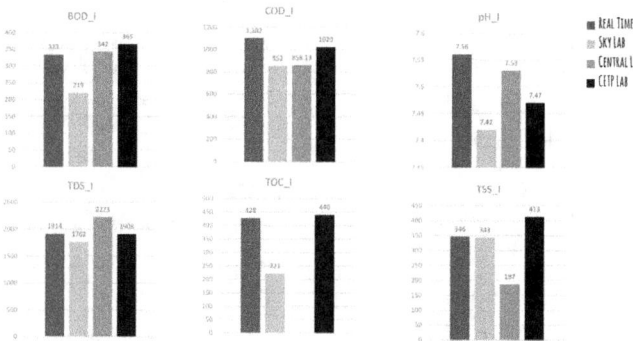

follows.

"We monitor environment (air quality, water quality, noise etc.) to understand the state of environment, establish trends, detect violations and communicate results to public, decision makers, implementers."

"We however conduct environmental monitoring at pretty low frequencies. We also operate relatively sparse density of monitoring stations. On the Ganga basin for instance we sample water quality at fewer than 100 stations (over its 3000 kilometers of length) and at each station, sample water quality only once a month."

"Do you think this kind of data is adequate for understanding water quality trends or detecting violations over the prescribed standards? This data is simply not sufficient for showing improvements (if any) in water quality due to the Ganga Action Plan – II. I told the Prime Minister that he is going to have a tough time proving that the investments he is making have actually improved water quality in Ganga." He paused. "We should be having many more stations and much higher sampling frequency if we are serious about environmental monitoring. Either do the job well or just don't do it. People don't understand statistics". His voice was now louder.

The monitoring stations we have are often not well sited. That leads to a bias. Do you know that the so called ambient air quality monitoring station sited in city of Pune was at Nal Chowk– a busy traffic junction– which actually reported air quality of pedestrian exposure and not ambient conditions. Data from this station declared Pune as one of the 10 most polluted cities in India and the city was put under the scanner of the Bhurelal Committee. And the Professor was right, as I had visited the monitoring location myself and had advised the Pune Municipal Corporation and Maharashtra Pollution Control Board to relocate the station.

The Professor continued to speak "And then look at the vagaries of how the sample is taken, preserved and transported to the laboratories. The QA/QC related situation is of concern. You know the BOD test we do in the labs is so unreliable for levels less than 3 mg/L that it often makes me wonder about the reliability of our river BOD data. Recently, I was provided with results of synchronous monitoring of industrial effluent at a Common Effluent Treatment Plant (CETP). This monitoring was carried out by 3 reputed laboratories and by an automatic water quality monitoring instrument. The arithmetic means of all the 4 were different and the Z-test hypothesis failed across all the parameters! *Isn't this frustrating? See a snapshot of the results.*"

He passed on to me one the sheets.

"Again what do we do with the data collected? We simply report means, maximum/minimums, time series graphs (that we call as "trends") and report compliance (over poor frequency data!). Much more can be done."

I nodded. "Yes Professor, we all know this reality is sad, but then where is your random number innovation?"

"Aha!" the Professor said. He lit a cigarette and put his spectacles on.

"I realized that there is NO great advantage in doing actual environmental monitoring. The kind of monitoring we do is as good as generating random numbers! The monitored data is neither representative nor reliable. So why bother? Why should we build and operate such an expensive environmental monitoring infrastructure? Why spend money?"

CONTROL CHARTS – SKY LAB WITH REAL TIME DATA

So I thought of generating random numbers. But cleverly!

All I do here is use past collected data, prepare quality control charts, and then toss random numbers in the range of one, two, three and four sigma – sigma being the standard deviation. The random numbers I generate follow an intelligent algorithm that almost mimics the behavior of the past data (to bring in credibility) but with some deviations *as needed or desired.* So the dots in the figure are my synthetic environmental monitoring data. In this case BOD. Sorry, I won't tell you how I generate these random numbers – a patent has been already filed. So hold on till then."

Look at the advantages. If you use my algorithm, you don't need to spend money on collecting and analyzing the actual sample. There is no need of laboratories, no need to employ staff and you directly get environmental monitoring data sitting right in your office! The data I generate is not too far away from 'reality' and cannot be easily questioned. Importantly, the randomness in the data can be controlled depending on what you want to prove – whether the environmental status is improving or deteriorating. When I explained to the

Minister this feature of the algorithm, he was so pleased!

I was shocked! "This Professor, is nothing but, data manipulation!" I said mustering all my courage, emotions and concern.

The Professor smiled. "Think deeply Prasad. In either case, does this matter? In both cases, i.e. actual monitoring and monitoring using my random number algorithm, we don't take decisions on environmental improvement anyways! In India, monitoring is not linked to management. And don't forget how much money and effort we save using my algorithm"

I left the Professor's office both depressed and disturbed. One thing that intrigued me however, was how come the Professor had not thought about the loss of jobs at PCBs, redundancy created in the field and regional laboratories, and loss of the business of equipment manufactures & chemical suppliers etc. The Professor certainly missed looking into the social costs (or benefits?) of environmental monitoring - the Committee at the Ministry should have thought of this downside of his random number innovation before bestowing the Award!!

23

Chitragupta's Apprenticeship at the EPA

Lord Chitragupta was bored in the Heavens. He was tired of keeping records of *paap* (bad deeds) and *punya* (good deeds). There was nothing exciting in his job as most souls that arrived had a *'punya* deficit' and were sent directly to *Naraka* (hell), with 100 lashes to begin with. Very few were sent to heaven.

So Chitragupta went to his master *Yama (Dharma Raja)* and asked for a leave of two weeks. Yama was startled. "How can I grant you leave? What will happen to the thousands of souls whose records you provide me every day to deliver fair judgment? There is no replacement for you. I wish Lord *Brahma* had thought about this earlier and had given birth to two Chitraguptas with one being the stand-by" (For those of you who don't know, in ancient Indian mythology, Chitragupta, son of Brahma, is the scribe who records all actions of every human being. These records are reviewed by

Yama for judging the soul after death.)

It is said that Yama would become confused sometimes when dead souls would come to him, and would occasionally send the souls to heaven/ hell wrongly. Lord Brahma, determined to solve this problem sat in meditation for thousands of years. Finally, when he opened his eyes, Chitragupta stood before him. Chitragupta, sometimes referred to as the first man to use letters, is known to be incredibly meticulous, and with his pen and paper tracks every action (good or bad) of every sentient life form. These perfect and complete documents are referred to in mystical traditions as the 'Akashic' records. Each year, Chitragupta is supposed to start his new book of accounts in the month of Chitiraj (April 14-May 15). The time had come to open a New Book[29].

Chitragupta said "Not to worry! April-May is a season in India with least number of deaths because most travel abroad for vacations where the environment is less polluted." He then provided guidance to *Yama* on how he could judge souls without seeing records e.g. a politician – should be sent to hell right away with no hesitation; an IAS officer with more than 10 transfers in 2 years – a case to heaven as he must be too honest etc. Yama was surprised to hear Chitragupta's insight. "And when I come back, I will cross-check your judgments with actual records and 'adjust.' I am sure there will be very few cases of reversals or changing the level of rewards and punishments." Chitragupta assured.

Yama agreed. This should not be a problem to Indian souls as they are quite used to courts changing judgments and making reversals especially on environmental clearances. He was not wrong.

"OK, I will let you go but what will you do for the next two weeks?" he asked Chitragupta

"I was thinking of doing something different. I plan to join one of the Pollution Control Boards in India or a Green Bench as an apprentice, helping create environment-related records of *paap and punya*. Perhaps my meticulous record-keeping can help the decision-making bodies in India towards sound environmental judgments."

"That's an amazing idea," *Yama* said "Tathastu!" (God bless)

Chitragupta closed his eyes and with his divine powers appeared at the newly-constituted office of Environmental Protection

---

29 See http://en.wikipedia.org/wiki/Chitragupta

Authority in Delhi. There was a long queue at the counter for making applications for the position of a replacement clerk for two weeks. This position required keeping records of consents, environmental clearances, quarterly monitoring reports, cess returns, environmental statements etc. and presenting these records to the judging committee when required.

When Chitragupta reached the counter after two hours of waiting in the queue, the man at the counter asked. "Where are the attachments? *Aadhar* card, proof of residence, last three years of Income Tax returns?" Chitragupta had none of these and did not know anything about them. The man at the counter glanced at the filled-up form – under experience, it was written – over 10,000 years; more than 10 billion cases handled. "Is this some kind of a joke"? Chitragupta explained and ended by saying that he was prepared to work for 2 weeks with no salary expectations.

We don't know what finally worked, whether his vast experience or the offer to work for free, but Chitragupta was ushered into the cabin of the Member Secretary(MS) within the next one hour by Joint Chief Environmental Engineer

(JCEE)

The proceedings were on. A committee of six experts was sitting. The MS took a look at Chitragupta and told JCEE "*Theek lagta hai* (looks alright)" ask him to join office in the next two days – get him trained on records and familiarize him with our filing system". Chitragupta did not want to waste two days, especially walking around in the polluted air of Delhi. "Can I start right now?" he asked. "OK," the MS said reluctantly, "sit down on this stool and just listen. Today, our JCEE is managing the records".

The case being heard was that of M/s GoodEarth Chemicals Inc. This case was about renewal of the consent to operate. The Environmental Consultant to the company was wearing a black suit and a red tie. He presented the records on all the environment-related matters in all earnest and elegance. "We have been 24×7 compliant, sir. All parameters are well within the limits and in some cases even below the detectable limits. We have competent staff and a sophisticated laboratory that is NABL certified. We have been paying cess regularly. The energy and water consumption per ton of product is reducing every year at the rate of 5%". The MS and the Committee members nodded and glanced at the records provided by the JCEE to countercheck "Good, looks OK. Go ahead."

"We are ISO 14001, OHSAS 18000 and SA 8000 compliant, Sir. We have been named the greenest company in India for the last year. We have started publishing a Sustainability Report as per GRI Version 4. And we practice CSR in both letter and spirit." The MD of the company got up and placed 7 copies of beautifully-designed Sustainability Reports on the table "with our complements, Sir", he said in a husky voice.

The Committee was clearly pleased.

Chitragupta closed his eyes and with his divine powers looked at records that could NOT be seen by the Committee. GoodEarth Chemicals wasn't as good to the earth as it claimed. Pollution parameters on average were within limits, but there were many occasions of spikes and on a contiguous basis, especially at night. Most of the COD was vaporized from the VOC and released from the aeration tank where there were no stipulations. Most of the sludge generated was hazardous but was shown as non-hazardous by carefully reporting concentrations/ kg below the thresholds. The 14001/18000/8000 certifications that were mentioned were obtained from lax and easy-to-influence certifiers, who charged the least in the market. The Green award that was received was from an NGO that got grant from GoodEarth's CSR budget!"

Chitragupta was therefore not comfortable with the records presented. With his divine eyes, he looked at the company representatives waiting outside, in the lounge. He saw that there were some genuine companies but they looked more under stress and worried despite their good deeds. There were more GoodEarth-type companies who were accompanied by Environmental Consultants. They did not look worried. They looked confident.

After ten such case hearings, Chitragupta stepped out with an excuse to go to the loo. He could not resist. He called *Yama* using the special mobile phone that was provided to him by the dead soul of the late MD of one of the 2G scam telecom companies.

"My master" he said (breathing heavily). "The environmental records at EPA in India are a real mess. Most of the times, the records are neither complete nor trustworthy. The judgments made on this basis are going to be clearly wrong and unfair. I think I should stay here a bit longer to fix the problem by showing the Committee (and more so to the people) – what real records are. Instead of rewarding and punishing souls after death (which I feel is too late!), we should start the process upfront – and here on the earth itself".

When *Yama* had picked up Chitragupta's call, he was on his way to meet Lord *Brahma* to present his business plan for FY 2015-2016. "Let me add to my plan, an opening for an overseas office of environmental justice in India. But I cannot spare Chitragupta. Instead, I must put there a clone. I will ask Dr. Joshua Lederberg, who came to us in 2008, to create one. Let me put in my budget his consulting fees and a couple of travels to Delhi"

Chitragupta returned to heaven the very next day cancelling his remaining 13 days of leave.

(Joshua Lederberg, May 23, 1925 – February 2, 2008 was an American molecular biologist known for his work in microbial genetics, artificial intelligence, and the United States space program. He was just 33 years old when he won the 1958 Nobel Prize in Physiology or Medicine for discovering the bacteria can mate and exchange genes)

LIVING GREEN
Sustainability

24

When the New Year comes, everyone plans to make a resolution. And many like to talk about it.

I was thinking what resolution should I make, that will reduce the mess in my life, decrease work entropy and bring better health and peace of mind. My wife pointed to me a chart of resolutions. "Do something you can, and do what you badly need to do – such as losing weight," She said

I did not find this list exciting. "This is all *simple stuff*," I told her "which anyone can do. Let me think differently and about *sustainability*," I said.

But instead of deciding for myself, I thought I'd better ask people around first – their New Year resolutions will give me ideas.

On December 31st the doorbell rang early in the morning. I opened the door to find Raju, our newspaper boy standing there. I asked Raju about his New Year resolution.

"*Saab*, I am a small guy" he said. "I don't understand this resolution business – but if you ask me, I would not like to deliver newspapers that carry the 'bad news'. It's terrible to wake people up in the morning with something sad and depressing. And in your case *Saab*, I will certainly don't want to deliver newspapers that carry pollution and corruption related news in which names of some of your friends in the industry and the government are cited. I know reading such news will hurt you badly". I thought Raju was right. Many of my friends were engaged in "unsustainable" activities and were still my friends.

When he left, I realized that I will need to find a new job for Raju as most of the newspapers today give only bad news. They keep repeating news about air pollution in Delhi, noise made during Diwali, effluents discharged into the Mithi River in Mumbai etc. and make us so insensitive about the challenges we face! I wish there was someone from the media resolving to publish only a "good news" newspaper! Won't it be nice if we could read news that could inspire? Then it becomes worth paying for the news!

I got into the car with my driver Ganesh. I asked him about his New Year resolution. "Well Sir, he said, I would like to drive an eco-friendly car. A true environmentalist like you cannot drive this diesel-driven Skoda and I really feel ashamed. I have heard about Toyota Prius – world's first mass produced hybrid car that runs on petrol and electricity. Sir, please buy this car. Let us make this resolution for 2016"

I explained to Ganesh that Toyota Prius costs 3.2 million INR, as against Skoda, which costs half that amount. "We will make this resolution for 2017 and drive Prius to public meetings to show off" - I assured him "Hopefully by then the price of hybrid cars will fall". Ganesh was disappointed to see that I did not value his advice on sustainability.

I reached my office and called my secretary Kermeene for a dictation. After I finished, I asked her to order a plate of *Patrani Machhi* from *Jimmy Boy* for lunch. What's your New Year resolution Kermeene? I asked.

"Oh I have decided to become a Veggie from January 1," Kermeene announced. When she saw my startled face, she said "Sir, Haven't you read the article, *Top 10 Reasons Why It's Green to Go Veggie?*[30] Being your secretary, I thought I must do my bit for going "green" and for the environment".

I thought of telling her not to trust claims made by such articles.

But Kermeene continued "Sir, by the way, tomorrow onwards, I will not order any non-veg food for you either. I want you to follow vegetarianism like me for the interest of this planet's sustainability. Hope this is OK

---

30 See https://www.do wntoearth.org/go-veggie/environment/top-10-reasons

with you"

I explained to Kermeene, that while she is free to have her own Veggie resolution to protect the planet she should not interfere with my life. How can I miss the box lunch of *mutton biryani* from *Karims* in Bandra and Tiger Prawns from *Excellencee* on the Mint Street? Talking about sustainability is different from putting sustainability into practice. I saw some disappointment on Kermeene's face. I felt I had lost her respect.

We had a group meeting in the afternoon with an agenda on Sustainability Reporting. Three of my senior colleagues attended this meeting who had flown from Delhi, Chennai and Ahmedabad. When we had a smoking break in between, I asked my colleague from Ahmedabad about his New Year resolution. He said that he will not travel by airplane in 2016. "No air travel anymore except when on holidays" he said. I want to reduce the carbon footprint of the company. "You know we will soon have a bullet train between Ahmedabad and Mumbai – thanks to our PM's recent meeting with the Japanese Premier) and so I will prefer to come by the bullet train instead." I thought this resolution was great as it would cut down both our travel costs and emissions. I changed my mind however when the same colleague said that he will arrive one day earlier for the meetings and book a room in Taj President. I realized then that "up" and "down" flights would be cheaper. In fact, the net carbon footprint of this journey could be even higher given the carbon emissions resulting from night stay Taj (especially because of the air conditioning) and accounting for the embodied energy spent on the food and drinks there. Sometimes Life Cycle Analyses (LCA) can be rather telling and dissuade you from doing anything different. LCA is such a cheeky tool that you can prove what you want by choosing cleverly the *system boundaries* of the analyses.

In the evening, there was a Seminar followed by dinner at the Oberoi that I went to attend. Hon Union Minister of Railways Mr. Suresh Prabhu was to address the participants. Before his speech, I bumped into Environmentalists Deepak Apte and Rishi Agarwal "Friends, what are your New Year resolutions" I asked. Both of them said that their New Year resolution was to stall the Coastal road and the Trans Harbor Sea link projects. "These two projects in their present form will be a disaster for Mumbai". They said this so loudly that CM Fadnavis sitting at the round table in the first row could clearly overhear (May be that was the idea). But I don't know whether the CM actually heard us. Perhaps his New Year resolution was to commence these two very projects. We *mumbaikars* do not have the time or sensitivity to understand the importance of the mangroves that protect us or the migratory flamingos around *Sewri* that are a treat to our eyes.

After Mr. Suresh Prabhu delivered his address, I met him and asked him about his New Year resolution. A clever man that he is, he said "I don't have any personal resolutions as my life is now public, but I have a resolution for my Ministry. From January 1, 2016, Indian Railways will go *green*. All railway coaches will now be painted in green to start with." When he saw my startled face, he smiled and said that he was only joking. He explained that there were many items in the agenda like bio-toilets, solar powered canteens, monitoring and controlling indoor air quality in the AC coaches with CO_2 concentrations on display". "Thank God Sir you were only joking" I said. "But I am sure one of the earlier Railway Ministers would have just done that i.e. painting the coaches green!"

I liked Mr. Prabhu' s idea on monitoring indoor air quality in AC coaches. Today we simply don't know what the air quality is like on the long-distance trains! Ignorance is often bliss.

Finally, I spoke about the New Year resolution to my Professor friend. He was busy examining a recently-launched app on iOS called Strides. **"It's not important to know what you have resolved, the key is to know whether you are actually implanting your resolution"** He said this in his characteristic serious tone. *Strides* is an elegantly designed app, flexible enough to help track multiple goals and it has built-in templates to help you meditate, save money, lose weight and so on. You type in the goal's name, enter data about your target (like a dollar value to save, or target weight to achieve), select a meaningful time scale, then set up regular alerts and reminders. *Strides* shows all of the goals on a dashboard with an at-a-glance indicator. To log your progress, tap the goal's checkmark in the dashboard. Selecting the goal's name takes you to a page that shows your historical progress, as well as statistics like the number of days you have kept up with your resolution and your percentage success rate so far. The app is free and runs on iOS only[31]

Coach.me is another goal-tracking and habit-forming app that's free for both iOS and Android. This app has a social networking aspect that lets people share their progress towards goals with a community and earn praise, as well as ask other users for advice. You can also use the app to find and hire a real-life coach to keep you motivated.

"I am working on these apps to set up a Sustainability-based New Year Resolution Dashboard" Professor said. A blend of coach.me and Strides seems promising to get people on the sustainability track. Our PM will be talking about this new app during *Mann ki Baat*[32] tonight requesting everyone to download and use it.

"Wow, this will surely transform India. Imagine nearly billion of us making New Year Resolutions for the planet's sustainability." I congratulated the Professor.

When I returned home, my wife asked me "so what did you decide for the New Year?"

I said "Let me get back to your standard list of resolutions". With so many people pledging on sustainability, I don't think I need to do much – I would rather focus on reducing my weight"

My wife wholeheartedly supported this simple New Year resolution!

You may like to read the article by Dr Ajit Ranade[33] on New Year resolutions.

---

31 See http://www.nytimes.com/2015/12/24/technology/personaltech/video-feature-apps-for-keepingnew-years-resolutions.html?_r=0 to know more about Strides

32 See http://www.narendramodi.in/mann-ki-baat

33 3 3 See http://www.mumbaimirror.com/columns/columnists/ajit-ranade/Resolutions-fit-for-2016/articleshow/50327427.cms

25

Greening the World of Finance

My Professor friend was once again in the news. He became an Advisor to the Governor of the Central Bank last month and was asked to take on the Green Agenda. The Governor had apparently attended some UN meeting on *Greening* and had found that a lot was happening in the financing world on this topic and India didn't have much to say. That was shameful.

So the Professor was appointed. After his taking over, the finance world in India simply changed towards Green.

I went to withdraw money from the ATM next to my home and there was a long queue. Most in the queue were reading newspapers. Some were patiently solving crosswords. Some had started eating their lunch. Clearly the queue was moving slowly. I asked the gentleman next to me why there was such a crowd. "Oh!" he said, "don't you know that the ATM now

asks a lot of questions on green. How much water do you consume in a day, how much diesel is consumed per kilometer by a 10-year-old bus etc. are few opening questions. Questions are also asked on your general knowledge such as what is the name of the chairman of the Tripura Pollution Control Board, or what is the significance of 2 degrees, and a few more questions at the end such as what did you do today on the Swatch Bharat Abhiyan etc. When you answer all these questions and get at least 70 marks out of 100, only then your ATM card becomes active. This takes time. Most people fail so they keep reattempting and since each time the questions asked are different, they keep failing again and again. I am planning to go to another ATM machine now where I believe there are professionals loitering outside who help field these questions for a small fee. Apparently, some advisor to the Governor

of the Central Bank has come up with this idea to promote green. Crazy!"

I was simply aghast. Although it generated Green Jobs, this was terrible. So I left the ATM machine and went straight to meet the Professor at the Central Bank. The Professor was giving a press interview at that time. "Yes, we propose to change the mindset of Indian citizens towards green living. This credit card (and he flashed a bright green credit card which had a shape of a leaf) will let you shop only green. If you attempt purchasing any "brown" product, then the card will not simply work". One journalist stopped him and asked who decides what is a *green* and a *brown* product? The Professor smiled and said that this work was already done and a master database of key green consumer products was created at a national level. New entries were however most welcome". Another journalist quipped "why should one buy this green credit card if this is so

restrictive?" The Professor was already expecting this question. "We will track the shopping done using this green credit card and give you "greenie" points. With these points you can shop more green as a bonus…. And remember that there are no annual fees charged for the use of the green credit card – don't confuse this with Green Card my friends," and he winked.

When we went to his cabin, I complained to the Professor about the ATM mess. I further added that the green credit card idea could be controversial as it is really difficult to ascertain what is a green product", But the Professor did not agree. Soon people will understand what is green through the ATMs and spend responsibly using the green credit card – he said. The product makers will shift to the mission of making green because this will be the only way that they will survive. This will lead to reduced GHG emissions. The Central Bank will thus change India's consumption and production patterns. This should have been the job of the Ministry of Environment and Forests (and Climate Change) but you know that this Ministry has been only focusing on management of residues or pollution …with no strategies towards sustainable consumption and production". He sighed and I nodded. On this we had no disagreement.

He then paused and asked me "Have you recently been to any of the commercial banks to ask for a loan?"

Next day, both of us went to a local commercial bank. I filled up a loan application form at the counter that used paper that was recycled, unbleached and had seeds embedded. When I went to the desk of the loan officer, he served me water from a rainwater harvesting unit and in a clay jar. I was carrying the supporting papers in a plastic bag. He took the papers, tucked away my plastic bag "no plastic my friend – this is against the Central Bank's directive". He then walked across and inserted my plastic bag in a plastic to diesel machine. "Thanks for your contribution for the national 'plastic to diesel' program," he said while sitting back on his chair and handed me a flower as a token of appreciation that came from an organic garden. My Professor friend was standing behind me with great self-admiration and a proud face.

When I explained to him about my interest in securing a loan for a vehicle, he asked me why was I purchasing a vehicle. "Can you not take a public transport? We must follow sustainable lifestyles and reduce your carbon footprint. We are importing crude oil my friend that affects our BoP" He then showed me couple of videos on YouTube that said how we should avoid using private vehicles and take public transport. "I am sorry," he said, "but if you still insist on taking a loan, then I will recommend you a bicycle. In the Netherlands, most people use bicycles." I tried to tell him that public transport in the city is not good and I get late, weary and tired. Besides we don't have bicycle pathways like in the Netherlands, so safety can be an issue, but the officer wouldn't pay heed to my protests. We spent another 30 minutes discussing my loan. According to the officer, sanctioning of my car loan would severely affect India's and world's sustainability and bring in adverse and irreversible change.

We left the Bank, I disappointed and the Professor triumphant with joy. I said "I will go to another

bank – perhaps a cooperative bank where Central Bank directives are often flouted". The Professor said, "Sure – try your luck". We have ensured that all banks follow our principles of sustainable finance in letter and spirit. The financing world in India now fully understands the importance of sustainability in investment decisions.

"But then how will the economic development in India happen? Especially the financial flows in the infrastructure sector and the foreign direct investments that we want to attract? Your requirements are so stringent," I struggled to say.

"Oh I am working on that, the Professor said while signing some important documents using a green pen. There are so many shades of green that I am sure we will find a way. After all, what is green is what we decide. So we will stay green for the world but fix the shade we want to – somewhere dark and somewhere pale".

"Aha!" – I exclaimed. I visualized my Professor friend like the scallywag boy of Asian Paints with a paint tin and brush in hand and a large pallette of green, busy painting the walls. Very clever!

26

City of Beards and Deodorants

I landed Mumbai International airport after three months of travelling in the United States. When I got out of the aircraft, I saw the local airline staff with wheelchairs on the connecting bridge. All men standing there had long beards. I reached the immigration desk. All immigration officers were sporting thick beards. At immigration I breezed through the customs. All customs officers had white beards matching their white uniforms. Soon, I realized that all men at the airport had grown beards – the policemen, the *taxi wallahs*, men receiving their folks, the McDonald staff at the counters … I was astonished!

When I got into my car, and asked my driver (who also had grown a beard), what's wrong? He said "Mumbai is in a severe water crisis and there is 60% water cut. The city administration has banned shaving for men to save water. All hairdresser shops have also closed."

As we were exiting the parking lot and paid for the ticket, I was given a deodorant spray – with complements of the Municipal Corporation of Mumbai. The spray was with a flyer. The flyer urged you not to take a bath every day but once in three days – as there was no water in Mumbai's water reservoirs. That hit me real hard.

When we reached my apartment, the driver parked the car at spot different from my usual parking place. When I asked him, he said that the locations of parking were chosen such that the cars were under the air conditioners. The drops from the air conditioners fitted in the apartments would fall on the cars and this water would be used for cleaning. No use of freshwater was allowed for washing cars.

I checked my mail box at the ground floor. The box was full of flyers on saving water and notices from the Corporation on new water-related rules, do's and don'ts and punitive actions that will be taken. There was an inspection report from the Municipal Officer who had visited the flat in my absence. The report said that he found 4 taps in the bathroom, 2 showerheads and 2 wash-basins. I was told to shut down 2 taps, one showerhead and remove 1 wash basin with immediate effect. This was all the Corporation would allow. There was no question of having a tub in the bathroom. A model of a tub was now placed in the Prince of Wales Museum for people to see and remember.

I did not take a shower but sprayed deodorant on my suit and went to office. The office smelled of deodorants – a few colleagues were sneezing and some had watery eyes due the allergy of the spray.

There were a few plumbers moving around the toilet. "These guys are changing our toilet to waterless urinals," my colleague said. I thought this will be smelly. But our office was told so by the building

society. Then I saw a big heap of paper napkins. This was because no hand washing was allowed after lunch. I realized that the city would produce huge quantity of tissue paper waste soon.

We decided to go for lunch at the nearby restaurant. The food items were limited. Only dry vegetables were served. No spicy food was provided as it would lead to more demand for drinking water. No finger bowls were allowed. Only small volume glasses of water were provided for drinking. Just one glass per person was allowed. For the second glass, the charge was equivalent to a bottle of coke. So many were drinking coke. Everyone at the lunch table was talking about

the water cut and was thinking of moving out of Mumbai.

The price of bottled water was now nearly three times as before –yet truckloads of water bottles were being brought to the city. The menace of used plastic water bottles was certainly going to increase, there were more water tankers now on the streets and queues outside the city wells were longer than the one on the *Chaturthee* at the *Siddhivinayak*.

I noticed that the greenery in the city had reduced as there was no water available for gardening. There were now plastic lawns at the Turf club and the Chembur Golf Club. The golfers were having a hard time to adjust to the new "roughness" of the turf.

The next day I was lecturing at IIT Bombay. My colleagues told me that a major scientific committee was formed consisting some of the senior professors. They were looking at tapping moisture in the air to produce water. Besides the challenge of technology, there was the issue of pollution in the air. The water so derived required purification to remove the air pollutants and this was where the economics of the project was failing. I wished the city air was not that polluted.

There was another big project that was getting discussed. This was about converting the city sewage by tertiary treatment into water. This water could be used for washing, cooling, drinking etc. depending on the level of treatment provided. The idea was to stop sending the sewage to the sea and instead build sewage recycling plants at various locations. This project required land, investments and some 10 years to implement. Some said that such a project should have been conceived and planned much in advance. Today, in Mumbai sewage recycling happens in some multistoried buildings and industries like Rashtriya Chemicals and Fertilizers. There are by-laws on sewage recycling but they are not seriously enforced. Some said that there will be risks in recycling as the sewage characteristics today are rather complex and not easy to treat, especially the micro-pollutants. The transportation of treated sewage for use was also going to be challenge.

Never too late, we could at least start with a pilot project – I said to myself. Sewage recycling plants will certainly work on a decentralized basis.

The corporation was also looking at identifying a new source of water. These sources were far away at some 150 km distance. This would require huge energy to pump. Indeed this was not going to be a very sustainable solution. Till then the building proposals department was asked not to approve new buildings. That made the officers working in the proposal department a bit upset as there were not going to be any *transactions*.

Rainwater harvesting could be a good strategy – While rainwater harvesting is mandated in Mumbai, its implementation is not seriously taken. There aren't many good professionals. There are space constraints and people generally neglect operation and maintenance. Of course, rainwater harvesting will help only if it rains – I thought.

Given the grim situation of water, I was generally impressed with the efforts taken by the corporation. I spoke about this to my Professor friend.

He looked at me and laughed. "We are really out of the mark. The first thing we should do is to address the water loss and pilferage happening at our pipelines. Mumbai has the highest rate of water loss. Its nearly 50% today. If this is fixed on priority we will address half our problem.

No need then to look for new water sources or levy severe water cuts"

I thought he had a point.

We often don't do things that are sometimes so obvious!

Sure, we don't want to see cities with people with beards and using deodorants. Stopping leakage from the pipes conveying water to the city makes a lot of sense!

27

Let us not just Build Green but also Live Green

Green buildings mainstream sustainability in planning, layout, orientation and design, and while making choice of material, source of energy, fit-outs and technology. The idea is to reduce life cycle impacts and risks.

Several green rating systems have emerged in the last decade that guide and inspire architects, planners, builders and material/equipment suppliers to come up with buildings with various *shades of green*. Focus has also increased on low-carbon buildings wherein greenness of the building is assessed based on Greenhouse Gas (GHG) emissions. These buildings are also called *climate responsive.*

In the early years, constructing green buildings was thought to result in cost overruns by factors as high as 20% but today because of the favorable policies/ regulations, market demand/ recognition, technology/ material innovations, the cost differential between a green and a "conventional" building has greatly reduced. When cost over the life of the building is considered, green buildings are in fact more competitive. A recent report on the evaluation of 22 green buildings post construction has shown significant operational savings[34]

We should by default build every building green.

While much attention is given to the greenness of the building on its "built form", **communication of its green features to the occupiers is often overlooked**. The *'use phase'* of the life cycle of the building thus faces a disconnect and sustainability is confined to 'half of the circle'.

---

34 See: http://www.gsa.gov/graphics/pbs/Green_Building_Performance.pdf

Green buildings typically have a rainwater harvester, a vermi-compost pit and a grey water recycling unit amongst several other features. You sometimes find the use of rainwater harvesters getting discontinued as they become mosquito breeding grounds. Also, compost from vermi-compost pit does not get used in the gardens or the practice of grey water recycling is abandoned due to foul smell. Reasons are several – some of these are low understanding/sensitivity, lack of ownership and many times sheer neglect and poor maintenance.

Efforts are needed to ensure that occupiers of a green building understand how to live green! Living green actually changes an occupier's mindset and lifestyle so as to make staying in a green building more meaningful. This is where the term sustainable habitat comes in taking us beyond physical form of a green building or green infrastructure and bringing in sustainable lifestyles.

Several years ago, I visited Hammarby Sjöstad, an exciting district in Stockholm where the City imposed tough environmental requirements on buildings, technical installations and the traffic. Accordingly the Stockholm Water Company, Fortum and the Stockholm Waste Management Administration jointly developed a common ecocycle model.[35] I spent the whole day walking around the district and speaking with the residents.

While there were several innovative materials and technologies, used one of the unique initiatives of Hammarby Sjöstad was the Environmental Information Center. This Center has been built to educate the occupiers of the green buildings and make them aware on how to live green. The Center showcases green materials, green gadgets/fit-outs and green technologies. It holds short seminars, screens films and arranges exhibitions for residents as well as district neighborhood. The Center called GlashusEtt plays the role of a hub or environmental community centre.

Indeed, every green building township we build should have a GlashusEtt. Mere physical green form is not enough. Green ratings or

---

35 See: http://www.hammarbysjostad.se/ and download the "environmental map" at
http://bygg.stockholm.se/Web/Core/Pages/Special/ServiceGuideFile.aspx?source=
constructionProjects&fileid =b5311122f3d04665af51e0e74141a19f

certificates may not be given one time on a permanent basis but renewed based on how the green buildings are actually used by the occupants. It's like asking for a *green occupancy* certificate.

If we really intend to promote sustainability in our built forms, then let us not just build green but also learn to live green!

28

FOUR TIERS OF SUSTAINABILITY

(This article was originally published in Green Prospects Asia in Malaysia)

Many stakeholders today want to understand organizations' commitment and performance on sustainability. But then Sustainability as a term is always hard to define. Communicating sustainability is even harder. A bigger challenge is how to put sustainability in practice.

Sustainability in an organization is generally pursued in tiers. At the minimum, the journey towards sustainability must start with compliance. Every organization that aspires to be a champion on sustainability needs to take all efforts to ensure that laws of the land are fully complied with. This may require complying with procedures, doing associated documentation; investing in mitigation measures, deploying qualified staff and conducting required monitoring and reporting.

Any organization that is not compliant should not be considered "sustainable".

The next tier of sustainability is to go "beyond compliance". Here the organizations undertake sustainability-related initiatives as driven by its vision/mission and goals/objectives and not solely directed by needs of compliance. So under the interest of resource conservation, the organization may install rainwater harvesting units or undertake vermi-composting of wastes or implement solar water heaters in the canteen to reduce consumption of fossil fuels. The organization may follow a policy of using only CNG-powered vehicles for its material transport to reduce GHG emissions. The idea is to minimize the footprint of the business operations. Many of these initiatives however provide returns or operational savings given the rising costs of resources (water and energy) and help improve resource security. Going beyond compliance is therefore more about practicing "smart sustainability". Strategies and tools such as "cleaner production" and "green productivity" help in this endeavor.

The third tier on sustainability involves expending the "boundary beyond the factory gates" and addressing a wider set of stakeholders across the supply chain or even the life cycle. For instance, here the organization needs to engage suppliers, on how to improve resource efficiency and waste recycling. Accordingly the technical/financial assistance may be provided. Further, vendor selection criteria may be developed and imposed asking for a code of practice on sustainability. A supplier may have to commit for instance 20% of energy use from renewable resources or recycling 50% of its water use. On consumer side, the organization may operate a "take-back policy" and promote recycling of packaging and used goods by setting up collection centers. Used mobile phones for instance could be deposited to earn reward coupons. These efforts may fall into the realm of organization's "extended producer responsibility". This strategy of practicing sustainability often adds a brand value to the organization, reducing risks and adding to its competitiveness over the long run. Generally at this tier, organizations follow the practice of 'sustainability reporting'. This helps in improved internal and external communication and builds record keeping.

The fourth tier on sustainability is to widen the 'social frontiers' of the organization by addressing the 'catchment area' i.e. 'going beyond project boundaries' but without any direct commercial motives. Here the organization addresses the needs of its neighborhood (or catchment area); works with interested partners and implements projects that help improve the livelihoods and natural resources of the region. These projects are often conceived and implemented under Public Private Partnerships (PPP) focusing on 'social inclusion'. Supporting school education and primary health centers, carrying out afforestation and watershed development programmes are some examples. These projects may well be form part of organizations efforts towards 'corporate social responsibility'. The returns on these investments are however received over a long term. Addressing global issues like climate change is also considered at this tier – especially financing projects that assist communities in adaptation. On mitigation, the organizations expand sustainability reporting of the earlier tier into specialized reporting such as on GHGs e.g. by subscribing to projects such as "carbon disclosure ".

Most organizations today in India belong to Tier 1 and struggle even to get there! Tier 2 is generally practiced by medium to large scale organizations that have technical capacities, financial resources and enjoy support of the top management. Multinationals with global supply chains are leaders in Tier 3 and their sustainability driver is the market and competition. Tier 4 is practiced by medium to large industries. This tier is conceived, inspired and driven solely by top leadership. These leaders understand sustainability in its true sense and are recognized nationally and globally.

The figure below shows the sustainability journey for an organization in tiers with associated strategies. Normally, sustainability should be implemented in this succession. Check which tier you belong to and aspire for the next one.

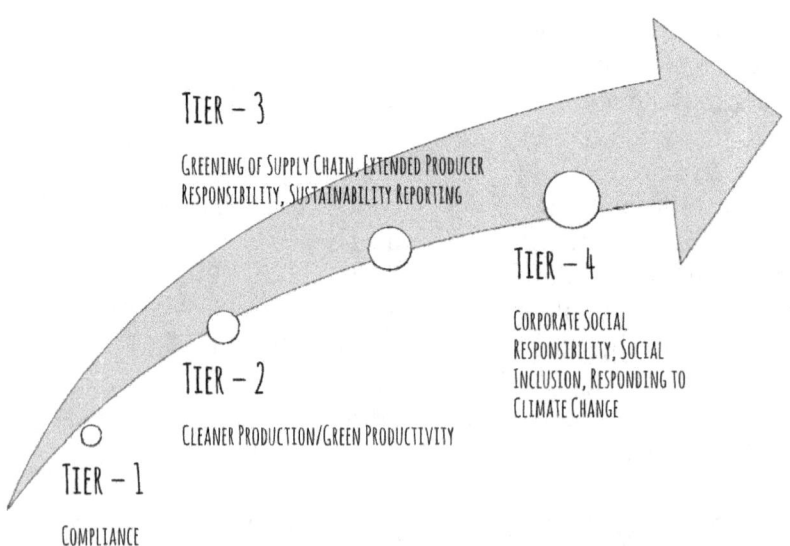

TIER – 3

GREENING OF SUPPLY CHAIN, EXTENDED PRODUCER RESPONSIBILITY, SUSTAINABILITY REPORTING

TIER – 4

CORPORATE SOCIAL RESPONSIBILITY, SOCIAL INCLUSION, RESPONDING TO CLIMATE CHANGE

TIER – 2

CLEANER PRODUCTION/GREEN PRODUCTIVITY

TIER – 1

COMPLIANCE

SUSTAINABILITY IS MOVING IN TIERS

29

Sustainability – Make it Smart and Simple

Sustainability is a *buzz*word that has spawned industry-wide interest and led to the emergence of several corporate sustainability initiatives in the recent times. However, many enterprises struggle to achieve significant tangible outcomes from sustainability based initiatives. Sustainability is perceived to be more of a *branding* strategy and many skeptics look at sustainability as just *green wash*.

While some say that *sustainability* pays, it is hard to find clear evidence that shows material or economic gains or advantages. Most ask – *we understand the importance of sustainability but how do we put sustainability into practice? And what is the advantage?*

This question was put to me by the Chairman of one of the group of industries near Mumbai. He put this question more as a challenge. We met over dinner then and went through a long conversation on how to make

sustainability happen! This dinner conversation led to a roadmap. We were not fully clear whether we were on the right track but we decided to make a beginning and remain open for any changes.

The first thing we did was to develop a policy statement that enshrined sustainability. We did this by inviting a small group of top management members, worker union representatives, company lawyers and principal company investors. The policy statement was simple, not ambitious and it drew upon guiding principles such as *'do no harm'*, *'conserve natural resources'* etc.

These guiding principles were then discussed with the company's operational teams to develop projects that best reflected the policy commitment. *'Conservation of natural resources' principle* for instance led to identification of projects on rainwater harvesting and vermi-composting. The *'do not harm' principle* led to a mission on replacement of Ozone Depleting Substances (ODS) and *'promotion of renewable resource'*s as a principle led to a project on solar water heating in the canteen.

All these projects were designed and evaluated for cost-benefits where benefit calculation included both tangible and non-tangible returns; and on scales both local as well as global such as reduction of GHGs. Some projects on a standalone basis had a relatively long payback period but some projects did have high economic returns. On a 'basket' basis, the projects were financially sustainable.

A project implementation plan was then prepared with financing arrangements. There was also a need to update company operating procedures, especially in the ISO 9000 documentation and impart associated training. This required a communiqué on the basket of projects to the third tier of the company team – giving them the genesis or the *project finding process* – and importantly its sustainability-based policy root. The teams were accordingly sensitized and involved in implementation on a departmental basis. An

element of competition was brought in.

The projects were implemented gradually with evaluations done to report project effectiveness and innovation e.g. water and energy saved, wastes avoided, wastes recycled, hazard reduced etc. In this process the overall environmental performance of the company improved and moved closer to the industry benchmarks. A catalogue of project sheets was developed, and shared through company newsletters and notice boards. This led to a comprehensive communiqué to the staff and the shop floor workers

I suggested that Chairman take the sustainability story further ahead to the families of the employees and the neighborhood. We organized an outreach programme on a Sunday where children of company employees and neighborhood visited the factory to see the projects implemented. Some children were excited to do a school project on vermi-composting using the data on vermi-pits and some college youth wanted to look at options for use of treated wastewater for gardening. All these engagements and interactions led to generation of more field data and better understanding of the technologies.

Some people in the neighborhood decided to replicate solar water heaters. So the message on sustainability spread! A feedback session indicated that the stakeholders were convinced that sustainability is not just to be believed in but to be put in practice with results and experience shared. I asked the Chairman to put aside funds that could help entrepreneurs in the neighborhood to set up businesses on solar water heaters. This fund was linked to Corporate Social Responsibility (CSR) and routed through a local commercial bank. There was an excellent response. The company put its logo on the solar heaters that were supported and this led to co-branding.

This is a story – some 15 years ago. Today, we use sophisticated management systems, reporting guidelines and mechanisms to express and demonstrate our commitment towards sustainability. In this maze however, simple approaches often get lost. The internal and external communications are poor or neglected. A kind of green-*washing* happens – though not intended!

Let us focus therefore on demonstration and practicing – and less on preaching on sustainability. Let us be smart and simple!

Corporate sustainability reports have been around for four decades. The first reports were perhaps published by the chemical industries that polluted the environment and faced bad reputation and penalties. Sustainability report was more of a savior!

Since then, more than 10,000 companies have published more than 50,000 reports, according to CorporateRegister.com, which maintains a searchable database of reports.

The Global Reporting Initiative has basically cornered the market on sustainability reporting, with 78% of the companies applying the GRI guidelines. This statistic rises to more than 90% in some countries, like South Africa, Chile and Sweden. India has seen the biggest rise in reporting, from 20% in 2011 to 73% in 2013. **But who really reads sustainability reports?**

I was speaking last week at one of India's leading corporate's Sustainability Conclave. The Conclave was attended by 50 sustainability champions of the company. When the Chief Sustainability Officer (CSO) asked – how many of you have read the company sustainability report – only 5 showed up their hands. The number was astonishingly low but I was surprised to see their candidness.

The CSO then asked, on page 3, we have featured a group photo where we have our Managing Director (MD). In the photo, is the MD sitting or standing? One sustainability champion ventured and said "sitting". The CSO smiled and said that there is no such photo on page 3!

Sustainability is not yet woven into the fabric of the corporations. Sustainability reporting provides increased knowledge on sustainability-related efforts taken by the company but this has not yet changed the behavior of investors, R&D and product designers or regulators. Regulators continue to focus on non-compliance, investors on the financial performance and the product designer's limit to the conventional designs and large-volume markets.

And how good are these sustainability reports? KPMG rated the reports of the top 250 biggest companies worldwide, and gave them an average score of 59/100. Construction and building materials did the worst of any sector, with an average score of just 46/100. So indeed there is a need to improve the way we write sustainability reports.

Time and again, research, data and information that goes into the sustainability report is not put to the best use. Often a company's most interesting sustainability work is left buried in these dull but important publications that no one really reads. You do see a new era of 'sustainability designers' who use their skills in choosing fonts and colors that are appealing, present info-graphics and plug in touching photos of the poor, underprivileged women and children. The paper used is FSC-certified elemental chlorine free and even with seeds embedded in it. That makes the report look special.

The reports contain annexes with time series data, indicators and benchmarks – especially for those who want to see details.

But most readers are not interested in tables and graphs and such statistics. They are also tired of the touching photos. Readers are looking for 'sustainability stories' to understand the company's true sustainability credentials. Stories tell a lot – and they sometimes get more viral than the numbers. But then not many companies have good stories to tell. And to get the stories you need to talk to people.

Some companies are taking a lead in communicating sustainability more innovatively. The Co-operative 2012 Sustainability Report is one good example. It exemplifies a new trend in video storytelling to illustrate sustainability reports. Other such examples are Novo Nordisk – The Danish healthcare giant that uses hand-drawn animation to explain its commitment to fighting diabetes – a major theme of the company's 2012 Report. SAP has created a dedicated Twitter hash tag #sapintegrated to help shepherd conversation around its 2013 integrated corporate and sustainability report.

Visit the new SMI-Wizness Social Media Sustainability Index update that is available online[36]

Sustainability reporting is a "process" that must involve all the concerned stakeholders. The report itself is not the only objective. The reporting 'process' brings in collective ownership, data flow optimization, identification of improvement projects and fostering of innovation. Everybody in the domain knows that. But in reality the reports are mostly consultant-driven with low involvement of the company staff. So reporting becomes more of ritual.

I asked my Professor friend about these concerns on sustainability reporting – especially that these reports are not prepared the way they should and are hardly read.

The Professor said that he just received a contract from a large corporate to fix this problem. "The company has two large halls for lunch. I converted one of the halls into a reading room. In this room, I keep several copies of the sustainability reports that the company produces. Employees are made to wait in this hall before joining the second hall where lunch is served. They browse and read the reports as there is nothing else to do"

I wasn't sure whether this was going to work. So I asked. "Are you sure they will? They may not even pick up the copies…"

The Professor smiled as if he expected this question. "The lunch coupons are kept inside the sustainability reports and at random locations. You really need to browse pages of the report to find these".

36 See: http://publisher.wizness.com/reports/the-smi-wizness-social-media-sustainability-index-2012

31
Think Out of the Box

(This article is a modified version of my column published in Green Prospects Asia in Malaysia)

When we look at the *'greenness'* of a product; its type, extent and material of packaging should also be a part of the perspective. While a product might be green, its packaging may not. Packaging accounts for almost 10 % of the environmental impact of a product. In estimating the "environmental impact" of the package, we assess the material (i.e. embodied intensity), its biodegradability and recyclability, the label and method of printing (e.g. ink used).

The considerations of Green House Gas (GHG) emissions has also influenced packaging design and the logistics. Grocery Manufacturers Association (GMA) in the United States has committed to eliminate 2 billion Kgs of packaging waste nationwide by 2020. If GMA reaches this target then GHG emissions will reduce equivalent to removing 815,000 cars from the road or to cutting of electricity from 363,000 homes for one year! Environmentally-sensitive packaging on a nation-wide basis can thus help in combating climate change.

Today, increased consumer demand has compelled many companies to make packaging as sustainable as possible. An ASSOCHAM study on Domestic Green Packaging Industry showed that 'rising environmental concerns about carbon emissions, dearth of natural resources together with increased health awareness and waste reduction targets' are the key drivers of green packaging in India[37]

The Global packaging industry

---

37 See: http://www.thehindubusinessline.com/industry-and-economy/article2543529.ece?ref=wl_opinion

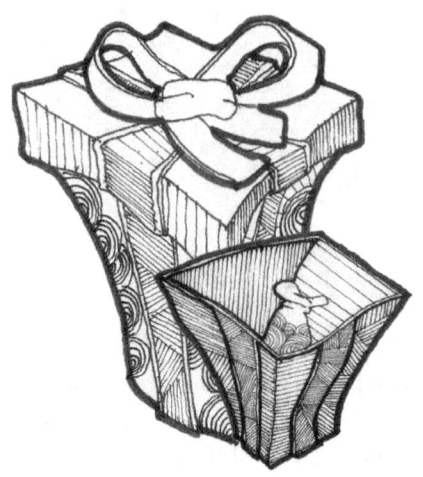

is estimated to be $429 billion. According to a study from Pike Research, sustainable packaging is a fast-growing segment of the global packaging industry, and will grow to 32% of the total market by 2014, up from just 21% in 2009.

It is not surprising therefore that you see commitments and innovations in eco-friendly packaging. EnviroPAK in North America for example uses complex recycled paper pulp for packing electronic goods. By opting for paper pulp in the place of expanded polystyrene, the company has claimed to save 70% in packaging and shipping costs.

Sustainable packaging often leads to innovation. While the use of recycled paper in packaging is one of the common options, Dell has pioneered the use of bamboo to protect certain devices[38]. Two-thirds of Dell's portable devices will ship in bamboo by the end of 2011. Bamboo is local (hence has less GHG emissions), grows quickly and is strong and durable. Plus, bamboo packaging is biodegradable and can be composted after use.

But then "under packaging" is also not desirable. A recent report by the Global Packaging Project states that the environmental risks of under packaging can be greater than excessive packaging. By reducing packaging excessively, products get damaged in transit, requiring re-manufacturing and re-distribution in order to replace the original products. Further, there are costs and liabilities for disposal of off-spec, discarded or foul products. Thus, by trying to reduce the environmental impact of packaging, companies may simply be shifting, and potentially increasing, the adverse impact to the environment. So a careful balance is needed. Let us not overdo sustainability.

For coming up with a sustainable packaging design

---

38 See: http://content.dell.com/in/en/corp/d/corp-comm/bamboo-packaging

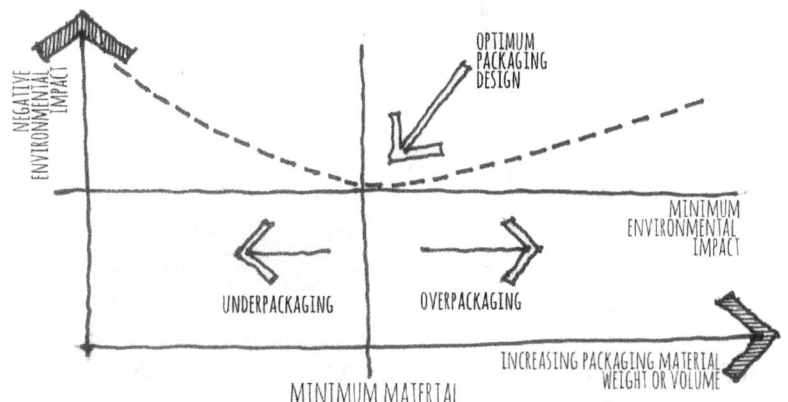

therefore, every manufacturer has to think 'out of the box' and yet be practical. This is done through clever choice of materials, design and a communiqué that tells that while environmental impacts are reduced, the product security is not compromised. You as a consumer will now judge a product in its *totality* – not just how green it is but in *addition* how smart and sensible is the packaging.

We got to think Out of the Box!

32

PLASTIC, PAPER OR REUSABLE SHOPPING BAG?

(This article is a modified version of article published by Green Prospects Asia in Malaysia)

Plastic bags are still used at shopping malls. A plastic bag can be 'in principle' reused many, many times. If collected, plastic bags can be melted and transformed into products, as an additive for road asphalting and even to make diesel.

Plastic if not recycled can be burned to generate electricity. Burning of chlorinated plastics can however lead to emission of dioxins and heavy metals. If incineration is not done at right temperature and appropriate control systems are not in place. Plastic does not readily degrade in a landfill. Biodegradable plastic bags are now coming up that are 'corn based'. Biodegradable plastic is however still quite expensive.

There is a popular misconception that paper bags are more environmentally friendly than plastic bags. Paper comes from trees and unless sustainable forestry is practiced, making paper leads to depletion of green cover – affecting local ecosystems and extent of absorption of GHG emissions. According to a 2007 study by Boustead Consulting & Associates, it takes almost four times as much energy to manufacture a paper bag as it does to manufacture a plastic bag. Paper bags use twenty times as much fresh water v/s plastic bags. These facts are just startling!

If we want to recycle paper, then the paper must be collected and converted to pulp. This is done by use of several different chemicals including sodium hydroxide, hydrogen peroxide and sodium silicate. The pulp must be washed with clean water to "deink". Ecological footprint of a recycled paper bag is therefore no different from a plastic bag. Both are equally sinful.

The best choice overall is perhaps to use a reusable

bag. Most reusable bags last for 5-10 years and beyond. Reusable shopping bags are often made out of waste materials - so in some sense – help convert waste to a resource. In Australia, most green bags are made of 100% non-woven polypropylene which is recyclable but is not biodegradable. 'End of life' impact of such reusable bags can therefore be complex.

An unpublished report from the UK's Environment Agency found that when compared to a traditional plastic bag, a canvas or cotton reusable bag would have to be reused a total of 171 times to offset the GHG emissions. So reusable bags must be used sufficiently enough to claim the environment advantage.

If a reusable bag is made using waste materials e.g. discarded textile fabric then it is much better. Making of such bags is often done by providing employment to women and the underprivileged so there is a benefit of livelihood creation especially for the poor. The apparel industry promotes reusable shopping cotton bags today as *sustainable fashion.*

Many fashion czars and supermarkets have introduced incentives towards use of reusable bags. Some supermarkets give points to customers when they bring their own shopping bags. When the customers collect a certain amount of points, they can usually get discount coupons or gifts, which motivate customers to reduce plastic bag use. Some

retailers such as Whole Foods Market and Target offer a cash discount for bringing in reusable bags. This makes the adoption of reusable bag an even smarter choice.

There are however concerns about the use of reusable bags as well. Shoppers do not wash their bags once they return home and the bags may lead to food poisoning. Because of their repeated exposure to raw meats and vegetable there is an increased risk of food-borne diseases.

Since reusable bags are often made out of waste, there are contamination risks. In January 2011, USA Today ran an article based on a report from the Center for Consumer Freedom, that bags sold in the U.S. by Walgreens, Safeway, Giant, Giant Eagle, Bloom and other grocery chains and retailers contained levels of lead in excess of 100 parts per million, the maximum amount allowed under law in many U.S. states. These findings are however not supported with adequate data.

To conclude, life cycle impacts of paper and plastic bags are roughly equal in terms pros and cons. When faced with the question of paper or plastic, the answer should be neither. Choosing a high-quality reusable bag will make you the real 'green shopper'. But remember that reusable bags must meet certain product quality and safety standards. You must also clean or wash the reusable bags prior to each use. And most importantly, you must actually practice reuse!

33

WHY SHOULD GREEN PRODUCTS COST MORE?

You walk in a supermarket in the section of green products and often get intrigued by the fact that the prices are a wee bit higher than the equivalent *brown* products. For some, this price hike is justified as these products have a 'brand' so to say. Sporting an organic T shirt in a party or serving an organic coffee post a celebrity lunch has that 'distinguishing' feel that you are essentially paying for! But fundamentally, why should you pay more for green products?

Many believe, and rightly so, that the market size of green products is rather small today and economies of scale do not simply come in as an advantage to the manufacturer or retailer. Green products get produced in small lots, more like boutique items and hence tend to cost more. It is weird that manufacturers go out of their way to make green products that cost more money – consumers do not buy them and then the manufacturer says "See, no one wants them!"

A green product should ideally be resource-lean and should generate low wastes/residues. So it should provide an advantage of less cost of inputs (water, energy, materials) and that of processing outputs (wastes or residues). All this should improve competiveness and provide an incentive to make more volumes.

Again, a green product, if truly green, must cost less, if accounted in a life cycle perspective. The problem is that life-cycle costs and

benefits are not generally computed and demonstrated to convince the buyer or the consumer. Price is often the driver for the decision. Further, life cycle costs and benefits are unevenly shared and are often hidden.

Some argue that green products are bound to cost more if they use frontier technologies and materials that are yet to be commercialized. If green products use recycled materials then cost of recycling is sometimes more than cost of virgin materials because of disproportionate costs of reverse logistics and often due to perverse pricing of resources. Green products are expected to be compliant across the supply-chains that may have informal segments. So you pay more for organic food ingredients as here the manufacturer will ensure proper wage to the labor.

There are companies however who have set prices of their green products comparable to those of conventional products and in some cases a wee bit lower! Examples of such companies are Sierra Nevada Brewing company, that uses fuel cells; Stonyfield Farm and Trader Joe's yogurt, that have reduced packaging; General Mills, which reduced the shape of noodles in Hamburger Helper to reduce

packaging volume by 20%, and Procter & Gamble and Unilever, in association with Wal-Mart, that changed liquid detergents to concentrated formulas to reduce consumption of water, plastic, and cardboard. So what works is the innovation in greening.

So when you next visit the Supermarket, look for companies that maintain or lower the price of a green product. These companies represent hallmarks of innovation and long-term interests in influencing the markets towards ensuring business with sustainability.

(Blog based on article I published in Green Prospects Asia in Malaysia. You may like visit report prepared by Green Purchasing Network of India on Consumer Perception of Green Products. Visit http://www. gpnindia.org)

34

MINISTER'S GREEN MOBILE PHONE

Last week, India's Environment Minister Mr. Prakash Javadekar got a gift from President Obama's office on his birthday.

The gift was an advanced mobile phone with several green features.

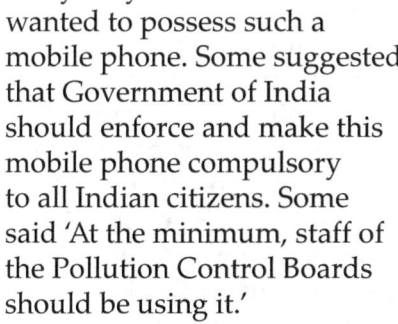

All in the Ministry were excited and everybody wanted to possess such a mobile phone. Some suggested that Government of India should enforce and make this mobile phone compulsory to all Indian citizens. Some said 'At the minimum, staff of the Pollution Control Boards should be using it.'

The Minister called me to his office. He was very excited to show me this new mobile phone.

"Do you know Dr Modak, this phone will lead to a green transformation in India – the Minister said while opening the leather case of the mobile that had a punch line in small fonts – "this case is eco-friendly – Made in the USA."

(I wanted to know what the term eco-friendly meant. Quite an ambiguous term I thought)

I said "Sir, I think you trust the Americans too much. Americans are very clever when it comes to marketing. They will call any product as green. I wonder what makes this mobile so green." I said.

The Minister smiled "Don't get so nervous Dr. Modak. Do you know that this mobile contains least quantity of metals? An average mobile phone contains 24 mg of gold, 250 mg of silver, 9000 mg of copper, 3800 mg of cobalt and 9 mg of palladium[39]. This mobile phone contains only half of

---

39 See http://www.metalminemedia.com/p/gold-in-cell-phones-average-mobile.html

these amounts. Less metal content means less extraction of rare earths, reduced risks to mobile phone users & the environment and lesser costs of treatment and disposal of the discarded mobiles. And low content of metals makes this mobile phone really cheap.

That's good to know I said "But less metal content could also mean poor performance of the touch screen, weaker signal detection and network frequently falling down." Imagine you are speaking to the Minister of Environment of Germany for lobbying on climate change and the phone hangs especially when you are about to change your stance! Won't it be very embarrassing? And what's more – your sudden silence could give a wrong signal. I suggest you don't use this new phone for important international conversations. For national talking this may be OK"

But the Minister was not in the mood to listen.

"Well, let me now tell you about the charger. The Americans have made the phone charger solar powered. So you don't consume electricity to charge this mobile. You therefore burn less of coal, hence generate lesser GHG emissions. Further, there will be less import of coal, less transportation and again less emissions…

"Oh Minister, such solar battery chargers are already in the market and not doing well" I said this while inspecting the solar cover of the Green phone.

The solar cover generally requires high-maintenance. As long as it's latched onto the phone, it will convert direct sunlight into electronic energy, but it isn't effective through glass. Further, the battery will get charged only if you hold the phone at a 90-degree angle to the sun. It is estimated that you'll receive only 20 minutes of talk time after an hour of sun worship. Do you expect to stand for an hour in the sun holding this phone at 90-degree angle just to show that you are eco-friendly? You'll have to be outdoors for at least 30 minutes on a sunny day. I know you have a lot of free time now as you have introduced self-regulation on environment in the country (meaning less enforcement) but for the sake of impressing others you cannot say that you can spare so much time – although this will be of interest to the environment."

"And remember that most people will use conventional chargers in addition, as a standby. So solar-powered charger will be more of a fashion and in fact add more burden on the environment."

The Minister was not pleased with my protest.

"You are so negative" he said. "Do you work with Times Now?"

I said "No"

Now let me show you something revolutionary.

The Minister opened a miniature secret slot using a toothpick on his table.

Look here – this is the slot where special nano fibers are plugged into this mobile set. These nano fibers can detect key air pollutants in the air.

He then pressed a blue button on the mobile phone. I saw a chain of digits scrolling over the screen. The digits were so erratic that it resembled the stock prices of the Bombay Stock Exchange, especially

when the RBI Governor and the Finance Minister simultaneously speak.

"These are not stock prices" The Minister seemed to have read my mind "These are the levels of PM2.5 that are in the air right now. These are the fine particulates that we are breathing"

I was shocked with this part of technology. "Very impressive," I said. "This means anyone using this green phone will be able to know the air quality around him"

"Indeed," the Minister said this in a triumphant voice.

All the users of this phone will not only be able to view the air quality data but will also be able to transmit this data to our NIC Central server. A real-time GIS based map will be created for every city. This data polling can happen every 10 seconds if you like.

Millions of mobile phone users in India will thus send billions of digital data on air quality they breathe. We will analyze this data and issue warnings. If the values exceed the standards, then the mobile phone will beep and alert.

As the Minister said this, the green phone started beeping I got up and opened the window. The sound of the beeps started increasing. Both of us however ignored the increasing beeping.

The Minister continued:

"I have asked Obama's office to include two more additional channels – one for carbon monoxide and another for noise."

I started wondering about the impact of such a nano mobile device.

Imagine people carrying such a mobile phone in movie theaters, A/C buses, A/C railway coaches etc. These people will be really upset if they come to know what poor quality of air they are breathing. This would lead to fewer people going to the theaters.

I couldn't resist saying "Yes Minister, this will simply revolutionize air and noise quality monitoring in the country. You can even shut down the Pollution Control Boards as they perhaps don't matter."

"But processing of 10-second data pouring from a million mobile phone users in the city like Mumbai alone will be so challenging. Also won't it make the price of the mobile phone a bit higher? Plus there will be issues on the accuracy, upkeep and maintenance of such a sophisticated device etc. How perfect is the

nano-technology?"

"I have thought over your concerns already." The Minister said.

"I have told the Americans to put a routine of random number generation instead of attempting actual measurements with the nano-fibers. When you will press the blue button, the screen will show so called 'air quality data' that will be essentially randomly generated. The basic idea will be to raise awareness of people and feed them something to discuss about in seminars and parties."

"And what was the response of the Americans?" I could not resist but ask

"Oh, they said – that's what they currently do!" The Minister said with a smile.

Indeed, design of mobile phones is getting *greener* today considering the significant environmental and social impact they cause in their life cycle.

Innovations are happening to cut down the metal content without any functional compromise. Low-impact batteries have also been the focus. Research and application of nano technology for environmental monitoring is also catching up.

The days of such a revolution are not far away. So one day Mr. Prakash Javdekar will actually launch India's first Green Phone.

I would highly recommend reading about the **Citi-Sense** project[40]

We should be building a pilot Citi-Sense in India. It fits into Prime Minister's vision of Smart Cities. Anyone interested in joining me?

See some of these useful links[41]

---

40 Download one of the newsletters at http://www.citi-sense.eu/Portals/106/Documents/ Dissemination%20material/CITI-SENSE_Newsletter%20No4.pdf

41 http://www.compoundchem.com/2014/02/19/the-chemical-elements-of-a-smartphone/ http://www.cnet.com/news/are-mobile-solar-chargers-worth-it/ http://cseweb.ucsd.edu/~earrowsm/TR.pdf

35

Green Washing: A Step towards Sustainability

The Mayor of Mumbai called me urgently on a Sunday morning. His interview was scheduled in the evening with Times Now. This interview was to be big breaking news.

In the interview, the Mayor was to make a major announcement on actioning sustainability for the city of Mumbai. The proposed action was a secret and no one knew the Mayor's mind. Before giving the interview however, the Mayor wanted to consult me. After all, he was to face Times Now's Arnab Goswami.

After the initial pleasantries, the Mayor asked "Dr Modak, do you have a washing machine at home?" I said "Yes, I do but it's rather old now. I need to buy a new one".

The Mayor asked "In that case which washing machine would you buy?" I did not understand the relevance of this question to the interview or to Arnab Goswami.

I said "I would buy the cheapest. Or the one that gives a deal or a discount e.g. Buy a Samsung washing machine and get 50% discount on a microwave"

The Mayor wasn't pleased with my (practical) answer. He looked a bit disappointed.

"What if I were to ask you to choose between a top-loading and front-loading washing machine? he asked.

Given my problem of back pain and bending difficulty due to spondylitis, I said that I will prefer to buy a top-loading washing machine. But I wondered how come the Mayor picked up these technical terms. May be an LG salesman visited him recently.

The mayor continued "Did you know that front-loading washing machines use 40 to 60% less water, 30 to 50% less energy and 50 to 70% less detergent than the top-loaders! These machines cost a bit more but if you considered 'life cycle costs' then the front-loading machines will be cheaper and environment & energy friendly"

I told the Mayor that this fact is well known. In Europe, more than 90% of washing machines are front-loaders, compared with less than 5% in the U.S. Americans are essentially dumb or insensitive or consumptive people. Europeans are not, because they simply cannot afford to be ignorant. Indians are everything of the above.

Currently, the washing machine market in India is estimated to be about 30% of the total INR 160,000 million home appliances market i.e. is of about INR 50,000 million. An estimated 2.5 million new washing machines are sold in the market every year. The front-loading washing machine category accounts for only10% of the overall washing machine market.

The Mayor read out this statistics from an IFB flyer that was there on his table. IFB is one of the major manufacturers of front-loading washing machines.

Imagine if all washing machines were of front-loading type in Mumbai. Mumbai has some 5 million families. Let us assume that 20% of these families have washing machines. If used every day, this would amount to a water consumption of 50 m3 a year per family. Now instead of a top loading machine if front loading machines are used, then this would lead to a reduction of at least 10 m3 of water consumption a year. This would mean saving of at least 10 million m3 of fresh water and a reduction of 8 million m3 of wastewater. Incidentally, we supply 250 million m3 of water every year in Mumbai. So overall, there will be at least 4% water use reduction. If front-loaders are promoted or made mandatory then this saving could easily reach a double digit figure crossing 10%.

The Mayor was ready with such calculations. Impressive I thought.

I told him that he should highlight the energy benefits as well. Front-loading machines consume 30 to 50% less energy per load. So there is less consumption of electricity, lower emissions of Greenhouse Gases (GHG) and more importantly saving in terms of money.

A typical top-loader machine spins at about 600 rpm (revolutions per minute). Many front-loading machines spin faster -1000 rpm to 1600 rpm. This forces more water out of the washing. Therefore, front loaders reduce drying time and energy input needed for drying. Of course natural drying should be preferred to save electricity.

"So what's going to be the breaking news Mr Mayor?" I asked

"Well, I am proposing the following. For the next 6 months, front-loading washing machines will be promoted. Taxes on these machines will be lower than top loaders. In the next six months, I will organize a ban on the top-loading machines. No white goods retail shop will be able to stock a top-loading machine. There will be surprise raids and if a top-loader is found, then there will be heavy fines levied. In a year, you would find that 80% of the washing machine users will be in the front-loading category. Instead of preaching sustainability at the concept level, I'd rather like to be focused and specific."

"That's an amazing move Mr Mayor," I said. And it's rather bold. No city in the world has such an action plan. Tell Arnab that **Green Washing should be the first step towards Mumbai's Sustainability.**

The Mayor was pleased with my statement – he liked it and noted it down. "I will say exactly this – and you phrased it very well for me." He thanked me profusely.

I left the Mayor's bungalow and was driving home. On my way, I saw an outlet of Vijay Sales – one of the large white goods retail chains in Mumbai. I stopped by to see how people select washing machines.

In the section of washing machines, I saw mostly women. Men were somewhere else – in the TV, mobile phone and computer sections – watching TV programs for their entertainment and asking some stupid questions to the salesmen.

I asked the woman who had decided to buy a front-loading machine. "Madam, what is the advantage of this machine?" The woman first looked at me suspiciously and when convinced of my innocence said, "Only this model fits into the space I have in my 'passage' between the kitchen and the toilet. No other model fits! I was disappointed as I thought she would tell me the advantage of reduced water and energy consumption and her commitment to sustainability

I reached home and called my Professor friend. As usual he had a new point to make.

"It's not just the machine, but

a lot depends on how you use the machine," Professor said. "This matters significantly in a machine's '*use phase*'. Men in the house in particular need to be trained. A recent study reveals that more than half (58%) of British men 'can't use a washing machine properly' because they find the panel of the machine 'confusing'. According to this research, 16 to 24 year olds are most reluctant to do their own laundry, the most popular excuse being not knowing what buttons to press (40%). So even the best washing machines with good water and energy efficiency do not get optimally used! Tell me how many of us read the book of instructions (that is written in six languages) or ask for a demo of the washing machine – whether top-loading or front-loading[42]."

"We often make a wrong choice of the capacity of the machine, forgetting family size and requirements. We tend to underload or overload the machine and generally latter. Overloading damages the drum bearings and belt. An overloaded washing machine fails to clean fabric properly because there is not enough room for movement in the washer and so detergent and water cannot reach evenly to every garment."

I thought the Professor made an important point. We need to learn how to use the washing machines properly – mere technology perspective is not enough to practice sustainability.

The Professor continued.

"And did you know that the type of detergent is different for front load and top load. Wrong detergent choice can lead to multiple wash cycles to wash clothes properly leading to wastage of water and electricity. Always use the manufacturer recommended detergent to wash clothes."

"Conventional detergents are comprised of a concoction of fragrances, endocrine disruptors, neurotoxins and potent cancer-causing chemicals. Most detergents have signature fragrances which are designed to impregnate and stay in clothes. The so called "aroma" of the washing chemicals can be hazardous. According to research by the University of Washington, when scented laundry detergents and fabric softeners are used, dryer vents emit more than 25 Volatile

---

42 See http://www.dailymail.co.uk/femail/article-2340216/Half-men-use-washing-machine-properly-quarterfigure-switch-on.html

Organic Compounds (VOCs) per load, many of which are classified as hazardous air pollutants. Oddly, detergents with less hazardous chemicals have lower cleaning efficiency (See Comparative Study of Detergents in India-A Step towards More Sustainable Laundry Meena Khetrapala et al.)[43]"

I was amazed at Professor's inputs. I decided to call up the Mayor and update him immediately with this information so that he can make interesting points in the interview. But by then the interview had already begun.

Arnab was asking questions to the Mayor on the water and energy related woes in the Mumbai city. The threat to city's sustainability was brought out. Mr. Mayor fielded all these questions. He then elaborated about his idea of focusing on the washing machines, reasons why front loading machines were important and how the switch could help to achieve major reduction in water and energy consumption with the co-benefit of reduction in the GHGs. He made a strong environmental and business case. Finally, he rolled out his one-year plan of the 'phase

out'. He even made a case that his suggestion should be included as a part of India's INDC (Intended Nationally Determined Contributions) that will be discussed in the COP meeting in Paris. I was really impressed with the Mayor's extrapolation of the idea to the national and international scales.

He ended with a statement *Green* **Washing should be the first action step towards Mumbai's Sustainability.**

I however saw that Arnab Goswami was not impressed. He said he does not like impositions to the public on which washing machine to use. "That's utter infringement of consumer's freedom," he said. "Sustainability cannot be forced upon or legislated."

Then with his characteristic pause, he asked "May I ask you Sir what happens to the top-loading washing machines that you will phase out? Where will they go? Will they find a place in Mumbai's slums or suburbs or at the landfill? Do you have an end of use of washing machine plan in place?"

The Mayor was really uncomfortable with this question and was not able to

---

43 http://journals.du.ac.in/ugresearch/pdf/J15.pdf

answer. He looked stunned with this 'googly'.

As if this was not enough, Arnab asked the mayor in his high-pitch voice. "And what about the fact that your son-in-law is on the Board of Directors of front-loading washing machine maker – IFB? Are you not hand-in-glove with IFB to promote their front-loading machines in the garb of sustainability? This is not green wash – but indeed *hogwash*. The Nation would like to know," he demanded.

Mr. Mayor's face turned white with sweat on his forehead. He muttered "there is something wrong in the transmission of sound." He opted to exit the interview.

And that turned out to be the real big breaking news!

36
The Interview

The Chairman of the newly-constituted National Environmental Protection Authority (NEPA) in India was finally appointed.
The selection process was rigorous. Every top expert and administrator of repute in the country had applied. Besides there were several applications from overseas.

A high-level committee was appointed consisting of Group of Ministers. Further, the PM took personal interest when it came to shortlisting. The Chairman's post was considered to be very important as his/her decisions will either 'make or break' India's journey towards economic development and/or sustainability.

The process of search and selection of the NEPA Chairman made big breaking news in the media. Arnab Goswami ran two episodes on *Times Now* on consecutive Saturdays as an exception.

"The Nation wants to know," he said (and this he said many times). And this time indeed, everyone wanted to know who the Chairman will be.

Apparently, my Professor friend had some hand when the final choice was made. He had never met the gentleman in person but was instrumental in recommending his CV, personally to the PM. That mattered.

When I called on the Professor to understand what went behind the scene, he was rushing out with a video gun. "I have to reach Chairman's house in the next 20 minutes for an interview". He said. "This is his first interview. Apparently he is a stickler for punctuality, and so I would not like to be late even by a minute."

"Why don't you come along? You handle this video part so

that I can focus more on the questions in the interview." I could see him pretty uncomfortable and clumsy in handling the videography equipment. So I readily agreed. Besides, it was a great opportunity for me.

We reached the apartment complex well in time. "Fourth floor and on the left," the Professor said and we reached the door that had no name plate. "Looks like this guy does not like to show off or remain 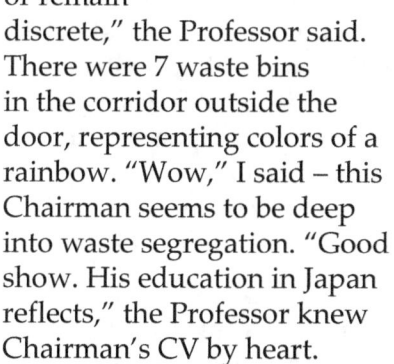 discrete," the Professor said. There were 7 waste bins in the corridor outside the door, representing colors of a rainbow. "Wow," I said – this Chairman seems to be deep into waste segregation. "Good show. His education in Japan reflects," the Professor knew Chairman's CV by heart.

We rang the bell and the door was opened presumably by a servant who ushered us into the drawing room. "*Aap Jara Joote Nikaliye*" (kindly remove shoes) he said this politely and we removed our shoes and then sat on the sofa. "*Saab ooper naha rahe hai*" (My boss is taking shower upstairs) he said. "*Abhi ayenge*" (He will be with you shortly). We said fine.

I started to look around the drawing room. The first thing to notice was a huge painting on the wall that depicted a thick forest with a road cutting across. "Interesting," the Professor said. "Gives me an impression that the Chairman will follow a balanced approach to the protection of forests and infrastructure development. See how lush the forest is". I wasn't convinced with the Professor's interpretation however. I thought that when the Chairman will take over NEPA, the next version of this painting will be a concretized road with forest trimmed down on both sides. We have so many such examples to cite in India of before and after. But I didn't want to be that pessimistic.

In the meanwhile, the professor was investigating the room further to read the Chairman's mind. He spotted a packaging box dumped in the balcony that carried a sticker 'Solar Cooker'. "Look at that,,The Chairman is actually practicing use of renewable energy at home. – even I don't use these devices though I preach about them". I wholeheartedly agreed. We see more people today who don't walk the talk – especially in the sustainability space. I went to the loo and found that the water faucets were fourth-generation water efficient.

During that time, the Professor took a stroll around the drawing room and returned to the sofa with more excitement. He whispered – "This is a real Green Home. Curtains are Oeko-Tex certified; Wall paints are low VOC, Furniture is Green Guard certified and the carpet is made from waste fibers". "How did you know all this, Professor and so quickly?" I was simply astonished. The Professor smiled and pointed me to a certificate that was placed on the Bar that said "This house is Green as it has ...."

"This guy when he takes over as Chairman, India is going to change. All homes will be directed to go green" Professor said.

I walked towards the bar to take a close look at the certificate. Indeed this was true. I was tempted to open the bar to expect to see locally-produced organic wines. But I resisted.

Our later inspections in the room led to more inspirational findings like a motion-detector based lighting system, indoor pollution absorbing plants and a vermicomposting unit with enzymes working in the balcony. "It will simply be a revolution if this Chairman runs NEPA". I said "Firstly we will shift our narrow focus of managing only the emissions and residues to management of resources. He will promote sustainable consumption and production".

"For years we are used to frame only residue-oriented pollution control related legislation," the Professor said lighting his cigar "We should look at what New Zealand did years ago by passing the Resource Management Act. In New Zealand, you need to take *consent to use resource and not consent to pollute* as in India.

"You did a great job of finding this Chairman for NEPA – Professor" I said this with full of respect towards my Professor friend. "Sustainability will now be on the rise."

As we were exchanging our impressions, and warmly so, a tall and bald gentleman descended the staircase. He was wearing a cotton Tee-shirt (must be an organic I thought). He looked at both of us with a

question mark on his face. "Yes please?"

The Professor introduced himself and me and said that this was an appointment taken to interview him as the newly-inducted Chairman of NEPA. I opened the videography equipment case.

"Oh, not again," the gentleman said in a weary tone. "The person you are looking for lives on the opposite side of this floor. I am in Flat 4A and he is in 4B. My door name plate has gone for repairs for the last two days and you are perhaps the third person to make this mistake!"

Both of us were shocked, dazed and embarrassed.

As we were putting on our shoes to reach the other side of the corridor, the gentleman said "Not only do we stay opposite, but we have completely different views – we are neighbors but just 180o apart"

I thought I should better tell the Professor now to stop his bad habit of speculations. And certainly not to make recommendations to the PM solely based on CV. I wish this gentleman applied for the Post.

This blog post draws inspiration from W.S. Maugham's short story "The Poet". It's a great read[44].

Students may like to read Resources Management Act in New Zealand[45] and compare with legislation in India

---

44 See http://pcenglish.weebly.com/uploads/4/9/0/9/4909164/thepoet.pdf and enjoy

45 See http://www.mfe.govt.nz/rma/ This dissertation is a must read.

147

37

Buy Nothing Day

The breaking news in all newspapers and TV channels was about India's adoption of the Buy Nothing Day (BND).

There were intense debates and opinions on the pros and cons of BND.

A few protested – especially from the industry and retail business, but several celebrations were held in the streets mainly by the environmental activists. BND is a great idea – they said.

What's Buy Nothing Day?

Buy Nothing Day is an international day of protest against consumerism. BND was founded in Vancouver by artist Ted Dave and subsequently promoted by Adbusters magazine, based in Canada.

The first Buy Nothing Day was organized in Canada in September 1992 "as a day for society to examine the issue of over-consumption." In 1997, BND was moved to the Friday after American Thanksgiving,

BUY NOTHING DAY
participate by not participating

also called "Black Friday", which is one of the ten busiest shopping days in the United States. Soon, campaigns started appearing in the United States, the United Kingdom, Israel, Austria, Germany, New Zealand, Japan, the Netherlands, France, Norway and Sweden. Participation now includes more than 65 nations.

I suspected that that my Professor friend played some role in advising and convincing the Indian Government to join the BND movement. I therefore called upon him and we met at our usual coffee shop. We settled at the round table in the coffee shop's verandah. An Ethiopian coffee was served with complementary ginger biscuits. The waiter got a large ash tray for the Professor.

"Well, observing BND was my suggestion to the Government" – the Professor said this and lighted his cigar. "It's a tactical move to show India's commitment to the Sustainable Development Goals (SDGs). However, there is bound to be some hiccups that we have to address. Some good ones– and some bad. I am working on these".

I looked at the 48" LED screen on the wall. The Times Now channel was showing shots of the streets of Mumbai – Live!

I saw a huge gathering at the streets of the junction of the Flora Fountain in front of HSBC. Advocate Deshpande, Chairman of *Grahak Sangh* was addressing the rally. He was proposing that we cut up credit cards on the BND to express our concern on the rising consumerism. All patrons of Mumbai Grahak Sangh will stand outside city's prominent malls with a pair of scissors and at sharp 12 am they will cut their credit cards.

I thought the idea was dramatic and really impactful. Besides, this action would mean helping people who want to put an end to mounting debt and extortionate interest rates thrust by the credit card companies.

But if the citizens who cut the cards ask for replacements later – then the cost of replacement would be quite high. And it will also lead to big inconvenience to the credit card companies – I therefore wondered whether it was the right action on BND.

In the meanwhile, the Professor ordered another round of coffee.

There was a group of people sitting on the larger roundtable next to us. A woman having Green Tea was talking about the "Zombie walks" to her friends.

On the BND, people in the United States and the UK take up "Zombie walks": These "zombies" wander around shopping malls with funny dresses and with a blank stare. When asked what they are doing – the participants describe what Buy Nothing Day is about. It's like a fashion parade of the crazy.

"We should go Zombie on the BND of India". The woman with Green Tea said. She suggested that in order to make a good impact, all should follow a certain theme e.g. a saffron dress. We could dress like Radhe Maa for instance, she said. This will bring in a new spiritual dimension. The woman made more such suggestions based on dresses she saw in some of the Page 3 parties.

Most folks at the table were excited and decided to meet once a week to plan ahead for the Zombie walks on BND. "This will be something special – and so different to work on. And it will keep us busy. Let me speak about this to my friends in the next Rotary meeting", the woman having fresh lime soda said.

In the meanwhile, the waiter at the coffee shop came and changed the channel to CNN-IBN as someone complained about Arnab Goswami. CNN-IBN was showing a clip of the pilot BND activity at the Ambience Mall in Delhi to get a kind of preview. This was a procession-like event carried out under Sunita Narain's leadership. Here, the participants silently steered their shopping carts in a long, baffling line without putting anything in the carts or actually making any purchases. The storekeepers were shocked to see this human chain moving. Sunita said that this was only a pilot or a dry run but on the actual BND, such processions will happen at 110 malls of India from 14 cities and already

10,000 people had signed up.

I thought that this was very impressive. To counteract, I was told that many retailers like Shoppers Stop, Reliance Fresh had come up with a strategy to give hefty discounts to the purchases made on BND and lure these people to "buy something".

The Professor said "this is nothing. Medha Patkar, Arundhati Roy and Vandana Shiva have come together to support BND. All the NGOs who listen to them, will not only ban buying for twenty-four hours but also keep their lights, televisions, computers and other non-essential appliances turned off, their cars parked, and their phones turned off or unplugged from sunrise to sunset. The BND will thus be remembered and talked about over another month because of all the inconveniences caused in this process."

"Very interesting strategy," I remarked.

The Professor continued.

"There are some issues however. Many women from Malabar Hill in Mumbai for example plan to get admitted in Breach Candy and Jaslok hospitals one day in advance to face the trauma of not being able to shop. These women for their health and peace of mind need to shop 'something' every day. Banning shopping could result in medical conditions such as high hypertension, heart palpitation, irregular breathing, profuse sweating, temporary loss of memory etc. Both Breach Candy and Jaslok have set up special BND wards for this purpose where such women can be admitted and treated. The charges are INR 100,000 that these women and their husbands are happy to pay. To them, BND could be dangerous."

I said, "I understand and I do have sympathies"

"Consumerism is too deeply ingrained in the society and culture to be eradicated in one day of abstinence. Everyone has simply become accustomed to this and it is one of those things that cannot be fixed overnight," I said

The Professor put off his Cigar and I continued

"Further, after a day when people can't buy anything, the next day people will spend double the amount, and also the day before, because people will buy things they think are necessary. The retailers, shopkeepers and businessmen will hike the prices one day before and day after BND and thus will make tons of money!

I hope that's not the idea?"

The Professor did not respond.

"It seems that there are around 1 million shopping transactions happening online. How would you handle this shopping on BND? I guess these portals will not operate and we will see the page Site Closed for Today. Is this the plan?" I couldn't resist asking.

"On the contrary" the Professor said. "These websites will remain open. They will let you book the orders but there will not be any deliveries of products on BND as a principle. And if you book the order on BND then you will be required to pay a surcharge of 10%. This surcharge will reach the Government's treasury."

"Wow! Very clever, Professor. I smell a rat here" I said this while settling the bill.

Thank god that BND is not made mandatory and that it is just for a day and not a week. Imagine what could happen if a BNW or Buy Nothing Week was to be observed. May be rich and consumptive nations need a BNW, would you agree?

38
BRUSHING TEETH, SUSTAINABLY

As Diwali (India's festival of lights) is approaching, most corporate houses are busy planning gifts. Every year, as a regular practice, these gifts are given to the staff, clients, and investors and of course to the government officers who matter. Everyone looks towards receiving corporate gifts that typically include leather pouches, boxes of sweets, a thermos or a ceramic decorated plate.

Given the buzz on 'sustainability' however, many corporate honchos such as Anand Mahindra, Kumarmangalam Birla, Cyrus Mistry of Tata and other such environmentally-conscious industry leaders thought of selecting gifts that can bring in a difference and distinguish them from others. "The gifts should communicate sustainability on a day-to-day basis and lead to some impact or a measurable change" – they said.

This led to flocking of many environmental consultants to the procurement divisions of the corporate offices. Several propositions were made such as an eco-friendly Tee shirt made from the farms in Maikal, table stationery set made out of waste from Dharavi, an organic jam or honey made by tribes in the hills of Matheran etc. The choice was difficult to make as many provided reports on the life cycle analyses of their products which were hard to believe and were generally built on data not relevant to India.

My Professor friend was simply in demand because of his expertise, farsighted vision and reputation. He was approached by several corporates and personal calls were made by the Birlas, Tatas, Mahindras and Ambanis. Everyone wanted the Professor to come up with some brilliant idea of a product that will show a great example of sustainability.

We met at our usual coffee place and I asked the Professor about what was on his mind as advice to companies on Diwali gift

"Well, I have to decide whom should I advise – as all these industry leaders are my good friends. But if I were to advice, then I would propose providing a pack of two tooth brushes as the Diwali gift."

"A tooth brush! Are you crazy?" I exclaimed. "A tooth brush cannot be a Diwali gift. What's the sustainability element in a tooth brush? In fact I suspect it may be reverse!"

The Professor lit his cigar. "It's not the usual tooth brush I am referring to. It is tooth brush made from Bamboo and with Nylon-4 as the bristles"

"There are about 18 million people in Mumbai. Let's say, as a very rough estimate, that 10% are little babies and very old people with no dentures and don't have teeth. So that's 16.2 million Mumbaikars with teeth,(including dentures, which still need to be brushed, so they count."

"We all know the dentist tells us to change our toothbrush when it starts to get shaggy; about every three months. We also know that we are lazy, and not aware that timely changing of tooth brush matters. We probably only change a tooth brush once a year."

"So every year, we should expect 16.2 million tooth brushes "bought and thrown" in Mumbai alone, buried in the landfills of the city."

"These toothbrushes are made of plastic (the handles) and nylon (the bristles), plus they come in plastic packaging – one of those single-use, disposable consumer items. As with most plastics, polypropylene and nylon are sourced from non-renewable petroleum and their manufacture is resource-intensive and more importantly these materials are not biodegradable. Just one person can create four kilograms of waste from disposable toothbrushes during a lifetime that will remain in the environment for at least 500 years."

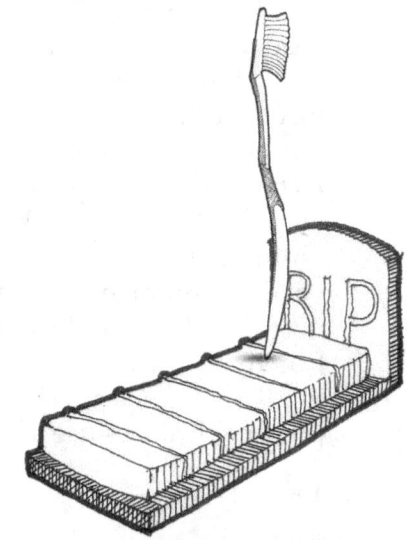

I said – "Agree, that tooth brush is a serious issue. But what is the option then Professor?"

"Sustainably-produced bamboo has the potential to be one part of the solution. Bamboo fiber can be used to completely replace the plastic used for toothbrush handles." The Professor said.

I remembered the electric toothbrush. These brushes are often touted as more eco-friendly than the conventional disposable tooth brushes because only the head needs to be replaced, which means less waste to the landfill.

The Professor had a counter argument:

"The materials used in rechargeable electric toothbrushes are similar, in fact with additional components including a plastic base, plug and power cord. The internal motor, which moves the bristle head, can contain nickel- and chromium-bearing alloys. Electric brushes are commonly powered by an internal rechargeable nickel-metal hydride (NiMH) or nickel-cadmium (NiCa) battery. Both have environmental impacts over their lifespan. Research from Bath University, England, found that electric-powered brushes use around 0.072kWh/day, equivalent to the energy use of a toaster. So electric tooth brush is not a good option!"

"An estimated 50% of the total 'ecological costs' of a manual plastic toothbrush, and 60% of the lifetime energy requirements of an electric toothbrush, are incurred during the manufacture and distribution phases, compared to the usage and disposal phases."

"In comparison, the handle of bamboo brushes are made from moso bamboo, a rapidly renewing plant which requires little water. This bamboo is farmed (not old-growth bamboo), has natural antimicrobial properties and no pesticides are necessary for growing it. Moso Bamboo is sourced largely from China and India has only recently started looking at Moso bamboo cultivation on a scale it deserves. A carbonization finishing process, which provides water resistance and prevents the growth of microbes on the toothbrush, is the only component of the ecological costs of using bamboo."

The Professor continued.

"The bristles of the bamboo brush are made from a nylon 4 blend. Bamboo brushes break down into compost, leaving no residue, including the nylon bristles. Japanese researchers have shown that nylon 4 breaks down in compost within four months, while nylon 6 that is used by the conventional tooth brush does not."

"Packaging is another consideration. Conventional manual toothbrushes, and replacement heads for electric toothbrushes, are generally packaged in a 'blister pack' of polyvinyl chloride (PVC) and cardboard, while bamboo toothbrushes come in biodegradable paper box with a compostable wrapper made of Polylactic Acid derived from corn. Being concerned about the issues in industrial corn production involving genetic manipulation, fertilizers and pesticides, some of the bamboo tooth brush makers are making the switch to a plant-based cellulose wrapper that does not use corn."

"By the way, only 50% of the Indian population is known to use modern oral care products and only 15% brush teeth twice a day. And so the market is going to grow. It is estimated that 700 Million toothbrushes are sold every year in India. HLL and Colgate-Palmolive account of 70% of this market but they only make conventional manual tooth brushes and now electric tooth brushes."

"I asked Cyrus Mistry to speak to Harish Manwani of HLL and Nambier of Colgate-Palmolive and convince them to start manufacturing Bamboo brushes in India. And if they didn't show interest then he could take on manufacturing Bamboo tooth brush as a Tata product."

"So this year, who will supply Bamboo tooth brush as a corporate gift in India?" I asked.

"Well, this year it will have to be sourced from China. Of course at the cost of added carbon emissions in the shipment. I only hope that the Chinese don't invade this market as then it will be too late for Indians to get in" the Professor said.

"Interesting point of caution," I said.

The Professor put off his cigar.

"All those who will receive these tooth brushes as corporate gifts, will think of sustainability as the first thing in the morning when they start brushing their teeth.

And hopefully with such a start in the morning, sustainability will be practiced throughout the day. This is where the impact of the corporate gift will come in"

"Bless you Professor," I said "wish it was so simple"

Before the advent of the nylon bristle, our forefathers used to rely on nature for cleaning their teeth. While the Indians were known to use Neem tree twigs (*Datoon*) the Chinese preferred the tough hair off the neck of a Siberian Boar!!!

The Miswak sewak is the natural way people in the Middle East, Africa, and Asia have cleaned their teeth for centuries. The bark is peeled off the tip of the stick from Asian Arak or Peelu trees, olive or walnut trees and the end chewed to separate fibers to rub on the teeth. As the fibers wear, the tip is cut off and the end peeled and chewed. Miswak sticks get in between crevices in teeth, promote tooth remineralization and strengthen enamel. It is antibacterial and prevents infections, and promotes saliva and blood circulation as the sticks are chewed. The stick contain minerals, alkaloids, vitamin C and calcium.

Neem sticks are the version of the Miswak sewak that residents of India have used for centuries and many still do today.

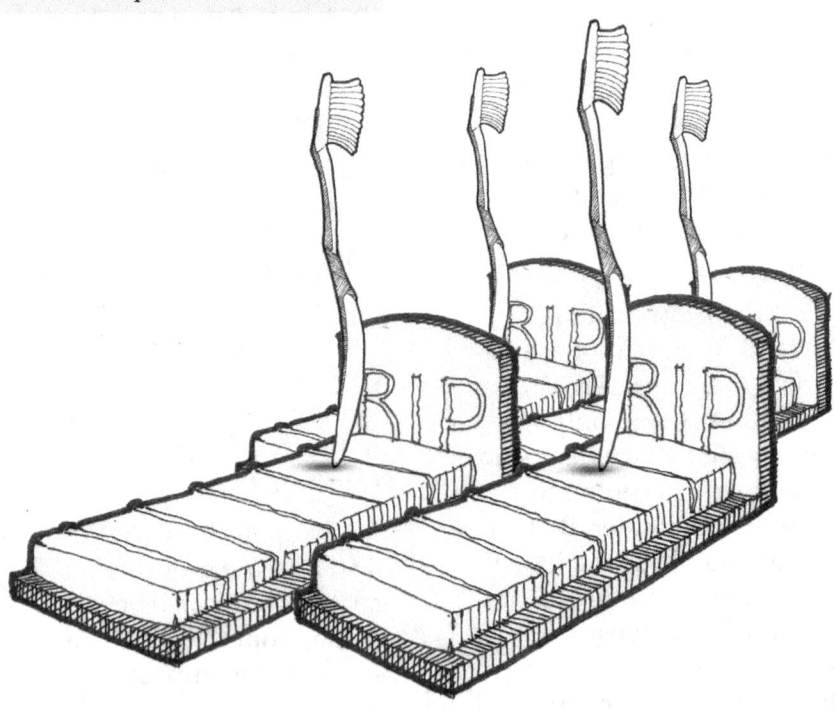

39

Make to Take

This Sunday morning I was having a cup of tea with diet *khakras* (Indian crunchy snack) and reading a newspaper. My Professor friend called me.

"Have you got any used tube lights to dispose?"

I didn't have one in the house (as I use mostly CFLs) but remembered that my garage had 4 used tube lights of Elips brand. I hadn't figured out how to dispose these used tube lights. My usual kachra lady (waste picker) had not shown much interest.

When I told about this to the Professor – he said – "Well then, here is a deal for you. Elips Tube lights have an offer – give them your used tube lights and they will give you a brand new free. No strings attached! It is part of Elips Extended Producer Responsibility (EPR). There is a tube light collection centre opened at Shivaji Park and today is the deal day between 11 am to 5 pm. Just rush." Elips wants to demonstrate

to the citizens how they care about their used products and about the environment.

I liked the deal and told my wife that I will drive right away to Shivaji Park with my used tube lights. I thought of calling a few friends as well. Apparently, you could get a new tube light for a used tube light of any make. That I thought was a very generous gesture by Elips. The Professor was to join me later at the Barista Coffee shop after the exchange was done.

The EPR concept is not new. It's been around for the past two decades and practiced by corporates in the developed world. The idea of EPR was formally introduced by my good friend Thomas Lindquist in 1990 in a report to the Swedish Ministry of the Environment. In subsequent reports prepared for the Ministry, the following definition of EPR emerged.

Extended Producer Responsibility is an environmental protection strategy to reach an environmental objective of a decreased total environmental impact from a product, by making the manufacturer of the product responsible for the entire life-cycle of the product and especially for the take-back, recycling and final disposal of the product.

Thomas did his doctoral dissertation on EPR[46]

There are many examples of successful and impacting EPRs. A very recent report on the status of EPR in EU countries should be seen[47]. This report is from Bio Intelligence Service.

EPR is now legislated in many countries and brought into national policy frameworks[48] for one of the most recent overviews.

In India, EPR is often practiced by involving and supporting the informal sector i.e. the waste pickers. This makes the Indian case unique. E-waste is one of the most popular waste streams in focus. In 2010, Indian lawmakers passed an e-waste policy that included EPR.

The Indian EPR law requires electronic manufacturers' partner with recyclers, including the informal sector, by setting up collection centers. This is perhaps the first time in the Indian environmental management framework that participation of an informal sector is sought. This should lead to creation of green jobs and support the livelihoods of the poor.

You may like to read the 2007 report commissioned by Greenpeace on India's E-waste and EPR[49]. Incidentally, Thomas was one of the authors of this report.

It was again Greenpeace who assessed the extent of EPR actually practiced by the Corporates in the E-Waste sector. This report prepared in 2008 showed that companies that practice take-backs in other countries did not do so in India. There was a clear

46 See: http://lup.lub.lu.se/luur/download?func=downloadFile&recordOId=19692&fileOId=1002025. This dissertation is a must read

47 See http://ec.europa.eu/environment/waste/pdf/target_review/Guidance%20on%20EPR%20%20Final%20Report.pdf

48 See http://www.calrecycle.ca.gov/EPR/PolicyLaw/#World

49 See http://escrap.com.ar/descargas/extended-producer-resp-non-OECD.pdf

disparity[50]. Indeed, we need to take a stock of the situation on EPR practiced in India today.

There are other examples of "take-back practices" in India. See take-back program from Tetrapack India in Bangalore in partnership with a social enterprise[51]. Samsung runs a STAR program[52] and so does Dell[53]

When I reached the collection center at Shivaji-Park, I was greeted by the Marketing Manager of Elips. On collecting 4 of my used Elips tube lights, he handed over to me 4 brand new, slim and efficient new tube lights.

When I was writing my contact details in the fat register kept on the desk, he asked "Sir, do you have used CFLs? – well if you have them then come in next month, as we have a scheme for replacing used CFLs. For a pair of used CFLs, we give you one free! And the used CFLs do not have to be of Elips make"

I was impressed. This is perhaps TEPR I thought i.e. Too *much* of Extended Producer Responsibility!

I started worrying about the Elips Company. Are they crazy? While environmental stewardship is fine, it cannot be at the cost of business. If Elips starts such campaigns of "take back" on their products, they will sure get bankrupt one day.

When I told all this to the Professor at the Barista Coffee shop, he lit his cigar and took a deep puff.

"You know what you just did? You walked to Elips with free raw material to help them make 9 more new tube lights. The amount of mercury in a fluorescent tube light typically varies from 3 to 46 mg, depending on lamp size and age. The kind tube lights you carried may probably contain 30 mg of mercury and in the new tube lights that Elips makes the mercury content is close to 3 mg. So Elips on collecting say 1000 used tube lights of high mercury content today will get free mercury good enough to make 10000 low mercury tube lights; plus of course the social good to boast of and a record of EPR delivered"

---

50 See http://ewasteguide.info/files/take-back-blues _2008_Greenpeace.pdf.

51 See http://saahas.org/campaign/tetra-pak-collection-recycling/.

52 See http://www.samsung.com/in/samsungrecycle/

53 See http://www.dell.com/learn/in/en/incorp1/dell-environment-recycling

"Oh", I said, "I did not realize the underlying 'economics' or the 'business case' of EPR. Did you advise Elips on this strategy, Professor?" I couldn't resist but ask.

"Well, I did – at a modest fee! But keep this as a secret. Right now I am advising APson Office Products. The deal will be 'bring your used printer and take a new one for free'. Any make will do. The logic of this EPR scheme is to ensure **continued consumption** of cartridges of APson make. A cartridge today costs one third of the printer and gets consumed on an average once a month. So, we will leverage on our free printer in a very short time. In addition, we are setting up a printer repairs workshop by training the youth (job creation) and provide the refurbished printers to underprivileged schools as CSR"

"You are a genius, Professor," I said while settling the bill. Indeed it's a game of make to take!

40

LUNCH BETWEEN OBAMA AND MODI – A DEEP SECRET FOR INDIA'S SMART SUSTAINABLE GROWTH

One of the prominent newspapers covering the recent visit of President Obama to meet Mr. Modi featured the lunch hosted by Government of India at the Hyderabad House. The lunch menu included *Shatwar ka Shorba, Shrimp Karavalli, Neza Kabab, Mahi Sarson, Bhuna Gosht Boti, Mixed Vegetable Kalonoji, Gujarati Kadhi, Matar Pulao, Gajar ka Halva, Gulab Jamun, and Fresh Fruits* ending with South Indian Coffee/Herbal Tea.

Some said that this Menu was a reflection of Modi's geo-political preferences and deserves a deeper analysis. I was also told that the menu was fast becoming a model for all high-level weddings in Gujarat. All top chefs in Gujarat were practicing hard to do a fine job with these menu items. Books were written and videos were produced especially for housewives who wanted to please their husbands' bosses with the Obama-Modi or the OM Lunch Menu. I called on my Professor friend to discuss the menu in these perspectives.

The Professor pooh poohed my observations. He said that a lot had gone behind the lunch and very few know about it. He then asked me to come to our usual coffee shop for a long session. "Come with a pack of cigars for me," he said. "I will give you some amazing dope – all top secrets."

When we took our seats, he lighted his cigar, took a deep puff and said- "Pra-sad, I was the Chief Consultant appointed to plan this lunch by none other than the PM himself. As soon as Obama's visit

got fixed, I was called by the PMO to work on the Lunch Project as an important National Mission. My institute relieved me from all teaching responsibilities. The PMO gave me unlimited budget to hire staff, take on travel or conduct or sponsor any studies or research as needed. I had to meet the PM every week in his personal gym while he used to be on the tread mill and therefore would only listen and not speak"

I could not comprehend how a Lunch Project could be equivalent to a National Mission. Looking at my jinxed face, the Professor continued

"Please understand the gravity of the Lunch. Take the venue itself. Obama is used to eat only in Green Rated Buildings. Six months ago when the lunch was fixed the Hyderabad house, it was not a Green Rated building. So

I commissioned an agency of national repute to assess the building and come up with an action plan for Green Retrofitting. This plan got actually implemented and today we are saving at least INR 1.5 million in electricity bills every month. This experience has led to a national program for building retrofitting following an aggressive business model. Do you know that four metro cities of the country are implementing this program, saving around 10,000 MW of power and 50,000 tons of GHG emissions on an annual basis? The Green Building programs earlier focused only on green-field or new constructions – successful greening of Hyderabad house triggered retrofitting of the existing buildings – that was most needed."

I was impressed.

"Now take the Lunch Menu itself. For this lunch, all the vegetables sourced for cooking were brought from local organic farms. Obama eats only organic food and gets a skin rash and an upset stomach if non-organic food is served. So I went to the organic farms personally to check. I realized that many of these farms did not have formal certification. So I developed a national program. This program included development of criteria, establishment of laboratories for testing, raising consumer awareness, imparting education and providing financial incentives for promotion of organic food etc. Next week, after the Obama lunch, Mr. Modi will be announcing the National Program for Organic Farm Certification that will be operated by the Agricultural Ministry. In the next 10 years, Indians will get only organic food!"

I was about to say that getting just food was more important than getting organic food, but the Professor was in no mood to listen.

"Design of the menu itself was a complex mathematical exercise. We were told that the total calorie intake for Obama was to be 1500 and the bread units were to be between 7 to 8. (I later found out that bread unit parameter was relevant as Obama has mild diabetes). So I set up a 0-1 Mixed Integer Programming optimization problem with Multiple Objectives. My problem statement considered 107 possible dishes or food items and picked only those 11 that added to 1500 calories and 7.5 bread units! With this application experience, I got a mobile phone application developed. Given the rising number of incidence of diabetes in cities in India and the growing serenade lifestyles, this application will help the citizens immensely. In the next two years you will see that all Lunch and Dinner menus in India will be based on my optimization algorithm. There will be a fall in diabetes incidences in urban India".

I was overwhelmed by Professor's national vision. Taking an ordinary lunch (that's what I thought) to the mode of national missions was

something too far-fetched.

The Professor was extinguishing his cigar – "and many more such things, Prasad" he said. "The napkins used on the Lunch table were as per the GOTS standard. If a conventionally bleached and finished napkin is used then formaldehyde sitting on the fabric gets leached as you sweat. Obama is very allergic to such fabrics and sweats profusely even in a room with 22^{0}C. So I flew to the GOTS headquarters in the Netherlands and got the napkins GOTS certified. I then developed with the Ministry of Textiles a National Eco-labelling Program. This program is expected to help the textile industry (and especially those coming from Gujarat) to meet the international eco-labelling requirements. This will lead to increase in exports to the EU and Americas by a whopping 30% over the next 2 years. As a side benefit, health and safety of the consumers will also improve".

I could now clearly see how one lunch with Obama was triggering smart sustainable growth in India. Sadly, few knew that my Professor friend was behind this transformation.

I had a number of questions though and wanted to learn more about other ramifications. So I called Professor's office. "Oh he is not available. And not for the next six months," his secretary said in a tired voice (must be telling this to the numerous callers asking for her boss). When asked about his whereabouts and reasons for a sudden disappearance – she said "Actually, he has strict instructions not to tell anyone – but only to you Dr Modak. Government of France wants to get on with smart sustainable growth. To achieve this goal, the French Government is hosting a lunch for Mr. Obama and Professor has been appointed as the Chief Consultant. He will stay in Paris for the next six months."

"God knows how many such lunches Obama will need to join if the United States of America wants the world to get into sustainable development," I exclaimed!

Note: This piece is fictional and NOT a real story. No offence to Obama, Modi or the PMO. I am writing this note as some of my blog readers wrote to me asking whether 'the Professor' was indeed hired by the PMO! I wish he was!

TEACHING GREEN

For the Academia

41

Do we have enough trained human resources to address current challenges in Environmental Management?

Environmental and Social (E&S) Governance is becoming increasingly complex today. Earlier, project developers had to comply only with the regulations imposed through various acts and rules – but now there are requirements from investors and lenders, supply-chains & markets and the neighborhood. These requirements, in many cases, go beyond the laws of the land.

Furthermore, concepts such as shared value and benefit sharing have come up as also 'CSR' – and more and more transparency is being demanded in the project implementation and operations. Recognition and integration of E&S perspectives is now becoming central or pivotal in strategizing and managing business. E&S management has thus become "material".

Given these changing paradigms, Project developers are in some sense caught in a cleft-stick. How to be consistently compliant with the Government, Investors and Markets (GIM) and yet be competitive has been the daunting question. This requires commitment from the "top", operation of proactive management systems

and culture of knowledge management towards fostering innovation. Without *eco-innovations*, one just cannot meet the targets that otherwise seem impossible!

But the key is to have the right kind of trained human resources who understand the complexity of the E&S Governance and importance of eco-innovation. We need E&S graduates who are exposed to the emerging topics with additional skills such as communication, conflict resolution etc. There is an awful deficiency of human resources in this arena. *"We would like to hire – but where are the right kind of people?"* companies often ask me – and so do the financing institutions and regulators. And there is no easy answer.

The courses offered at most universities today are still traditional, primarily focusing on 'end of pipe' and do not address topics on contemporary E&S governance. We don't see courses that cover environmental management, environmental economics, market regulations, responsible investing, social impact assessment, CSR etc. It's not just the issue of topics or courses, but also that of faculty. We simply don't have teachers who are well exposed and resourceful enough to teach such topics. And that's my serious concern.

All of us in the E&S profession need to work collectively to address this issue.

'Modernizing' the course curriculum is one option. But this takes time. We need to move step by step over the next 5 years as we build faculty. Every major graduate program in Environment in India for instance should brainstorm and prepare a 5 year curriculum transformation plan. This plan will also guide recruitment of new faculty. Such transformation plans are unfortunately seldom made. The student body should press upon the department head to ask for such plans. The Alumni should also get actively involved. I will be most glad to help if any department is interested.

And how do we get faculty? One idea could be to 'identify' potential faculty who are 'outside the academic campus' but are both resourceful and interested in teaching. There are many such 'gems' around but not connected to academia. We need to engage them in the teaching of the courses – even few lectures – giving them as much flexibility as much possible. If any of you are interested, please let me know and send me your CVs and topics of interest and I will hook you up with the graduate teaching programs I am connected with.

We could also run summer and winter schools over 3 to 5 days for teacher training. I did one such training event at Suratkal this year where we had 80 faculty and doctoral/masters students participating. I will be most happy to repeat such programs at other locations. Those interested in joining me are most welcome.

Another possibility is to conduct what I call as 'Finishing Schools'. These Finishing Schools can be conducted on the university campus for graduating students and cover some of the 'missing' and 'essential' topics. The school can be open even for young professionals. I conducted one such Finishing School over 4 days at NITIE in Mumbai where around 60 'students' participated. We received a very positive response.

Of course we need to float a number of continuing education programs – both open house and in-institution – in the form of 'modules' addressing contemporary topics. These modules could be a blend of Face to Face

(F2F) and e-learning platforms and interspersed so as to allow for implementation. You can, for instance, teach a 6 week module on CSR, with F2F sessions on Friday half day, fully supported over 6 weeks by the e-learning platform, providing access to knowledge resources, group interactions, mentoring and assessments. The course could be designed such that at the end of 6 weeks, each participant is able to prepare a CSR implementation plan for his/her organization. That's another take away, apart from capacity building. I have designed a few such programs in the past and plan to launch them shortly through www.ekonnect.net By the way, on this website, you will be able to access reports of the Suratkal and NITIE training events. Please do take a look.

Let us work together to come up with a multi-pronged strategy to upgrade or improve our environmental education and training programs. I would like to form a National Working Group to steer this strategy. Through this post I would like to invite all those who would be interested to join. Please write to me at prasad.modak@emcentre.com

Look forward to your ideas and support.

42

TEACHING ENVIRONMENTAL MANAGEMENT DIFFERENTLY

The subject of Environmental Management is both exciting and challenging to teach.

Blending real world experiences in environmental management education is necessary. But it's often an art as much a science. Further, you need to complement teaching with discussions and innovative assignments to *brew* the subject. It has to be a well-designed and executed strategy.

It's hard to get faculty who can 'blend' and 'brew' theory with practice. I am writing this post today to make some suggestions and offer ideas.

The world is changing rapidly. Understanding of environmental science is continuously evolving.

And environmental education needs to reflect these changes. **We may therefore need to teach environmental management differently from what we did some 30 years ago.**

And we need to recognize here, the power of multimedia, web collaborations, search engines and increasingly smart mobile devices.

Don't teach in silos – emphasize a holistic and integrated approach

Earlier, environmental management was taught through *topics* generally placed in silos. Topics were typical – like air pollution control, wastewater collection, treatment and disposal and solid waste management.

Faculty specialized in each of these silos and did a great job teaching the details. But students rarely received an integrated understanding. The very interdisciplinary nature of the subject of environmental management requires a 'rounded' and 'integrated' approach. Details are now available – plentiful and in a variety of forms.

Take for instance, teaching the 'subject' of effluent

management in an industry. Conventionally, one would teach *sub-topics* such as sources of effluent generation, effluent characteristics, applicable effluent standards, technology options, economics, case studies etc. Give the current and future perspectives, you may like to 'expand' the sub-topics and bring in a more systems or integrated understanding to the effluent management problem. This may require touching upon topics such as air pollution (e.g. due to release of VOCs from aeration tanks), energy optimization, water use reduction, substitution of hazardous substances, elimination of hazardous processes, health & safety of workers at the effluent treatment plant. A feature of resource recovery may help the effluent treatment plant to turn into a profit centre.

To emphasize the importance of such an integrated understanding, I have prepared a one slide presentation pasted below, showing changing *system boundaries.*

Teach not by topics but through events and issues

Introducing basics as well as applied aspects can best be done through *posing issues.* The issues could be structured according to tiers such as *local, regional, national* and *global.*

The table below provides a sample list of issues selected from diverse areas that a Professor could build on. Students may be taught how to dissect the issue, carry out research to deepen their understanding, express opinions and share views. A well sequenced stack of issues then becomes the body of the curriculum on environmental management thereby leading to an issue based series of lectures.

Blend and brew the

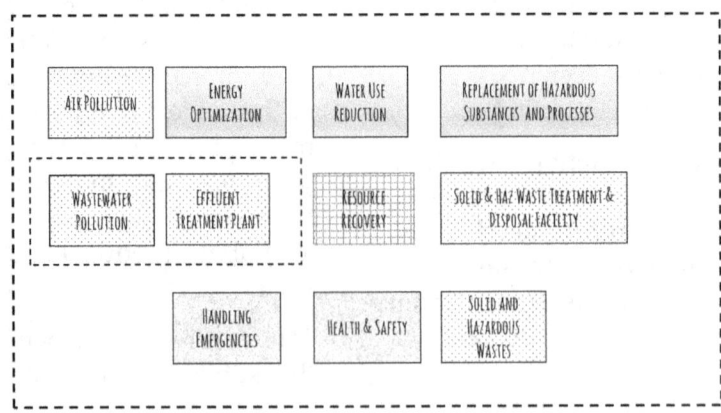

Local	Regional	National	Global
Was CNG substitution the right decision to tackle Delhi's air pollution?	*Why do we worry about the protection of Western Ghats Ecosystem?*	*Is Ganga Action Plan the right model to address India's River Water Quality Management Problem?*	*How can the strategy of producing Low Carbon Goods and Services help India meet its voluntary commitments to GHG emissions reduction and become competitive in the market?*

learning through innovative assignments

Information in the environmental domain is dynamic over time. Data, Hypotheses, Evidence, Conviction and Learning changes as we progress. Research must be a key ingredient of the assignments. A Professor will need to devise class assignments and group work accordingly.

Students may be asked to undertake specific literature review (e.g. state of the art), conduct interviews of some leading and inspiring personalities (for understanding trends and perspectives) and carry out field work (where you show students the interface with 'practice').

The assignments for the subject of "water management" on the issue of arsenic contamination could be

- Prepare a State of the Art review of treatment of Arsenic in groundwater

- Do a Skype interview with Prof Prosun Bhattacharya of KTH in Sweden on his work on Arsenic Removal

- Visit the ARUBA arsenic removal plant implemented by Dr. Ashok Gadgil of Berkeley and prepare a field note

In a class of 30 students, such *blended* assignments could be given on 15 topics (two students working together). A two day seminar/roundtable event will help the class understand the 'dynamics' of 30 key issues on water. I would place at least 30% of the class engagement on research based teaching and assignments. In the evaluation of the assignments, I would highly recommend a **Peer Assessment** approach that involves both students and externals.

Use flipped classrooms to promote active learning

The traditional pattern of teaching has been to give students the tasks of reading textbooks and working on problems, listening to lectures and taking tests in class. In flip teaching, the students first study the topic by themselves, typically using video lessons prepared by the Professor or third parties. In class, students apply this knowledge by solving problems or discussing issues and doing practical work (assignments).

Thus a Professor will video record presentations for instance *on modelling fate of pollutants* and provide key resources (publications and software tools). The students are expected to go through this material prior to coming to classroom. The details are thus left outside the classroom. In the class, the Professor fields questions, clarifies doubts and presents some landmark application of models which have led to important decision making.

Thus in this flip method, the Professor tutors the students when they face a problem, rather than imparting the initial lesson in person. Further, students can also help each other, a process that benefits both the advanced and less advanced learners.

Flip teaching promotes active learning. Research shows that active learning improves students' understanding and ability to retain information. This method can be very effective in developing higher order cognitive skills such as problem solving and critical thinking. The essence of the flipped classroom is to shift from passive to active learning where the learning process is more visible, reflexive, and collaborative and engages the students in critical thinking. **Active learning is extremely critical for building understanding and skills on environmental management.**

Envelop your course, set up collaboration – crossing geographical boundaries

The subject of environmental management is highly contextual. Ecosystems we live in and manage have a spatial specificity which we simply cannot ignore. To understand the mosaic, we need global, regional and national perspectives. Knowing how crisis in water is addressed in the African continent and in the Middle East is important for a student studying in Tamil Nadu in India. Environmental education must therefore operate in a "spatial collaborative mode".

Management of environment involves diverse stakeholders both in terms of scale (local, regional, national and global) and characteristics (business, community, government). It is essentially a people oriented, nature (resource) based, political science.

We will need to make clever use of web platforms to achieve this objective. A Professor should therefore envelop the course with an online collaboration by inviting colleagues from other academic institutions and practice, representing different geographies, to contribute to the course. These invited experts could play the role of content contributors and peers/mentors to students. There are several web based collaborative tools available today – many of these are free.

I am personally very keen that we work together to discuss some of these ideas- may be through workshops – and build capacity of Professors in environmental management. Do write to me if anyone is interested to chip in and help.

43

Books that Matter!

I often ask young professionals and students the following question in 'interviews' (I prefer the term 'discussions') "Which book did they follow during their studies". In many cases, you will be surprised, that the student does not even remember the title and author of the book! That's terribly disappointing. I feel sorry.

Some students have an answer, but I feel that they could have followed some other book instead. And when I ask, if they possess the book as part of the collection in their 'library', the answer is generally negative. Folks don't buy books anymore. All Google or 'manage' the e-copies of books which are not printed to read over a coffee. The concept of building a personal physical library now no longer exists.

Books you follow (and keep following) build your pedigree. But a lot depends on who introduced the book to you and how the book was taught. You can judge the student by assessing what books were read and how passionately the books were followed in research and professional life. So books matter.

In this blog post, I would like to recall some of the books that influenced me in my student and professional life.

I recall Professor P Khanna, Head of the Centre for Environmental Science & Engineering at the Indian Institute of Technology (IIT), Bombay, called me one evening and said "*tomorrow morning onwards, you will start lectures on Environmental Microbiology. Prof Mrs. Mahajan who is taking the course has fallen ill because of spondylitis*". While returning home that day, I was thinking "How do I handle this sudden requirement of teaching?" and "Which book should I use?". I picked up the book authored by Professors Anthony Gaudy and Elizabeth Gaudy in 1980 – Microbiology

for Environmental Scientists and Engineers[54]. I had studied this book during my doctoral studies.

Professor Gaudy's book turned out to be a hit. Not only did the students enjoy the book but I realized I understood Environmental Microbiology a lot better than before. I strongly recommend this book as something very fundamental, with a blend of research & practice. It is so lucidly written. Prof Anthony and Elizabeth Gaudy taught in University of Delaware. A subsequent release in 2001 titled Elements of Bioenvironmental Engineering is also worth reading. It's a hardcover from Oxford University Press Inc., USA. The chapter on quantitative description of growth is simply a masterpiece.

Another great book on this topic is by Ross E. McKinney – Environmental Pollution Control Microbiology: A Fifty-Year Perspective. This book illustrates the application of fundamental concepts in microbiology to provide a sound basis for the design and operation of various biological systems used in solving environmental challenges in the air, water, and soil. I find the multimedia canvas of the book most fascinating and different from other books[55]. Worth a buy.

I remember that I was asked to teach undergraduate students of IIT, Bombay 'Environmental Science & Engineering' over 36 lectures. Earlier, there were three professors who cotaught this course splitting the course into compartments such as water pollution, air pollution and waste management. This was because these professors were specialized in these specific areas.

I realized that this way of 'siloed' teaching is not going to lead to an integrated understanding of the students towards the 'problem' and

---

54 See: http://www.amazon.in/Microbiology-Environmental-McGraw-Hill-environmental-engineering/dp/0070230358)

55 See: http://www.amazon.in/Environmental-Pollution-Control-Microbiology-Perspective/dp/082475493X

its 'solution'. So I started looking for a book that could help me in this direction. The book I hit upon was Strategy of Pollution Control by Paul Mac Berthouex and Dale F. Rudd published in 1977. Prof. Berthouex (Mac Bertho) is a civil engineer and his mentor Prof Rudd was a chemical engineer. A great combination.

Strategy of Pollution Control is one of my favorite books even today. It is not media specific and emphasizes that you need to know enough of ecology, microbiology, chemistry, separations and strategies to manage pollution in an integrated manner. The book is written differently, with a 'case study' approach and has an inspirational and challenging set of questions at the end of each chapter. I found that the undergraduate students could 'take on' this book pretty well and really enjoyed it. (IIT has the brightest students of India, and teaching with this book really kept me on my toes! To my relief, Mac Bertho was kind enough to send me a set of solutions to the problems)

(I met Mac Bertho in London in 1986. In 1992, I invited him to work with me on a book on Air Pollution supported by UNESCO. He is an amazing Professor now retired from University of Wisconsin, Madison. We are still in touch. He recently updated the Strategy of Pollution Control with Professor Linfield Brown of Tufts University[56].

Exposure to quantitative techniques and systems thinking are critical in environmental science and engineering. This area is weakly covered in current courses on environmental engineering. Three of my favorite books in this domain are

Environmental Systems Optimization by Douglas A. Haith[57] (You can sense a typical Cornell touch in this book)

Numerical Methods for Engineers by Steven C. Chapra and Raymond P. Canale[58]. (An extremely well structured book for both Professors and students)

Statistics for Environmental Engineers, Second Edition by Linfield C. Brown, Paul Mac

56 See http://www.amazon.in/Strategy-Pollution-Control-Paul-Berthouex/dp/0471744492)

57 See http://www.amazon.in/Haith-Environmental-Optimization-DA-HAITH/dp/0471082872

58 See http://www.amazon.in/Numerical-Methods-Engineers-Steven-Chapra/dp/007339792X

Berthouex[59]. Another great book from Mac Bertho.

I taught a full course on Environmental Systems Optimization using Prof Haith's book. The book, especially the solved problems, helped me in introducing systems thinking and exposes the students to optimization techniques.

Sometimes it is effective to refer to a set of 'linked' books for a more complete understanding. Let me illustrate this point with an example on the subject of water quality management. I was working on the Ganga Action Plan in India in 1984. I developed, in those days, water quality modelling software (captioned STREAM-I and STREAM-II) and conducted more than 10 training programs on

water quality management in the country. In addition, I was teaching a course on water quality modelling at IIT, Bombay. So a lot was happening and I was looking for a set of books that could best introduce the subject of water quality modelling and management to students and professionals. These were books I used at that time

- Models for Water Quality Management, McGraw-Hill series on water resources and environmental engineering, by Asit K. Biswas[60]. This book presents fascinating case studies on water quality management. Kudos to Professor Biswas for managing such a collection. Later, I had the privilege to author along with Professor Biswas, a book on Environmental Impact Assessment

- Managing Water Quality: Economics, Technology, Institutions RFF Water Policy Set Series, RFF Press Series by Allen V. Kneese, Blair T. Bower[61]

59 See http://www.amazon.in/Statistics-Environmental-Engineers-Second-Edition/dp/1566705924

60 See http://www.amazon.in/Quality-Management-Resources-Environmental-Engineering/dp/0070054819

61 See http://www.amazon.in/Managing-Water-Quality-Technology-Institutions/dp/0915707136

The analysis in this classic study ranges from basic economic and political theory to engineering and institutional practices, and encompasses case studies in England, France, and West Germany, as well as in the Ohio, Potomac, and Delaware river basins in the United States. Originally published in 1968 and a real treat.

For those interested in modelling per se, I recommend the following three classics

- An Introduction to Water Quality Modelling, 2nd Edition by A. James[62] (Sam James and I worked together between 1985 to 1989). A teacher par excellence and that is reflected in this book)

- Principles of Surface Water Quality Modelling and Control by Robert V. Thomann, John A. Mueller[63]. Numerous solved problems is the USP of this book.

- Surface Water Quality Modelling by Steven C. Chapra[64].

It would be immensely valuable if Professors introduce these books to the students as a 'pack'.

And then some of the landmark books we all follow and respect are

- Wastewater Engineering: Treatment Disposal Reuse, McGraw-Hill series on water resources and environmental engineering by Metcalf & Eddy[65]

- Handbook of Solid Waste Management by George Tchobanoglous, Frank Kreith[66]

- And the old classic Fundamentals of Air Pollution by Arthur C. Stern[67]

- Analysis of Water Distribution Networks by Pramod R. Bhave, Rajesh Gupta[68]. I would rate this

62 See http://as.wiley.com/WileyCDA/WileyTitle/productCd-0471923478.html

63 See http://www.amazon.in/Principles-Surface-Quality-Modeling-Control/dp/0060466774

64 See http://www.amazon.in/Surface-Water-Quality-Modeling-Steven-Chapra/dp/1577666054

65 See http://www.amazon.in/Wastewater-Engineering-Treatment-Resource-Recovery/dp/0073401188

66 See http://www.amazon.in/Handbook-Solid-Management-George-Tchobanoglous/dp/0071356231

67 See http://www.amazon.com/Fundamentals-Air-Pollution-Arthur-Stern/dp/0126665605

68 See http://www.amazon.in/Analysis-Water-Distribution-Networks-Bhave/dp/1842653598

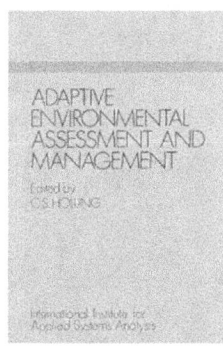

book as one of the most authoritative work in this area.

Finally, some books that are 'deep' and stand out, but are not commonly read. One such book is by Professor Holling– Adaptive Environmental Assessment and Management. This book develops an adaptive approach to environmental impact assessment and management in a systems perspective and ecology as the base. Professor Holling discusses how we can incorporate impact assessment studies with actual environmental planning and decision making[69]. I highly recommend this book if you really want to 'understand' the subject of impact assessment.

I remember I worked on a consulting assignment with ESSA Technologies, based in Vancouver, Canada, that specializes in Impact Assessment and associated Modelling and Expert Systems. When I was in a discussion with colleagues at ESSA – Tim Webb and Bob Everett – I could clearly sense the influence of the book Adaptive Environmental Assessment and Management. *"Are you by any chance students of Professor Holling?"* I asked. "Yes very much" they said with evident pride. I then realized how influential books are in life and how great are the professors who write such masterpieces.

My resolution for 2015 is to make a modest effort at writing one such book. And I do hope this actually happens!

---

69 See http://www.amazon.in/Adaptive-Environmental-Assessment-Management-Holling/
dp/1932846077

44

How to Plan Inconsequential Research?

My senior Professor friend dropped by my office when I was busy preparing a list of research topics for the master's students of the new academic year. Professor looked at my list and exclaimed – "Prasad, you are taking this task rather seriously. Identifying research that makes sense is relatively easy but have you ever thought of floating research topics that lead to inconsequential outcomes?" I was taken by surprise – I knew that my friend had radical thoughts and so I asked him why? *Isn't it crazy to come up with research topics that don't make sense?* I pulled up a chair for him to sit and passed on an ash tray to rest his cigar.

"Look at our department's last 10 years of research topics. Most of the dissertation topics have been well thought, well linked and organized to address the current and anticipated problems in the environmental industry and governance. Almost every dissertation has led to a

referred international journal publication – leave alone numerous presentations in conferences and seminars. Many of the research outcomes have influenced practice in the industry as these topics were identified in partnership" He went on, lighting up his favorite cigar.

I was wondering whether the Professor was serious or *sarcastic*. My own assessment was that research in my department was simply patchy, personality driven and addressing topics that were often irrelevant. And to add to it, there was no research planning or sufficient supervision provided to the students that would guide and inspire. Yes, papers did get published in journals but then this publishing activity was mostly driven by 'publish or perish' pressure. I always wondered what impact these publications had on practice, planning and policy making. I thought that the investment of time and resources in

180

dissertations could have been much better utilized!

I remembered one of the famous papers by Ettinger in 1965 titled "How to plan an inconsequential research project". This paper was published in the American Society of Civil Engineers, Journal of Sanitary Engineering Division. The paper was full of satire and had drawn a flurry of comments.

In his article, Ettinger noted that doing research with consequences was potentially dangerous, and the water profession had developed methods to protect it from consequences while maintaining funding. Among the 'techniques' he described was this anecdote:

A bystander passes a drunk on all fours on the sidewalk under a street light looking for a $20 bill. After failing to find it, he asks the drunk where he had lost the money. The drunk says "over there in that vacant lot." Bystander asks, "Why aren't we looking there?" Drunk says, "There are rocks and broken glass in the lot and the light is much better here on the corner."

Ettinger had come up with nine categories of inconsequential research. One of the categories was the 'data hungry' professor & student who were constantly looking for some data – no matter whether the data made any sense or had any practical relevance. So one could link data on ambient air quality in a city on RSPM to health records of 2000 employees working in Software Technology Park (who worked indoors over long hours and in an AC environment). Interestingly, results from this work showed a high correlation! The other research category was the platinum bridge where a double deck bridge at San Francisco was designed in platinum (since nobody had done such a design before!) knowing fully well that so much platinum was simply not available on earth and besides the bridge was not affordable!

I wanted to interrupt but the Professor continued.

Contributing research that is inconsequential has so many advantages. Firstly, to conduct such research is like a breeze and does not put too much load or stress on the student and professor. They can take it easy. The research topic may sometimes sound drab and questionable, but then you can always dress the dissertation up to make the outcomes look smart. More importantly, this kind of research does not interfere with the ongoing practices and policies of the world – so whatever we currently do – we keep doing it without any disturbance or disruption. Everything remains as is – and it can be so blissful. I really therefore, hate research that is consequential. Who wants to change?

I thought my Professor friend had a point and made a very interesting argument. I was silent.

The Professor took a deep puff and extinguished the cigar. While leaving my room he winked *"Do you still want to float your kind of research topics?* I introspected, looked at my list and realized that I better change the topics now.

I asked for a strong coffee from the pantry as changing the present topics to the topics of inconsequential research was not going to be an easy task. It was going to be a challenge! I realized that that's where I will need help from my colleagues. As they were more experienced. And so I walked to the faculty room.

PS : Dear Readers of this book, this post is clearly satire, don't take me as a pessimist, or a sadist– indeed a lot of consequential research

happens and we need to encourage more of this kind of research.

I would recommend an editorial by Thomas Walski titled "Consequential Research" – that is published very recently in the Journal of Water Resources Planning and Management, Volume 140, Issue 5 (May 2014)[70]

In his editorial, Walski notes

Not all research can be ground breaking or award winning or even consequential, but an excessive amount of what gets published seems inconsequential, primarily because it ignores real-world considerations. By looking at the way the aforementioned top researchers approached their work, young researchers can produce more consequential work.

He recommends the following 10 steps for consequential research (in the context of optimization of water supply and distribution networks)

1. Define the problem;

2. Talk with people in the real world;

3. Read literature;

4. Conduct experiments;

5. Simulate;

6. Better define the problem;

---

70 See: http://ascelibrary.org/doi/abs/10.1061/%28ASCE%29WR.1943-5452.0000430

7. Optimize (if needed);

8. Validate;

9. Develop lessons learned; and

10. Publish.

Do you think it will be good to create a webpage to encourage posting of research topics at Masters/Doctoral level as offered at various universities/institutions in environment as a "Research Gateway"? It may follow a simple format like title, abstract, student, professor, university, year with contact details. This information when available could help both students and professors, provide ideas, spur collaborations, strike synergy and avoid duplication. I will put up such a page on www.ekonnect.net.

And do read the article by Ettinger (1965). "How to plan an inconsequential research project." J. Sanit. Eng. Div., 91(4), 19–22. It's hilarious and rather thought provoking. You will simply love it.

45

HOW TO EXAMINE A DISSERTATION WITHOUT READING!

I was sitting in the room of one of my senior colleagues at the University, chatting in general. He suddenly looked at his wristwatch and exclaimed "Oh, time to go for the exam – I have to go upstairs to examine a Masters dissertation".

The Masters dissertation that my friend was to examine was in a sealed envelope on his desk. So clearly, he had not read the dissertation. But still just to be sure, I asked *"but have you read the dissertation at all?"* My friend just smiled and said "No, I haven't. And you don't need to read the dissertation for the examination". After seeing my bewildered face he said "You are too raw in this game Prasad, come along and I will show you how". I joined him right away as I was eager to learn the art of thesis examination.

"Hold on" he said. He opened the drawers of his table and pulled out a pad of colorful stickers that we use as page markers. He then put a number of these stickers across the pages of the dissertation randomly so that it really looked like a 'well read' and a 'well-marked' work! This looked both colorful and impressive. He then got up from his chair and took me along to the examination room upstairs.

The examination room was packed. The guide (another professor) and Chair were sitting in the front row. The student (poor guy) was on the stage with a nervous face waiting for the examiner. Other students were sitting in the hall – there was an atmosphere of silence punctuated with whispers. My friend was a well-known Professor in his field so when we walked in – the students stood up with respect and even the Guide Professor and the Chair acknowledged his presence. We went up to the front row to sit down.

But then my friend did a strange thing as he was sitting down. He banged the copy of 'the dissertation' on the desk with a sound like a thud– so loudly and hard that not only did it make an impactful noise but also raised a small cloud of dust! All looked towards the desk and noticed the copy of the dissertation with a number of colorful page markers jutting out. That was scary – especially to the student who was to be examined. It was clear that the Professor had read the dissertation in great detail, made page specific observations and was 'ready to kill'. Even the Professor Guide had a worried face.

The student was asked to start the presentation. I could see sweat forming on his forehead and his eyeballs gazing at the copy of his dissertation in front of my friend. The dissertation looked like a pigeon wounded with colorful arrows. I don't think the student spoke his best.

Once the presentation was over, the Chair Professor

turned to my friend and asked if there were any questions. And this was the real turning point for me.

My friend paused noticeably and said "Good attempt. I have many questions to ask but let me not get into details here" and while saying so, he kept turning the pages of the marked up dissertation.

He then looked up at the student and asked "Are you happy with your work?"

He said this casually but with a cunningness of a land mine. And there was silence.

The student did not know what to say. If he said, *he was happy* then what about those numerous questions the Prof already has (in the form of stickers) and if he said *not happy* then the next question would obviously be, why? He was in a real fix.

So he chose to be "safe" and said that he was not really happy. This led to the first crack on the door. As he "confessed" saying why he was not so happy, my learned friend dug in and came up with a volley of questions that the student found hard to answer.

After this bit was done, came the next question *"If you had more time, what else would you have done?"*

This was another tough one. The student realized that if he said that there was nothing more to be done – then he was clearly in trouble. So he preferred to explain how he missed doing X and would have liked to do Y etc. This led to another volley of questions from my friend.

Then came the last googly.

My friend asked *"All this is good in theory, but can your work be applied in practice?"*

While asking this question, his face was that of a CEO of a private sector company or of a picky investor– indicating that there were two worlds– one of the University and other the Real World. And that he came from both these worlds.

The student was apologetic when it came to answering this question – oh we did not look at the economics, we need more pilot runs, we assumed support of the following policies etc. This questioned the immediate usefulness of the work done.

Finally the examination round ended with my friend advising the student what should have been done and what was not needed … This part was both hard hitting as well as educative and I liked the latter part as my friend did – so cleverly. The Guide was grateful. The Chair Professor was impressed. Students in the examination hall were really floored to see the conduct of the examination.

When we got back to his office, my friend looked at me, smiled and said "Hope you got it!" And indeed, I had understood the "game" (as he had earlier said) and I had nothing much to add seeing that impressive performance. He then stood up and said "have to go home now" and then while putting on his coat exclaimed "now let me rearrange the stickers in the car on the right pages on my way home based on the students answers in the examination. I will then pass the copy to him tomorrow for fixing!" I simply gaped!

I was really awed and amazed with this style of examination.

Next time, when you examine a student, don't read the dissertation, follow my friend's style of conduct and ask the three key questions that matter!!

46

PROFESSORS WITH WARM EYES AND GOLDEN HEARTS

(Professors who work with you – matter. They greatly influence your lives. Most students tell me that there are not many Professors today at the Universities who can serve as role models. That's a pity.)

In 1981, I credited a course with Professor Fude on Environmental Impact Assessment of Water Resources Projects at the Asian Institute of Technology in Bangkok. Professor Fude was 65 years old then, with a PhD on water resources from the University of Iowa in 1939! He was a Taiwanese national, physically fit, an avid golf player and spoke in a Chinese American accent. He served in the army, fought in the Indo-China war and was recipient of the Cloud and Banner award – a military award of the Republic of China, instituted in 1935.

I recall Professor Fude walked into the classroom on the first day dragging a crate of Heineken beer. The class was at 7.45 am and we were shocked to see this crate of imported beer. Professor Fude then picked up a few bottles from the crate and said "Anyone interested?" And we simply gushed – free beer!! No one wanted to refuse this generous offer. We found the experience of sipping beer in the class while listening to the Professor very exciting and different! The next lecture, there was a repeat and so in the third lecture. In the third lecture however less beer bottles got picked up. We realized that though the beer was offered free, was it really worth it to have alcohol at 7.45 in the morning? Not good for health and not so good when we are 'learning'. So the fourth lecture saw even less number of students 'interested' and in the fifth lecture, none volunteered. Professor Fude first made a disappointed face, then smiled, warmly and said "Oh, it took five lectures for you to understand what is not the right thing to do". We then understood his novel way of teaching.

The class had assignments. Professor Fude asked us to write 1 page of our 'experience of reading' (not exactly a summary) of any book of our interest and that is aligned to the title of the course. The condition was that each student will work on different books and ensure that there was no duplication. I thought that Professor was too lazy to formulate an assignment. I expected to be given something more intellectual and challenging involving some calculations. Later, I asked the Professor about it and he said – well, the assignment is lot deeper than you think. First, it exposed the students to our library, what books we hold on the subject of EIA of water resources projects. Then it taught the students about how to choose a book out of a few – that compelled them to look at more than just one book. Since no student could write about the same book, they needed to talk to each other. This led to networking and making new acquaintances, and finally apart from learning what's in the book, they understood the subtle difference between a creating a summary and writing the 'experience of reading' where self-expressions are shared in your own language. And when all 1 page writeups were shared across 30 students, each got a dossier of 30 interesting books as a resource for 'essential readings'. I was simply amazed with this explanation. Very clever.

Once Professor Fude asked me how I use the library. I said that I go to the environmental section (628) and look at the books on the shelf and sometimes do a 'card search' (we did not have computerized database then) using author and subject index. Professor Fude said that this was alright but not good enough. He asked me to start with Alphabet A, at the first library shelf and spend time picking up almost every book and browse or look into – no matter whether the book concerned my doctoral research. "Pick up a book, turn the pages, take a deep breath to smell ... If you like the book, sit down and read more". And I followed his advice. My research was on optimization of ambient air quality monitoring networks and I discovered that the science was similar to the design and modeling of precipitation networks, petroleum exploration and even conducting of gallop poll! "This is how innovation in research happens" – Professor had said.

Professor Fude had a principle that books in his collection that he did not 'touch' over 6 months did not belong to him! So every six months he used to stack these books on his desk and put a notice for students to come and take away these books. That used to be a treat for us. He would then sign each book and hand them over. I did this practice when I taught at Indian Institute of Technology, Bombay. You should know how to part with and spread the knowledge – he said

I was to get married while studying and was really worried about how to handle the 'cost of married life'. Professor sensed some stress by the look on my face and called me to his room. He was the only Professor on the campus who had a small bar in the room where he would have a mix of rum and coke after returning from a game of golf and a shower. He was on his rum shot when I met him in his room. On explaining the reason for my stress, he offered me a job. He said "Can you wash my car before I drive back home every day. I will pay you 500 bahts a month". I was desperate for money and so readily agreed to the offer. The next day, Professor

Fude took me to his car. The car was parked right next to the main corridor where all the students and faculty were walking by. I was hoping to do the 'car wash' discreetly in the car park to remain unnoticed. But the Professor had another idea. Here all passersby looked at me, some even made comments and few talked about it to others. I was quite embarrassed. Professor Fude would sit on a stool next to the car and inspect the quality of my work, giving me instructions for doing a better job and later giving me a kind of discourse about 'life'. After the first month, he told me that rather than him paying me, I should be thankful and pay him fees for the advice he had given! Of course his sense of humor and when he gave me my 500 bahts, he said "Prasad – the idea was to teach you the dignity and pride of work – no matter what you do and to help you learn humility". I still cherish his words of wisdom.

When I defended my doctoral dissertation, Professor Fude was in the examination committee and I thought that he was the only member who actually understood what I was trying to say! He had a 'systems perspective'. When I was told by the Committee that I am through, I remember drafting a letter of application for a job. I ended my letter with 'Sincerely, Dr. Prasad Modak' and Professor Fude had just walked into the room then and looked at the letter I was typing. "Oh, you should not be saying yourself that you are a Dr... others should know and recognize your Ph. D from your work and not from you". Since then, I never write prefix of Dr. before my name.

When we parted, Professor Fude called me to his room. He passed on a woolen jacket to me and said "a small gift for you". While accepting his gift, I told Professor that I lived in Mumbai where the weather was never challenging enough for wearing a woolen jacket. Professor Fude then smiled and said "I know, you may not need this jacket and won't use it as much... so it will last longer and you will remember me for longer!" And yes, the jacket is still in my wardrobe. Of course, I still and will always remember him!

47

"Most believe that the Prime Minister supported the ban on beef due to religious reasons. Pity that none understood his real motive"

My Professor friend said this, lit his cigar and took a deep puff. We were sitting in his verandah enjoying the drizzle of the rain.

I said "Indeed, the reasons were religious. We have been worshiping cows for centuries in India and cattle are the pillars of our agro-economy"

The Professor smiled.

"The real reason for banning beef was to protect India and the World from water stress. Actually it was my idea"

I was surprised. I knew that Professor was SA (Secret Advisor) to PM – but then what was the connection?

"Do you know that 1 kg of beef requires an average 13,620 liters (13.62 m3) of water?

India produces nearly 5 million metric tons of beef annually. This means that producing beef in India amounts to annual consumption of 70 billion m^3 of water!!"

"On an average an Indian consumes 100 liters of water on a daily basis. So one billion people of India would need 30 billion m3 of water over a year for household consumption. Water consumed for production of beef is thus twice the water consumed by Indian households (covering both urban and rural).

Today, fifty percent of the beef produced is exported and so if consumption of beef is banned in India then we could save at least half or 30 billion m3 of India's precious water resource – an amount comparable to the annual national domestic water consumption! See the great impact of banning beef. This will help India save water, improve our dwindling ground water resources and meet the Sustainable

Development Goals (SDGs) in specific Goal No 6.

I realized that the Prime Minister had a much deeper thought on India's water sustainability – and the impression that he discouraged domestic consumption of beef on religious grounds was simply not true.

The Professor continued. "All these ideas essentially flow from the concept of 'virtual water', originated in Europe. In this concept we are talking about Embedded Water"

Embedded water is water used to produce food and non-food products. Beer, burgers, clothing, our cars and homes, and even electricity all have water embedded in them.

About 65 percent of the water that we consume is in our food. A tomato has 13 liters of water embedded in it; an apple has about 70 liters; a pint of beer about 170 liters; a glass of milk about 200 liters; and a hamburger about 2400 liters. It takes about 136 drops of water to produce one drop of tea, and about 1100 drops of water to produce one drop of coffee!

If present levels of consumption continue, two-thirds of the global population will live in areas of water stress by 2025. Increasing human demand for water coupled with the effects of climate change mean that the future of our water supply is not secure.

"Did you know that each Briton uses about 150 liters of tap water a day, but if you include the amount of water embedded within products then water consumption is around 3400 liters every day. An amount 20 times that of the water we "see" Professor said

"I am now working on similar Indian statistics. It's a complex task as Brits eat only Fish and Chips while Indians eat a variety of food items like Idli-dosa, Naan and Paneer and Chicken Biryani. I have commissioned five top IITs to work on this problem. We will soon come up with the true per capita water consumption for a North Indian and South Indian to begin with.

Much of the embedded water that we consume, about 70% of our water footprint, comes from other nations, as we import goods and services into our country. I am revising therefore, India's export of goods policy. Some items will be banned and some items that have large water footprints will attract higher export duties. I have already drafted a note for Indian Commerce Minister to present in the next WTO meeting"

"It's a great revelation

192

Professor. Are you providing any more advice, especially to the State Governments apart from the Government of India?" I asked.

"Well, I have been in discussion with various leaders of Indian States. In Maharashtra State for instance, if you ask for a fruit salad, you will not get to see a piece of apple. Selling apple or eating apple in Maharashtra is now banned as one apple has embedded water of 70 liters. Maharashtra is really a progressive State when it comes to banning. The College of Catering in Mumbai is now coming up with LEW (Low Embedded Water) Recipes to teach the students. That is food for thought."

"That's very impressive, Professor", I said. I decided not to order fruit salad in Mumbai restaurants anymore.

The Professor continued.

"One liter of wine or beer requires 900 to 1000 liters of water. When I released this data to the Chief Ministers, some of the drought prone States decided to take action and consider banning of liquor in their States on the grounds of Water Sustainability. Government of Gujarat is now issuing new justification saying how over the past several years they have contributed to water sustainability by banning consumption of liquor in the State"

"The concept is hitting the private sector as well. Hamburgers have a very high embedded water. All outlets of McDonald's will therefore need a water resource clearance (this is a new instrument of the Ministry of Water Resources). Each McDonald outlet in India will now be required to install a rainwater harvesting unit as a gesture to compensate for the water consumed in making of the hamburger. This step is forcing McDonald to set up outlets only at places where it rains"

"Wow" I realized that Professor was set to bring in a quantum change with the concept of virtual water. Banning beef was only the beginning.

I returned home. The News hour show on Times Now channel was on. Arnab Goswami was speaking as the anchor of super primetime.

"Breaking news – Delhi Government is now taking far bolder steps on water. The Government is asking the Delhiites to consume as much water as they want – with no restrictions – and all for free. The Government has realized that the virtual water consumption of Delhi is nearly 10 times of the real so why focus on conserving water at the households and charge people for water use. Let the water be used in abundance and for free.

The only condition will be that chocolates won't be available in Delhi anymore as 1 kg of chocolate requires 24,000 liters of water. Anyone found eating or storing chocolates in Delhi will be punished. Chocolates will also not be available at the Duty Free shops. The Delhi Government feels that this radical step will certainly help them win the next election and at the same time, align with the national water conservation strategy. Some believe that this move may also help (incidentally) in reducing extent of obesity and incidence of diabetes of the Delhiites"

Clearly this step must have been an outcome of the meeting with my Professor friend. I realized.

Arnab Goswami was ending the show– He said in his usual high pitched voice "Nation wants to know – why?"

I decided to call the Professor right away, and ask him to come online to explain the concept of embedded water to the Nation.

Interesting links to follow[71]

A nifty infographic at National Geographic, showing 'How Much H2O is embedded in Everyday Life'[72].

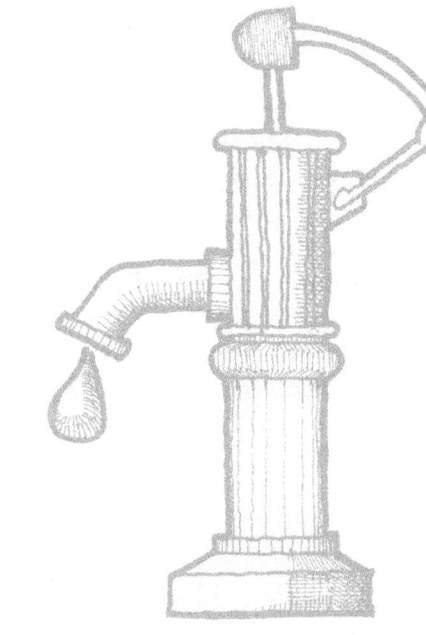

---

71 See http://www.waterwise.org.uk/pages/embedded-water.html

72 See http://environment.nationalgeographic.com/environment/freshwater/embedded-water/
http://www.iwawaterwiki.org/xwiki/bin/view/Articles/embodiedEnergyintheWaterCycle
http://www.waterwise.org.uk/pages/embedded-water.html#sthash.fuId0uo5.dpuf

48

The Project Case Work

Many say that Training is a great art and science. Training innovatively – can be a challenge. Not all professors are good trainers. They also need to be trained, sometimes along with the 'students'.

My good old friend, Dr Guenter Tharun introduced me to his training technique – Project Case Work (PCW) – years ago in Bangkok.

PCW was Tharun's invention and a passion. I am glad today that I became part of the PCW legacy as a PCW writer and PCW trainer. There are not many PCW trainers around – at least in the environmental domain. We need PCW breed of trainers.

What is PCW?

PCW is a method of training participants through a semi-real situation. Participants are divided into groups of 6 -8 and are supported by a facilitator. PCW is all about "problem solving" over 3 to 4 days working in a group, under pressure of time, competition and with limited information. Learning while doing is the principle.

PCW is generally conducted at a place away from the buzz of the city, preferably at a resort on a residential basis. The idea is not to have any interruptions, no boundaries of time and enough opportunities for intense and extended interaction amongst faculty and the participants. A PCW must put forth a new concept, introduce a new paradigm or demonstrate innovative processes.

PCW is generally triggered off by an event e.g. a company receiving a notice from the Pollution Control Board. The notice could be about frequent violation of the effluent standards. This notice leads to an extraordinary meeting of the company's management board. The Managing Director of the company chairs the meeting.

The participants are provided

with a mock notice and transcripts of the management meeting. Sometimes, a video clip is created to make the situation look 'real'.

The meeting discusses various options and arrives at a decision of revamping the effluent treatment plant (ETP) ASAP. This seems a logical quick fix!

Just then, one of the Board members asks "How about checking whether we are generating excessive amount of effluent? May be we are overusing rinses, not recycling water enough or missing opportunities for recovery of solvents" This question leads to a twist. An intense discussion takes place and the Production head who was earlier only listening – gets into a volley of questions. The Managing Director decides to mobilize a team to look into this 'new perspective' immediately.

So each team working on the PCW is given the task of finding a 'solution' for the company that helps reduce effluents, reduce cost of ETP, save water, recover heat and materials and increase profitability. The focus thus changes from 'downstream' to 'upstream'. To do this, participants need to be trained while they are 'solving' the

problem.

Training is therefore provided in the form of a well-designed learning path. The problem solving process is divided into milestones. These milestones include preparing a plant layout, process flow diagram, setting material and energy balance, identifying focus areas, developing pollution prevention options using Ichikawa diagrams, conducting pre-feasibility, shortlisting and prioritizing options, carrying out extended cost-benefit analyses, preparing implementation plans, financing, monitoring and reporting etc.

These topics of the 'learning path' are covered in not more than 20 minutes (so we call them 'lecturettes') and are delivered through lectures spaced over 3 to 4 days. If the faculty crosses 20 minutes, then the participants are asked to clap!

The faculty are essentially the facilitators. Generally, they arrive night before and we conduct a faculty orientation workshop. A separate guidebook is provided to the faculty on PCW and the 'solutions' – earlier. The faculty do not refer to the problem at hand. Through the lectures, the 'students' are expected to understand the basics or fundamentals and apply the knowledge acquired to the problem that they are trying to solve.

The lecturettes are delivered in plenary mode where all participants sit. After a lecturette is done, participants move to separate rooms in groups for the PCW. Each room has a white board and flip charts. A central place is kept for tea and coffee.

After working on the PCW for say an hour and a half, participants reassemble at the plenary to listen to the next topic or the lecturette. So after the lecturette on 'How to set material and energy balance', the groups work on data provided for the case and attempt calculations. Learning thus goes in a structured way and the group work moves 'up the ladder' step by step. It thus becomes a blend of progressive and retrospective learning. By working in a group, the participants learn how to express individually, how to work in a team and how to reach a consensus. At the end of PCW, new friendships are made. That's the added value.

See below a diagram that shows the structure of PCW with four groups participating.

To do the PCW, data on the case work is needed. This data is provided in an implicit form (like field notes, pages from annual reports, water and electricity bills etc.). The data are often incomplete, forcing the participants to make assumptions or surf on the internet. Sometimes, a separate room is created

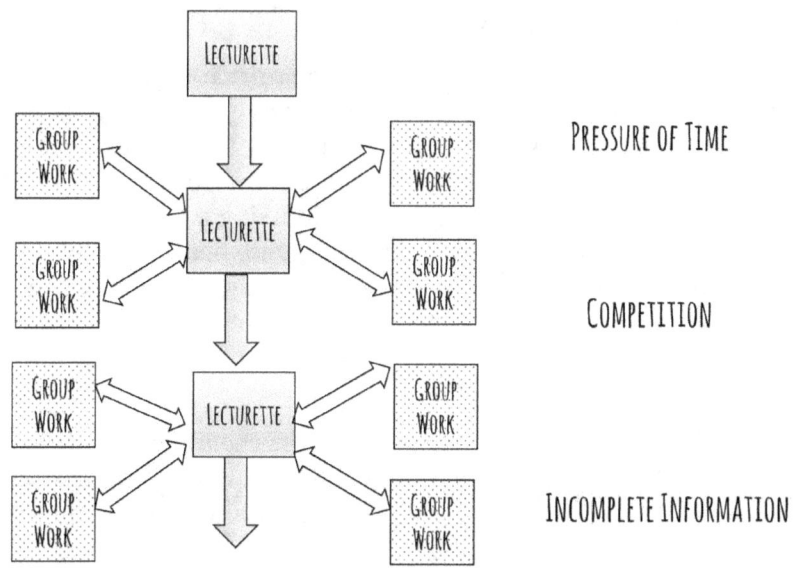

PRESSURE OF TIME

COMPETITION

INCOMPLETE INFORMATION

as a knowledge room where 'data' is kept for 'purchase'. Each team is given a budget to purchase data or procure information – This is an important facet of learning about what data or information to buy and what not to. Sometimes, a resource person moves around with a hat. This person provides 'knowledge' at no cost but the advice provided, may or may not be correct. The groups need to take a call. So it can be a challenge.

At the end of the 3 to 4 days of learning while doing, the groups prepare to present their 'solution'. PowerPoint presentations are prepared by each group. Presentations are made to the Jury consisting of the faculty and some external invitees. A winning group is then declared and generously rewarded (like bottles of black label whisky).

The program for the 3-4 days is full. After the day long sessions, additional sessions are conducted with games, karaoke, short films etc. Sometimes coaching is provided on how to make PowerPoints, How to use Excel efficiently etc. In some cases, a field trip is organized in one of the afternoons depending on the location.

Each PCW is customized to the topic and the participants.

I remember we ran a PCW for the students of Environment, Energy, Industrial Engg and School of Management at Asian Institute of Technology in Bangkok at Khao Yai resort over 4 days. The topic was cleaner production. Here the professors from these schools also participated. This PCW gave students an integrated perspective on 'production and pollution'. The faculty from the four schools got 'indirectly' trained.

A PCW was run on ISO 14001 EMS at Tagaitay near Manila targeting the Small and Medium Enterprises (SME). At the end of PCW the SME were both motivated and capacitated to implement ISO 14001 in their companies. A PCW on community based action plan was run in Laos. This PCW was based on the principles of Green Productivity. I trained 25 directors of National Cleaner Production Centers (NCPC) in Berlin using a PCW approach. The theme here was how to establish and operate Cleaner Production Centers.

PCW can be assisted by providing easy to use software tools. These tools help in creating quick scenarios and for discussions. Examples of such tools are SimAir,

Wisewater, and SimWaste etc. Write to me if you are interested in these tools.

Sometimes, PCWs are created based on a real situation. In Hong Kong, I created a PCW by spending a week at an electroplating workshop. When this PCW was conducted, the owner of the electroplating workshop attended the final presentations as a member of the Jury! Later, participants visited the electroplating workshop to see the 'real' situation. The owner rewarded the winning team by plating their wristwatch bands at no charge! Sure he got some bright and shining ideas from the PCW! And that was the deal.

I love the PCW approach. It's by far the most effective way I have come across for training simultaneously on concepts, processes and tools that we often look for in environmental management. Kudos to Dr Guenter Tharun. I fondly remember the numerous beer sessions I used to have with him at 'Papa's shop' in AIT in the 90s.

Let me know if anyone is interested to know more on PCW. I will be most pleased to help, conduct or participate.

You may like to sample a typical PCW content from the link below[73]

---

73 See http://www.kmutt.ac.th/ev/inmage/InTex%20Co[1].%20EMA%20Training%20 Scenario.pdf

49
CREATIVE FUSION

The subject of environment could perhaps be best understood and communicated when there is a fusion with art. If we want to enjoy a 360o learning of topic such as environment and sustainability, that touches and influences our lives, then we must be creative, unorthodox and willing to experiment. We need to brew and blend our communication.

How can you teach subjects like ecology in a classroom with concrete walls and ceiling full of artificial lights? I recall few lectures on Human Ecology that were delivered by Professor Indira Mahadevan in 1975 under a tree on the campus of IIT Bombay. This style of teaching in the open and natural environment was rather new to everybody – to us as students as well as to the passers-by. People walking around used to be often amused or sometimes even joined the 'lecture'! Why not?

During the lecture (which was more of a conversation), dry leaves would fall (and sometimes even crow shit!), or raindrops would drizzle on our heads. We used to feel that we were 'living' the lecture. Learning in natural sunlight with a gentle breeze and with the faint fragrance of flowers, helped us understand the importance of eco-systems much better. So that was the right setting to learn. Many of us don't experiment such types of sessions today.

In 1990, I was invited by

the students of Erasmus University in Rotterdam to deliver some sessions on Pollution and *Poverty Nexus – Case of India*. The students had organized a large lounge that had a long wooden table with tall stools. The room had dim lights and the walls were damp with old paintings hanging. Freshly brewed beer was generously served that had an *oaky* aroma.

I spoke extempore and the students flocked around me, crowding the area, some sitting on the floor. They listened patiently with eyes focused on me. Once I was done, a student got up and played on a box guitar *'Let it be'* by John Lennon. He did it very softly. A girl who had recently visited India played Anando Shankar's famous number *'The River'* on a long brass flute. The sound of the flute was sharp and deeply penetrating. Was it done impromptu or by design? – I do not know. But all this inspired me to speak more as if it was my further reflection or more of an afterthought. When I finished this second round, many students told me that this part of my expression was more from the bottom of my heart, rather candid but very delicately put at the same time. Certainly the music in the interlude had influenced

me and clearly made the difference.

Street art, apart from serving as a beautiful decoration, can be a powerful platform for reaching out to the public, drawing our attention to certain issues. Graffiti is gaining more and more popularity in urban communications. Dr. Love, one of the famous Georgian artists is known as the crusader of communicating on urban air pollution. This artist has expressed his protest against air pollution in the city through his paintings. Air pollution in cities is quite an important issue nowadays, since more and more green areas have disappeared being substituted with buildings.

Moreover, rapid increase in the number of cars has worsened the situation significantly, practically leaving the city without fresh air. Many have appreciated Love's work to confront air pollution as well as to make our society think about the problem through his art[74]. Artists in Delhi could take inspiration from the graffiti of Dr Love.

Dr Love's graffiti – a hospital patient receiving oxygen from a tree – was part of the three-day Upfest Festival in Bristol, UK. To illustrate the growing global problem of air pollution, Dr. Love painted the piece in his typical stencil style but added moss to give additional texture to his artwork[75].

In July, 1969, photographer Mark Edwards, was lost on the edge of the Sahara desert, and was rescued by a Tuareg nomad. This changed Mark's life. Bob Dylan's songs 'A Hard Rain's A-Gonna Fall': "sad forests", "dead oceans", "where the people are many and their hands are all empty" had lent a touching impression to the World. The World seemed to be on the fire.

Edwards thought of illustrating each line of the Hard Rain song. In the years that followed, Mark traveled around the world on assignments that allowed him to capture the photographs. The result became Hard Rain, an outdoor exhibition, book and DVD that brought global

challenges alive in a moving and unforgettable way[76].

Hard rain exhibition is an example of fusion between music and visuals. It has

74 See http://www.georgianjournal.ge/arts-a-culture/31599-more-than-street-art-fighting-air-pollutionthrough-graffiti.html

75 See http://www.upfest.co.uk/artist/dr-love

76 See http://www.hardrainproject.com/d

been seen by over 15 million people at over 50 venues on every continent including India (courtesy The British Council). It is a very successful photographic display that attracts huge public and critical acclaim, along with the support and endorsement of political and environmental leaders across the world. Mark's photographs illustrate every line of Dylan's prophetic song, setting the scene for a moving and unforgettable exploration of the state of our planet at this critical time. Hard Rain puts the puzzle together to show that there is ONE problem: aligning human systems with natural systems.

In addition to poetic and holistic interpretations of the environment, artists now regularly collaborate with scientists to exchange knowledge about water, air, energy and soil. This leads to a new expression of art. We as environmental professionals need to connect with the artists. But we seldom do.

I did an experiment of holding a workshop on Water in partnership with Mohile Parikh Center – MPC[77] in Mumbai. This was a part of MPC's project captioned the *"Geographies of Consumption"*.

The workshop was organized at the premises of Rachana Sansad's School of Architecture. It was attended by some of the famous artists of the city. In the opening session, three of my colleagues spoke on Mumbai's water woes providing highlights, statistics and the challenges faced. Once these short discourses were over, some of the artists worked on paper to reflect their understanding, their personal impressions and the messages they wanted to convey to the *Mumbaikars*. This kind of a 'studio' led to creatives. This is how I feel we could attempt a fusion of science and the art. Can environmental science departments at the universities conduct such studios involving students, professionals, government officials in the presence of local artists?

Right now I am working with Navjot Altaf, a famed artist[78] on communicating water situation in Mumbai. We are using the concept of pure and impure blood flow in the

77 See http://mohileparikhcenter.org/site/
78 See http://www.contemporaryindianart.com/navjot_altaf.htm

human body to depict water movement in the city – i.e. flows of purified drinking water and the wastewater drains that we generate. Here Navjot is using images from the angiography reports with the help of Cardiac Intervention specialists. The human body connection here is the message to citizens to take care of their city as much as they do of their own bodies. We plan to hold an exhibition in early January, 2016, once the narratives and photography are done.

And have you heard about *River Listening?* You should read an article by Dr Leah Barclay[79]

Dr Leah is an award-winning composer, sound artist and creative producer working at the intersection of art, science and technology. Her work has been commissioned, performed and exhibited to wide acclaim internationally, and she has directed and curated interdisciplinary projects across the Asia-Pacific.

Dr Leah realized the opportunities for hydrophone recordings as a measure for river health. The soundscapes of rivers can expose many qualities, including the active marine life. She found that the polluted and stagnant waterways were silent, often with a hum of anthropogenic sound from boats and machinery on the riverbanks. The healthy waterways were filled with sound ranging from dolphins, fish, and turtles to shrimp and insects.

According to Dr Leah, bioacoustics and acoustic ecology have emerged as extremely valuable fields for non-invasive environmental monitoring involving auditory recordings of the environment. While scientists have developed advanced software tools for species recognition, there is a growing need to consolidate the available tools and explore the value of *listening to the data* in new ways. There are also exciting possibilities to make this data available to a wider audience through digital technology and creative collaborations. Sound is so closely associated with the State of the Environment. I wish the Pollution Control Boards in India work on such exciting projects with communities and universities and correlate the water quality data with the bio-acoustics. How exciting such work would be!

---

79 See http://www.australianmusiccentre.com.au/article/river-listening

I would urge the readers to follow Dr Leah's work on Pamba river in Karnataka and Narmada in Gujarat[80].

Last month I delivered a keynote at the Global Conference on Sustainable Consumption and Production in Barcelona. Prof Don Huisingh was the Convener. Don connected me to Marco Casazza, a physicist and a violin maestro.

Marco Casazza got his academic degree in violin at the Conservatory of Music "G. Verdi "in Turin under the guidance of Maestro Paola Tumeo. He also has a master degree in physics from the University of Turin[81].

I shared my slides with Marco in advance and whenever there was a 'transition' or 'pause' in the presentation, my slide showed a different background color. Marco standing with his violin on the other side of the stage then played an 'appropriate' piece over 20 seconds. Once the piece was done, I continued with the next slide. I think the experiment worked well and I could blend my thoughts with Marco's musical reflection to deliver the message creatively.

Recently, Daniel Crawford composed the song, called 'Planetary Bands, Warming World,' to trace the rise of Northern Hemisphere temperatures since the 1880s. Four students from the music department—performed the song. Each instrument played the temperature range of a zone of the Northern Hemisphere and was tuned to the average temperature of that region. The cello tracked the equatorial zone, and the viola played the midlatitudes. One violin played the high latitudes, and the other traced Arctic temperatures. Each note corresponded to a year out of the 133 years data, and the pitch of the note represented the temperature. Higher notes thus corresponded to warmer years. One can 'hear' the Earth getting warmer through the music. According to Crawford, music is a better way to communicate Global Warming to people than maps, graphs or numbers. But probably, you need both[82].

I am all sold on blending art with the environment, especially when delivering

---

80   See http://www.australianmusiccentre.com.au/article/insight-sonic-ecologies-stretching-beyond-noteson-the-page

81   See http://www.marcocasazza.com/Marco_Casazza/Music.html

82   8 2 See http://www.smithsonianmag.com/science-nature/this-song-composed-from-133-years-climatechange-data-180956225/?no-ist

public lectures and while holding public events.

The other day I was invited to speak at a University to the students of environmental engineering taking them through the evolution of the subject. I asked the Chancellor – could we also invite faculty and students from the Department of Arts and Geography for my presentation? The Chancellor wondered why. Is that relevant? He said – they won't understand what you speak". And I insisted saying that I will speak in a *common language.* Creative Fusion is my idea – not a one dimensional delivery of a lecture!

50

WHY THE FUSS?

When we were offered dissertation topics for B Tech project in IIT, I remember I took the selection of the topic rather too seriously. My interest was in environment and the only topic offered was **Design of Sewage Treatment Plant for the IIT Bombay Campus.** This topic did not excite me as I thought it was too mundane. I wanted to take a topic that will be 'path breaking' and 'impact the world'. Probably I was making too much fuss.

Identification of a Guide was an equally daunting a problem. We had only one Professor in Environmental Engineering, – Professor S G Joshi – and he was the one who had offered the topic on Sewage Treatment Plant design. So obviously I could not approach him as I wanted to take 'some other' topic.

Professor J T Panicker was one of the senior most faculty at the Civil Engineering Department then. He was

the Professor of Hydrology, Deputy Director of IIT Bombay and carried an umbrella for the entire year – irrespective of whether it rained (may be as a true Professor of Hydrology!). He had his own lecture room and accepted only PhD students. I approached Professor Panicker as a Guide. Books on his desk always intrigued me such as a book on 'Cloud Physics' and photographs of some French Researchers (He did his doctoral research in Paris).

When I explained to Professor Panicker that I am not clear about the topic; and I want to do my project; and yet wanted him to guide me, he said "Take your time to decide, I don't think I can add value in the environmental engineering space – but feel free to drop in if you need any general advice." He then smiled and said "Well, do let me know your date of final examination in advance so that I can block my time!" So he essentially assured me the freedom to

207

choose the topic I want to pursue.

Having completed this part of 'housekeeping', I set out on my 'topic finding mission'. I thought about meeting Mr. V D Desai, the Deputy Municipal Commissioner (DMC) of Greater Mumbai for advice. It took a while to get an appointment with Mr. Desai – but perhaps my status of student of IIT Bombay worked. I was in his cabin one day late in the evening. He was winding up his work. When I mentioned I had come to meet him for guiding me on choosing a B.Tech. project, he was a bit startled and a bit angry. "This is hardly something that you need to see a DMC of Mumbai. Take something straightforward and simple. You are too young to think of something different and the topic at B.Tech level is not like deciding a PhD topic". But when I insisted, he ended the conversation abruptly and said – go and meet Dr. Deepak Kantawala at Environmental Engineering Consultants. He works for us on Mumbai Sewage Disposal Project and has an office in Nariman Point in Mittal Chambers"

Two things fascinated me. First – I had not met someone who ran a consulting firm in environmental engineering (So I wanted to see what a consultant's office looked like) and second – I had not seen someone who had a doctoral degree in environmental engineering from the United States!).

I went to meet Dr. Kantawala. The receptionist ushered me into his cabin. The cabin was filled with the aroma of tobacco. Dr. Kantawala was wearing Quadra jeans, a smart tie and had a pipe in his hand. His cabin had a window with a good view of the sea. He had an American-*Gujju* accent. He looked at me and said "We are working on a project of designing marine outfall for Mumbai's sewage disposal. We are setting up a one dimensional DO-BOD model for this purpose". The very term one-dimensional DO-BOD model impressed me (although later I realized that this one-dimensional approach for Mumbai's coast did not make any sense!). I felt this topic was a 'lot elevated' as compared to the design of a sewage treatment plant. While I was about to ask him how I could get involved in this exercise of one dimensional model, Dr Kantawala said " I would like you to join two of my young engineers – Saifee Attarwala and Nayan Khambati, get on to the sampling boat and do hourly DO-BOD measurements following the tidal cycle. You can then analyze the data, make plots and interpret. In this process you will also learn how to do sampling and analyses in the laboratory."

I was disappointed. I thought this work was too mundane and wouldn't be 'influencing the world'. I was expecting to work on a computer based math model and simulate DO-BOD concentrations for various outfall locations and tidal conditions. Sampling and analyses in the laboratory was perhaps just a routine. I thought to myself – why should I compromise my research by doing such routine tasks? I thought Dr. Kantawala was simply looking for some cheap labour! I politely declined the offer.

Many told me that I should approach National Environmental Engineering Research Institute (NEERI) at Worli in Mumbai to get guidance on the topic. I met the Head S R Kshirsagar and his colleague R K Pandit. Mr. Kshirsagar was known to be a very kind hearted and positive person and Mr. Pandit was always negative and would play devil's advocate. "Take a topic on treatment of distillery effluents – It is a real tough problem to solve and we do not have a good solution today" Mr. Kshirsagar said in all seriousness Mr. Pandit added "Do you know the typical BOD concentrations of the distillery effluent? Its over 30,000 mg/l. Distillery industries in Maharashtra and Uttar Pradesh have been polluting surface and ground waters over the years due to absence of suitable technology – and I don't think you will be able to handle this kind of a complex topic". He had a smirk on his face.

I was impressed with the 'problem'. When I read more about it, the topic further motivated me. **I saw myself getting felicitated by the Indian Environmental Community for solving this problem and protecting the country from the menace of distillery effluents. I thought**

like Walter Mitty – a character created by James Thurber who day dreamed. I decided on my topic as 'Treatment of Distillery waste'

When I informed my senior colleagues A D Kini, S L Naik and Hemant Jamenis in Hindustan Dorr Oliver, they supported the idea. Hemant said "Boss, if you cracked this problem, you will be making loads of money". This possibility further motivated me to stick to this topic.

Anaerobic pathway was the method for the treatment of distillery waste. So I started looking for a 'Guru' on anaerobic digestion. All cited the name of Professor A D Patwardhan at VJTI, Mumbai. So I went to meet him. Professor Patwardhan was in the laboratory wearing an apron. The laboratory carried the aroma of chemicals. Professor Patwardhan's doctoral research was ongoing at Nagpur University on Anaerobic digestion. He was attempting treatment of sewage sludge with shredded municipal market waste (i.e. cellulose substrate). When I expressed my interest on distillery waste to Professor Patwardhan, he recommended that I meet with Professor B Subba Rao at Walchand College of Engineering in Sangli. Professor Subba Rao

had completed his PhD on the anaerobic treatment of distillery waste. So I travelled to Sangli to see Professor Rao.

I remember I wrote a letter on a post card to Professor Rao before reaching Sangli about my research interest seeking his help. I wish I had kept a copy of this letter. I had written how passionate I was about this topic and how honored I would be if the Professor could guide me and enlighten…. And how this would influence my life and how I could help the country! I was sure Professor Rao was lost with my expressions and yet was kind enough to let me meet him.

I met Professor Subba Rao in his office and laboratory. After initial discussions, I requested him to give me a copy of his PhD dissertation which he gave me a bit reluctantly (I am sure I must have asked him rather rudely).

I read through his PhD dissertation over a whole night. The dissertation was centered around experiments that used 3 to 4 buckets simulating anaerobic lagoons. Sampling was done of the BOD/COD of the distillery effluent as it moved from buckets 1 to 2 and 3 and so on exhibiting different levels of removal efficiencies over a period of time. After such several experiments, an optimum configuration, retention time and BOD/COD loading was found and a design methodology was recommended. Professor Rao used this methodology to provide solutions to various distilleries around Sangli.

I remember – I was not too excited about this 'enumerative' research. I also thought that the approach taken was too empirical (input-output limited) and trivial. When I spoke about my impressions openly to Professor Rao, I don't think he liked my 'criticism' – especially from a 22 year old kid. I greatly appreciate that the Professor gave me a patient hearing and let me speak. He said "Go to the anaerobic lagoons at Ugar Khurd Distillery – I suspect that the four lagoons in series there show acid-methane segregation. You may like to investigate the phenomenon of "diphasic anaerobic digestion".

How do I reach Ugar Khurd? I asked. The Jeep is about to leave, the Professor said, "Ride on!" And I went to Ugar Khurd at the Karnataka border.

I stayed at the plant, did some assessment and picked up samples for analyses in Mumbai following the required sampling and sample preservation protocols. A chemist at the plant guided me. I boarded a train from Ugar Khurd to reach Mumbai via Pune with a carton of distillery waste samples.

At the Pune station, Railway Police came to arrest me on complaints from fellow passengers that I was carrying illicit liquor on the train! To them the distillery effluent was liquor as the carton was stinking. I had a tough time explaining and finally my IIT ID card and a phone call to Professor Panicker at IIT by the station master secured my 'release'. Professor Panicker asked me to see him immediately on return. What a mess you are doing – he said in a shrill tone.

We did not have an environmental engineering laboratory at IIT Bombay. So I requested NEERI for help that Mr Kshirsagar generously granted. I did my analysis work in the NEERI laboratory. It helped me in learning how to use instruments, follow the standard methods and interact with the NEERI scientists.

While all this recce and the mission to meet people was on, I dived into the literature survey. Again, the library at

IIT Bombay was not great in stocking environmental books and journals and so I had to look for other options. I spent most of the time in Matunga at the libraries of VJTI and UDCT. I still remember looking through the back issues of the Journal of Water Pollution & Control Federation, Proceedings of the Purdue University Industrial Waste Conferences etc. at these libraries. Those were treasures to me. Even now I remember some of the papers I read there. I used to walk home from Matunga (a 20 minute walk over Tilak Bridge) and not take the bus as it helped in pondering over what I had read in the journals. It used be my think-walk.

In one of the readings at UDCT, I came across a paper by Barker on the 'Evolution of Methane' (a classic 1938 article!) and the experience of Chicago Recirculation Pump (CRP) Company. CRP practiced gas based recirculation for mixing the digester liquor and found that the methane fraction in the gas could reach to 80% as against 65% generally found. This was called as the CRP process. Barker had argued the role of CO_2 in the evolution of methane.

By then I had realized that 'breaking of the propionate' in acid-methane segregation was the key and a thought came to my mind to conduct experiments with certain species of methanogens and propionate under CO_2 and 'no CO_2' bias with beakers placed on a shaker. The idea of doing such an experiment excited me. The question was where to do such an experiment?

My experiment needed a Gas Liquid Chromatograph (GLC), inoculum of methanogenica genre of species and a mentor who could teach me how to work with anaerobic organisms. I also needed to know how to handle a GLC.

I was told to approach Dr Gokhale at the National Chemical Laboratory (NCL) at Pashan, Pune and Dr S H Godbole at the Maharashtra Association for Cultivation of Sciences (MACS). Both Dr Gokhale and Godbole liked my 'idea' and supported me. Dr S H Godbole had a research group working on anaerobiosis.

I stayed in Pune for 30 days conducting the experiment at MACS after training on GLC at the NCL. Two doctoral researchers at MACS helped me with my experimental set up. The results were extremely encouraging. The breakdown of propionate in the flask with CO_2 bias was much earlier.

As CO2 bias was increased, the methane content increased too – unfolding the mystery of the CRP process. At that time, I came up with a concept of Biochemical Carbon Dioxide Demand (B CO2 D) for anaerobic treatment process. This was my own proposition. I developed the procedure to estimate (B CO2 D) over 10 days and design anaerobic reactors on this basis. To me it was the major outcome of my BTech project – It also satisfied my 'appetite' of doing research in my own way.

Well, the fuss I made to pick up my topic and working on my own – taught me a lot in the latter part of my life. I met very interesting people, visited different institutions and built skills that helped me immensely. In the process of this 'chequered research', I made new friends and established a network. Indeed it was struggle for me but I think the 'fuss I made that time was simply worth it'.

The other day, a student from IIT Bombay came to meet me while looking for a research topic. He almost interrogated me to assess whether I was worthy of being his Guide and said in a candid tone, "I want to find my own topic and I am not really sure what to do. But please don't think that I am making a fuss...."

And I said to him reassuringly – "No worries – Please do go ahead and make a fuss – I promise that you will enjoy and cherish the experience"

I was close to Mr VD Desai after his retirement and visited his house in Mahim, Mumbai several times, He is now no more. Dr Deepak Kantawala has always been my well-wisher, friend philosopher and guide. We have done several assignments together and when he 'sold' his environmental engineering consulting company, I was involved to some extent.

I am in touch with both Professor Patwardhan and B Subba Rao. Professor Patwardhan advised us recently on the training of effluent treatment plant operators. Mr S R Kshirsagar is no more. I took over the job of Hon Editor of the Journal of Indian Water Works Association from him. We had worked together for several years to shape the Journal.

213

I was asked to speak on sustainability at a Corporate of great repute. I was working on my presentation using PowerPoint just a few hours before the talk.

I normally keep a good stock of sustainability related slides and depending on the audience, pick and tweak as necessary. This approach is monotonous and kills creativity (as you live here on content that is dead!) but when you get into this rut of working on the presentation in the last hour– then you just give up and compromise. I was editing my PowerPoint slides with these mixed feelings and just then my good friend Professor walked in.

"When will you stop this practice of doing PowerPoint, Prasad" he said "Teaching an exciting subject like sustainability with PowerPoint is the most boring thing to do".

I knew that my friend always spoke his mind, was a rebel in this own right (especially when it came to teaching), but this time, I fought, struggled and argued to tell him that this was a presentation to a corporate audience, serious guys, who expect those glossy presentations, quotes from Big Shots and Business leaders, and some startling statistics / graphs are needed to show how sustainability makes a business case. My fiend pooh poohed my arguments and asked if I could give him the floor this time to teach sustainability in his own way. He said he would not be using PowerPoint.

I felt a bit uncomfortable. There was some risk of the 'unknown'. But my curiosity would not let me put his proposition aside. So as a compromise, I offered him to front end this talk and said that after his non-PowerPoint approach, I would do my usual PowerPoint slide presentation- as per what was promised to the Chief Sustainability Officer (CSO) of the Corporate.

"No messing around my friend" I said this a couple of times. And my friend smiled and said "No worries – leave it to me"

"I need to prepare a bit" he said. He disappeared for 15 minutes and returned with a ream of photocopying paper and a pack of 20 assorted pens of various colors. I became even more curious and also a bit nervous.

We reached the venue and some 40 participants were already there sitting in a large room. The CSO came to me, greeted us and asked for my pen drive for the PowerPoint projection. "Everything is set Sir – let us test however, whether your slides work". I passed on my pen drive, introduced my Professor friend and said that there was a slight change in the program. My friend would be doing a kind of introduction to sustainability first and then I will be following with my formal PowerPoint presentation. The CSO was kind enough to agree and I was indeed relived. The CSO announced this 'little' change and gave a brief intro to both of us. He simply introduced the Professor as my good old friend as he didn't know him. In any case he wasn't critical.

The Professor then took the charge of the opening session.

The participants were sitting in the room in 3 rows with each row of 12 people. The Professor asked all the participants in the second and third rows to leave the hall. He also asked the CSO to leave. This was rather odd and unexpected. But everyone followed his instructions and went out to the lobby.

The Professor then distributed to the 12 participants sitting in the front row, blank photocopying papers. Each participant was given a color pen. He then simply left the room and asked me to follow him. While closing the door he said to the participants "See you after 5 minutes!"

There were no instructions on what to do for 5 minutes. The participants were really startled. All they had with them was a paper and pen.

So most decided to do something on their own. Some drew pictures, some wrote their names and some even practiced their signatures. Then they chatted a bit generally showing their surprise on what was going on and speculated on what would happen next!

After precisely 5 minutes, my Professor friend opened the door. He said "Thank you"

"Please leave the papers and pen on your seat and exit the lecture hall". All the 12 participants left the room and went to the lobby where coffee was waiting for them with cookies.

The second batch of 12 that was sitting in the second row was now let in. My friend did the same stunt as before. As he was closing the door, one of the participants asked him "Sir, what are we supposed to do?" and he made an innocent face – equally confused and said "Honestly, I don't know! – do what you feel like"

The participants in the second batch also did 'something' with the left over papers and the pens. Some added more to what was earlier drawn. If someone in the first batch had drawn a hollow circle, the participant in the second batch filled it with a solid color to make it look better!

After another 5 minutes, the third 'batch' went in and my friend repeated the "performance". This time, as he was closing the door, one participant looked at the scribbled papers lying on the desks, and said " There is no space now to write on the papers anymore –please give us new blank papers so that we can write". And more participants expressed the same request. My friend did not say a word. Just closed the door and let the third batch do what they could.

Participants in the third batch were not happy with the used or abused paper. They still attempted to do some writing. There was a dustbin in the room with a sign 'use me'. "This paper is now useless" one participant said, throwing the paper in the dustbin. Some thought of doing something more interesting. One participant knew origami so he made interesting products like a giraffe, a house and an airplane. Few copied.

Once the five minutes were over, the Professor asked all the participants come into the lecture hall and take their seats. Once all were settled in, he spoke.

"Thank you friends for your participation. I gave you a paper and pen with no

instructions. You decided to use the paper and pen to write. Was there any need to write? You could have just let the paper and pen be there and spent 5 minutes to chat with each other or even meditate! One of you perhaps started writing and others followed. You wrote on the paper to express your thoughts or put down your identity"

"The paper is like the mother earth – it's a finite resource you have. Pen is the technology, economic activity – the business. Most of you used or spoiled the resource you had for your own interests – interests that were not even clear to you individually or to the group as a whole"

"Each batch that followed – continued what was done by the earlier batch-mechanically and more intensively. The paper now had less 'white

space' left. The resources were depleted and degraded –more and more. Each batch represented a generation ..."

"As generations marched on, you started asking for another paper. Another earth! Is this possible? – You just had one paper – you just have one earth to live on"

"We must think of sustainability when we use our resources – our consumptive thinking must be tamed, our wasteful use of resources must cease"

"And some of you threw the 'wasted paper' in the dustbin. Some created interesting products out of the wasted paper using their origami skills – you thus turned around wasted resource into useful products. That's the innovation you need towards reusing the resources – we need more of such innovations if we want to be sustainable"

With these words, my Professor friend paused. I saw on his face a complex set of expressions – a serious note, a gentle smile and an 'accidental revelation'.

"That's sustainability"

He ended his session with these words.

And there was silence.

I could see that the participants understood the message – and deeply. They had perhaps actually experienced or discovered sustainability.

The participants then spoke, expressed what they learnt and my Professor friend responded with case studies that were insightful and inspiring.

I realized that there was no need for me to give a PowerPoint presentation anymore. "Let us stop here" I said. I asked the CSO to return my pen drive and thanked the Corporate for inviting me.

The next day I received a call from another Corporate to speak on Sustainability. The CSO said "Sir, we will make all the projection arrangements – just bring your pen drive of PowerPoint slides".

I said, "No slides please

– All I need is a ream of photocopying papers and two dozen color pens!!" The CSO was startled. And I was never invited!!

52

Living with Assumptions

We often make assumptions when it comes to designing, modelling and taking decisions. Assumptions are made because sometimes we simply do not have credible data, or complete information about the subject or deep enough knowledge. Assumptions become our best guestimates. Often, time and resource constraints (both financial and human) compel us to make assumptions and move on with decisions. Nothing wrong with that.

Many analysts state the assumptions (often in an apologetic tone! but a good and ethical practice to follow), and some generate scenarios (optimistic or pessimistic as examples) that help us take better decisions. Unfortunately, some just don't care and leave the outcomes to the user or reader.

Sometimes, we keep making assumptions over a period of time; over decades of practice and so we don't even

realize what assumptions we are making! That is of some concern.

Take the example of designing of urban water distribution network. For designing this system, we first lay down a network of pipes and nodes along with road network and superimpose the land use. We then allot a zone around each node for lumping the water demand that has mixed land use of today (or the most recent one). This land use around the node is often assumed to remain the same for next 20 years for which a network is to be designed.

We account for this fallacy by projecting population in the zone using a model that mimics the past growth of the city (not at node level) based on some limited data. Inmigration or changes in Floor Space Index (FSI) are difficult to accommodate in these projections.

When it comes to projecting commercial and industrial demands, we run into difficulties and so we make further assumptions. Well, then we start assuming per capita water demand and follow the 'norms' as applicable. This factor (e.g. 200 lpcd) is often held constant over next 20 years irrespective of changes in water use due to technology, availability affordability and pricing of water.

We assume that the demands are concentrated at the nodes and are not exerted along the pipe (as is the actual reality). We apply a peak factor to get peak demand which is another major assumption. We further assume that all demands at the nodes are acting simultaneously! Finally, we use for hydraulic calculation (i.e. to calculate the flow in the pipes and pressure at the node) a model such as Hazen Williams with a magic coefficient C that is itself built on several assumptions!!

And one more final assumption we make– tacitly so– that water supply equals water demand.

The net result of all these assumptions can be elegant as we feel that we have solved the design problem finally –clearing all the hurdles through assumptions! We look at several software tools today that spew detailed outputs, plot pressure contours and provide 'what if' scenarios if pipe diameters are changed, valve setting is changed or reservoir height and location is shifted. We also have software codes that optimize the design for costs. I myself did one called LOOP Version 4.0 for the World Bank way back in 1990. But all this makes sense for only for publishing in Journals I suppose.

Design of urban water distribution network was one example of 'cascading assumptions'. But umpteen such examples exist in environmental systems such as modelling of pollutant dispersion, assessing health risks, conducting Life Cycle Assessment, designing common industrial effluent treatment plants etc. **I would urge students reading my blog to 'research' on some of these examples to pull out the range of assumptions we make. It can be both revealing**

and inspiring to address.

It's the learning from actual operation of the system that counts. The more you learn about the behavior of the system in practice, the more data we collect and apply analytics to, the more we discuss performance through roundtables and share the outcomes, the more we will become knowledgeable to make better assumptions. Imagine, if we processed the actual data from some of our operating water distribution networks, how confident we will be when engaging with network redesign, strengthening or improving on the operations. A practice we rarely follow today in India. This is where research and practice should merge.

There is nothing wrong in making assumptions. Assumptions are inevitable. However, we have to learn more about what we assume and their consequences and keep improving on our judgments by examining the reality. We need to be transparent and responsible in disclosing assumptions and learn how to live with them.

A PALETTE OF GREEN
Random Thoughts

53
The Conference Game

I went to see my Professor friend last week at his office. He was busy as usual answering two mobile phones at the same time. He was having a tough time skipping between the two conversations.

Behind his large desk, there was a wooden panel with hooks. A large number of conference registration tags were hanging there. Some with thick green nylon strings and a plastic pouch, some with a clip and a laminated cover. On the side of the desk was a chest of drawers. A heap of conference folders was placed on the top that seemed to be covered in dust. Some conference folders were of plastic and a few were made from jute that stood out. There was a large mug on the desk that was full of all kinds of pens– mostly ball points. I realized that the Professor was on a conference spree. No wonder I did not spot him at our usual coffee place of late.

I asked him and he said "Well, Prime Minister's Office asked me to attend all important conferences on Environment & Sustainability in India over past 3 months. Phew – it was a hell of a job. I had to travel to almost all the corners of the country as everyone seemed to be holding a conference on environment. And I realized that it was not just me alone who was travelling – it included speakers and participants as well. I found the same speakers and same participants at these events but at different places! It looked as if for some, attending and speaking at conferences was a profession or an addiction!"

"Oh I see" I said, wondering how large the carbon footprint of these conferences would be. Fewer such events would indeed help the cause of environment and sustainability.

"But how did you find the presentations and discussions" I asked. "Anything new, interesting, innovative?"

"Well well" Professor said lighting his cigar. Most topics were standard and repetitive like Waste to Energy, Corporate Social Responsibility, Business & Sustainability, Green Buildings, and Climate Change – the only difference being that some conferences are run by CII, some by FICCI, some by BCCI and some by IMC. These chambers and associations take turns and keep revisiting these topics. The titles are kept different because of the competition. The good part is that these organizations book different hotels as the venue each time so you feel that the conference is different although the topics are the same.

Sad part however is that these hotels offer the same lunch menu like *paneer tikka masala,* *jeera rice, mixed vegetables, naan* and *ras malai* even when the conference is held in South India. I developed indigestion by eating the food at these conferences over the past three months. I have been telling the organizers that I don't mind the presentations are repeated or drab but the food should be innovative and interesting to keep the participants engaged during the lunch breaks. FICCI and CII are seriously looking at this suggestion."

"But how do the sessions happen?"

"Oh, that's another story" Professor said. There is a chairman for the session, generally an IAS officer from the Government, or an Industrialist who has co-sponsored the event or a Professor from IIT if the first

two are not available. The Chairman generally appears to be redundant. Speakers are called one by one. Since the speaker profiles are often provided only minutes before the session, the Chairman struggles to read these profiles and ends up saying "Dr Modak is so well known that he needs no introduction – so without further ado let me invite him to the dais." Some Chairmen dominate the session and behave like speakers. Some Chairmen are strict on time and all they do is ring the bell after 8 minutes. The session ends with the Chairman saying "Sorry – we have already overrun the allocated time and I don't want to stand between you and lunch. So no questions please. Meet the speakers in the lobby and ask your questions bilaterally". In most conferences, sessions end on such a note. Participants don't mind. Who has questions and who has answers when it comes to the topic of Environment and Sustainability?"

"And what about the speakers?" I asked. (I was worried because I was a speaker at one of the recently held conferences)

Generally, the speakers are good. But many speak about what is already known or say something that is not relevant. They often forget to update the slide date – so we see presentations that they or their assistants prepared from a few years ago. Speakers come up with a 50 slide presentation for a 10 minute slot so they keep moving through the slides like a fast train – apologizing to the audience. And often there are slides that can be seen only by the first two rows because of the small fonts or poor quality pictures. The speaker apologizes once again. That's typical. Some speakers try to show video clips that don't run on the first click. It then becomes a 'technology issue' and a few minutes are spent to fix the issue with no success! The speaker then looks like wounded eagle who cannot fly!

A group photo is taken of the Session speakers along with Chairman. This photo reaches you in a week which you promptly put up on Facebook.

Then of course there is an important benefit of networking. This happens in the corridors and in the loos. You catch up on the business buzz and get an update on people who have changed jobs. New visiting cards are exchanged. As well as gossip. I find this the most rewarding part of the conference. Professor said.

I was wondering what if we had a

2-hour lunch (instead of 1 hour) and 1 hour tea/coffee break instead of the usual half hour cutting down the so called technical sessions. This may make the conferences much more effective.

What about the conference kits?" I asked Professor this 'material' question.

Well, most organizers now a days give you a pen drive with papers or presentations. Later you can erase this content and use the pen drive to store movies. That's the material benefit. Since the conference bag does not contain papers, it is filled with publicity material, information on tourist spots or coupons for discounts on shopping nearby. This is very useful. The bags are often made out of jute to show the commitment of the organizers/sponsors on environment. Participants however don't like these 'cheap bags' as they prefer a good quality leather bag or a pouch considering the high conference fees.

So given this scenario, why were you asked to attend such conferences? I could not resist asking.

Well, the Government wants to know what people discuss in conferences when it comes to Environment & Sustainability. This is in view of the modernization of Environmental Governance that the Government is busy with.

After attending 30 conferences over last 3 months in the country, my report conclusively shows that there is indeed nothing to worry about for the Government. Conferences do not bring out anything new, all mundane stuff, few ripples here and there but no storms. Conferences are not there to change India's outlook, infuse knowledge from practice, inspire or influence the world. Airlines, hotels and conference kit providers will continue to remain the principal stakeholders of the Conference Game.

54

SKD – A Procedure for Selective Knowledge Destruction

I woke up in the morning and decided to go to the Park for a walk. It was 5.30 am. As I stepped out, I saw an online display board flashing at the entrance of the Park that showed the Air Quality Index (AQI). The AQI indicated that the air quality was at alarming levels and that I should be either staying home or walk with a mask[83]. I decided to go back home.

Newspapers had arrived. I read the headlines. Pretty depressing, I thought. Can there be a newspaper that just gives good news and not (heart) breaking news? I thought of talking about it to my journalist friends.

I went to the kitchen to make a bowl of Eggie noodles. I like Eggie as it just takes little more than 2 minutes to prepare. In the busy life of Mumbai, every minute costs and counts.

When I opened the shelf, I did not see any packs of Eggie noodles. My wife said "Eggie is in the soup as the company violated the limits set on lead and Monosodium Glutamate (MSG) content[84]. No more Eggie noodles in the shop. There will probably be a nationwide ban.

I got ready for the office, picked up a couple of apples for lunch (I believe in healthy food) and walked to my car. Driving to the office in messy traffic was always a major pain of the day. I put on the AC and drove my way to the parking lot near my office with a scorching sun overhead. I always carry a bottle of water and keep it in the car. I took a few large gulps of water to wet my throat, took the elevator and reached my desk.

My colleague was reading aloud from a Cancer magazine

---

83 See http://blogs.wsj.com/indiarealtime/2015/04/08/how-indias-new-air-quality-index-works/

84 See http://www.hindustantimes.com/india-news/maggi-noodles-in-soup-everything-you-need-to-knowabout-the-controversy/article1-1354268.aspx

"Among a long list of other problems, drinking water from plastic bottles left to bake in your car will increase your risk of getting cancer, although the risk factor is a function of your current level of health, the relative quality of the plastic containing the water (There are no safe plastics, but some are worse than others), the temperature achieved, the length of time it was in the sun, & whether or not a person consumes water from hot plastic on an ongoing basis, not to mention the quality of the water pumped into the bottle to begin with.

ASIDE from the phthalate exposure, drinking water from hot plastics increases your exposure to Bisphenol-A (BPA), a potent hormone disruptor which is known to attack the body IN MYRIAD WAYS, including elevating one's risk of breast & prostate cancer"[85]

I was shocked. First of all, I dislike magazines on subjects like Cancer and don't know why our company does not subscribe to Filmfare or stock old issues of Debonair. This piece of information on Cancer due to plastic bottle water was particularly disturbing.

During lunch, I asked my peon to cut the apples for me and give them to me as a 'fruit platter'. Just last month, we purchased Zent Ozone Purifier that promised the removal of pesticides and chemicals retained on vegetables and fruits. This Zent Purifier brought a sense of safety to our family.

But one of my friends who had joined lunch had a story to tell – Apparently the ozone based purification technology was not fool proof. The claims made by Zent were rather tall. Research carried out at the University of Maine in the United States reported that there was no guarantee[86]

As I was left gaping with this new information, my friend said in a hush hush tone, Neha, the Actor who is the brand ambassador of this product is withdrawing her contract with Zent. She is worried that she may be sued for false claims!

I felt cheated and angry and then scared.

I decided to go the Gym on my way back home. Some exercises, especially on the tread mill will be good for my

---

85 See: http://www.quora.com/Can-drinking-from-plastic-water-bottle-left-in-a-hot-car-cause-cancer

86 See: http://www.plentymag.com/magazine/claim_check_ozone_infused_wate.php

health – I muttered.

Last week, I had purchased a nice Tee shirt, at a cheap price and with psychedelic colors on the streets of Bandra. When I changed into this Tee shirt, it caught the eyes of everybody in the Gym.

I was on the tread mill for 30 minutes on a speed of 5.5 kmph and 15 degree incline. Later when I went to the changing room, one of my buddies said "Boss, you are sweating so much as if you're standing under the shower. Hope your Tee shirt is of good quality. These street Tee shirts often contain high levels of formaldehyde (for anti-shrink) and when you sweat formaldehyde gets leached on the skin and can cause skin cancer[87]"

I gave up and decided to junk my jazzy Tee shirt.

When I reached home, I felt defeated, frustrated and scared. I wished I was born on some other planet. Every moment of living here on this Earth and particularly in Mumbai, was a risk proposition. The increasing strings of knowledge about these risks were looming around me like a spider web. I felt trapped.

The next day was the weekend and I called upon my Professor friend to vent my fears and frustrations. Professor was very busy as usual. "I am going to the Hospital" he said. "My day is blocked with patients – Want to come?"

I had no clue what the Professor was up to.

Well, you probably do not know my latest invention. I have come up with a medical procedure called Selective Knowledge Destruction (SKD). In this procedure, we simply 'wash out' or 'destroy' the person's knowledge about the chosen subject – in this case 'environment'. Once the SKD is performed, the person treated knows NOTHING about that subject. More interestingly, the effect lasts over a year – that means no new knowledge gets transferred to the person in this period. After a year you will need another SKD like putting on another stent. Procedure is very simple and straightforward but requires some training. It's like putting on a saline to the brain with my secret electrolyte.

But why should one go for SKD? I asked (as usual a stupid question).

---

87 See: http://www.nytimes.com/2010/12/11/your-money/11wrinkle.html

Oh, easy. It's the most sought after procedure now. I just launched it one week before and I am booked for the year already and there are requests all over the country to open up franchisee units. I may have to give up my teaching job at IIT.

The SKD treated person is blissfully unaware of the environmental risks he or she is subjected to. So one can live life normally without any tensions, fears or anxieties. If someone falls sick or dies, you don't know why – as there is simply no point in knowing. And these risks are never fully understood nor actioned upon. Knowing the probable cause is therefore irrelevant or inconsequential. So you can live life as you normally would – like going for morning walks, eating Eggie noodles to your heart's content, using Zent Ozone Purifier for making your fruits and vegetables healthy. Plus you can keep plastic bottles with water in the car to drink when thirsty and wear cheap Tee shirts because you like them…. Professor went on and on with more examples.

I said – My friend, can you give me an out of turn appointment for the SKD. I badly need one … **I am looking forward to living a normal life.**

55
ENVIRONMENTALIST AT A COCKTAIL PARTY

I was attending a cocktail party at a triplex apartment in one of the tall buildings on Carmichael Road, in South Mumbai.

Someone said that a famous Environmentalist was attending the party. I looked around for someone in organic cotton Tee shirt or a Khadi sling bag first, but couldn't locate anyone. Since many famous environmental NGOs are now 'rich and corporatized', I looked for someone wearing an expensive 'designer' saree, with large size Prada spectacles with a gold plated chain. Couldn't find such a woman either. Most people in the party looked normal. The environmentalist must be in disguise, I said to myself.

"Are you the Environmentalist?" a lady asked me with a glass of wine in her hand covered with diamond studded rings. "You must be Mr. Bittu Sehgal," perhaps this was the only name she had heard at these parties. No Ma'am, I said, Bittu treks in the Sanctuaries and does not attend cocktail parties, I am an Environmental Consultant. "Oh, then you must be making lots of money she said. Nowadays I hear that consultants in the environmental field are in heavy demand because everybody wants speedy environmental clearances". You are partly right and partly wrong Ma'am, I explained while sampling a *chicken tikka*. It is true that Environmental

Consultants are in heavy demand and are sought after for speedy environmental clearances but then they do not make much money. There is just too much competition and most of the money goes to those who grant the environmental clearance. The lady was convinced.

A stern looking guy, dressed in an Oxford suit walked across to me. "So you are that Guy, someone told me that there is an environmental activist amongst us. You must be the one since you are the only one not having any drinks. Are you Rishi Agarwal? I said no. Rishi Agarwal does not attend such cocktail dinners. He is in Aarey Milk Colony just now organizing a protest to oppose the Regional Development Plan of Mumbai. It's all crappy the newspapers say". That's the problem, the Man said. "You activists simply stall development of this city just for the sake of opposition. You never take a holistic and long term view on development. Good that the present Government understands this perspective" The Man was bitter and angry. He went to the bar to refill his shot of Glenfiddich.

In order that I was not labelled as an environmental activist again, I asked the waiter to get me a large Mojito "Sir, this person who spoke to you just now is one of the powerful builders of Mumbai who wants to develop a mega housing complex in the Aarey Milk Colony" the waiter whispered. "Oh I see" I said while sipping the Mojito and sampling a mini pizza. I was relieved that I did not live around Aarey colony.

I moved towards the balcony as there were fewer people there. I thought of having my drink in peace. A woman with a large chain of beads followed me. She was smoking a perfumed cigarette. You must be Rufus David. I said No, Rufus is with Green Peace raising funds for their activities. I work as a consultant to the World Bank on environment". Oh dear, how exciting she said. You must be globe-trotting and visiting places. My daughter wants to take on such a career. Can you give her some guidance and some leads? Please connect me with some international Environmental NGO where she could do some four weeks internship. She is keen to show some NGO type activities on her CV – like sanitation survey in Mumbai slums or a tree hugging campaign to save trees. Wouldn't that help? She was right I thought. I gave her my visiting card. Ask her to contact me I said finishing my mini pizza.

There was a discussion going on at one of the roundtables. It was about the cutting of two trees that were in the middle of the Veer Savarkar Marg in front of the Catering College at Shivaji Park. There was a divided opinion – some were of the view that the trees should be cut as there were accidents, especially at night when people (mostly from film industry) would drive drunk from the pubs in Bandra. Some were dead against the proposition of cutting as the trees were 80 years old. When they saw me, Man with rum and coke said "You must be Professor Sharad Chaphekar who counts the trees in Mumbai". No I said you got me wrong. "Professor Chaphekar does not attend cocktail parties. He is busy right now updating his book on Mumbai's tree inventory, I am Professor at IIT Bombay and I teach a subject on Ecology and Environment" "Oh, then you must give us your opinion".

I said "Both of you are equally right and equally wrong"

The Man did not like that answer. He wanted a solution. "You professors never say anything clear and concrete.

You just blurb" He said. "Why don't we dig a tunnel as an underpass to save the trees? The tunnel will also avoid accidents. We are going to build several tunnels in Mumbai anyways – so another one!" Man with gin and tonic said. I asked "By the way what kind of trees are they? And don't you think that the tunnel will cost a hell of a lot of money. Besides we will have to keep the tunnel illuminated whole night." There was silence – "Does this matter?" The Woman with margarita and a straw asked in an angry tone. "You are too academic to ask such a (stupid) question."

I decided to help myself to some cocktail samosas and paneer mirch from the bar counter. "Sir, are you from Delhi? Then you must be ABC of IICA" Man sitting on the bar stool having a large brandy on the rocks said. "I am sorry I am not A B Chakraborty of IICA" I said. ABC is busy conducting training programs for environmental NGOs on Corporate Social Responsibility (CSR). He travels all over the country looking for trainees (that is hard to get) and he has no time to attend such cocktail parties" I work as a Chief Sustainability Officer for a Corporate in Mumbai I said.

Oh then you are the right

person I should be talking to. The Man said. I run an Environmental NGO in Mumbai that specializes in CSR. We help corporates implement CSR projects, ensure that money gets spent in time – irrespective whether the projects make any difference or not. We get some nice photography done and record video clips of the interviews of the community representatives (who say how happy they are) and write a good story. We have worked with several Corporates by now and have ready templates of reports you can chose from. We own a great picture library of photos taken across the country (people with large eyes, people with chinky eyes etc.). This option is in case you are in a hurry and want to be costeffective. I can come to your office with a presentation and show you some of our 'CSR resources'.

I looked at the Man carefully. He hardly looked like an environmental NGO and appeared to me more like a businessman. "So he is the Environmental NGO in disguise – I said to myself. A new breed indeed! Someone, who I would have totally missed.

"Sir, I attend such Cocktail parties on a regular basis. It's more like a client meet for me"

The Man was certainly frank and a bit high in spirits. He asked the barman for a third round of a large brandy on the rocks. That explained it.

I left the party half way with a vow not to attend the next one.

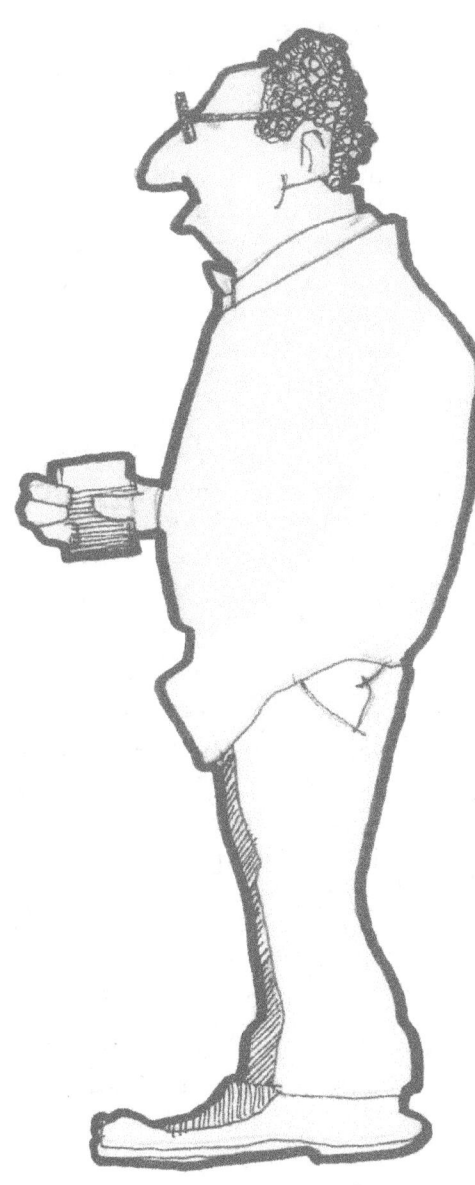

56

Game of Indicators

My Professor friend and I walked into the waiting room of the Minister of Environment in Delhi. The secretary asked the Professor to insert his Green Card into the slot machine. When the Professor did so, the machine made a chuckling sound like R2D2 of Star Wars and flashed a number. That number was the sequence number for us to meet with the Minister. Professor's Green Card must be highly respectable or valued as we were ushered right away into the Minister's Cabin.

When we finished our meeting (which was typically inconsequential) and reached the elevators, I asked Professor about the Green Card. Professor explained that this was the Minister's pet subject and a pilot that he is thinking of launching all over the country soon.

The Green Card was proposed to be linked to the *Aadhar* card and pooled into the central database, covering all the environment related parameters or attributes of the person. The Card when used for transactions (e.g. for purchasing goods at the stores, making payments at a hotel or restaurant, purchasing fuel at the petrol/diesel station, buying an air ticket etc.) will assign appropriate "green points" and calculate the person's Green Index and rate between 0-10. If your Green Index is less than 5 for example, then you will be considered an *irresponsible citizen*, and penalized so that you are coerced into behaving responsibly. Thus your Green Index should always cross the minimum of 5.

The other day, one of the top executives of a Company (who was in the pilot project) realized that every time he went to the restaurant to dine, his bill was taxed 10% more as his Green Index was less than 5. When he started ordering organic food on a regular basis and chose restaurants who had energy efficient fixtures, the Green Index moved a bit beyond 6 and he got out of the 10% surcharge. So to save money and at the same time protect the environment, he had to make a behavior change. Imagine the impact once the first lot of 10 million Green Cards is issued to India's rich and high middle class citizens. The launch of the Green Card with Green Index will 'tame' our highly consumptive and carbon intensive lifestyles. Professor said.

I thought this was rather visionary and very impressive. Perhaps, Professor's Green Index must be close to 9 and that's why we were given priority while visiting the Minister. (I was later told that Visa and MasterCard companies were already holding talks with the Government of India on how to bring in these elements on their card chips on a universal basis.)

"You know, this Environment Minister is very fond of indicators. He likes to bring data together and make a number out of it as an Index and disseminate the Index to people so that they become aware. Have you read about his an-nouncement on Air Quality Index (AQI) in Indian cities? This index has been developed by IIT Kanpur. It provides one consolidated number after tracking eight pollutants and uses color coding to describe the severity in terms of associated health impacts"

I looked up on the web and found the description of AQI and also articles that say that the Indian AQI is not as easy to understand and is not too action oriented[88].

When I mentioned this observation, Professor said that making complicated indices is the current state of the art (or science). How can you have a simple index for complex issues on environment?

I suggested that why don't we show data on the sale of respiratory drugs and inhalers instead of measuring PM_{10} and $PM_{2.5}$? Higher is the level of $PM_{10}/PM_{2.5}$, more will be the sale of the respiratory drugs and the inhalers. So the sales statistics will serve as an Index. I continued.

We could speak to Cipla Pharmaceuticals as they have nearly 50% of the market share on such products and would be happy to sponsor a number of display boards that will

---

88 See: http://www.thehindu.com/opinion/blogs/blog-datadelve/article7083985.ece

post their sales each day. We will save money on expensive automated air quality monitors and in fact earn advertising revenues. In any case, the veracity of the data collected at the automated air quality monitors is rather questionable and data is as good as random numbers" I said.

But the Professor probably did not hear me. He continued.

A few years ago, a Comprehensive Environmental Pollution Index (CEPI) was developed by the Central Pollution Control Board (CPCB) to rank India's industrial estates. This index was developed by IIT Delhi and made use of several complicated variables such as *pollutant, pathway, receptor and additional high risk elements*[89]. Indeed, CEPI was complicated to understand but was applied to 88 industrial estates. The index was actually used for policy and taking action. For example, the analysis showed that there were 43 industrial areas/clusters out of the 88 estates that had CEPI crossing 70. These estates were declared as *critically polluted*. These critically polluted industrial clusters/ areas were recommended for

further detailed investigations to assess the extent of damage and a formulation of appropriate remedial action plan. In this process, several action plans were created. Don't know how many were implemented though.

I recalled the criticism on CEPI, its questionable formulation of aggregation (e.g. additive function) and the poor quality field data that was used in arriving at the Index. The impact of publishing and using CEPI was however high, since a freeze was called on the expansion and modernization of industrial units in critically polluted areas. The Industry Associations protested. CEPI was pushed as a Policy without proper scientific debate and stakeholder consultation.

I was wondering why simple data points could not be used to develop indicators for industrial estates/clusters. These data points could have been – overall water consumption as against water available, energy and fuel consumption, materials brought in (with octroi collected as proxy), number of workers/staff in the estate and in the neighborhood of say

89 See the full report at http://cpcb.nic.in/divisionsofheadoffice/ess/NewItem_152_Final-Book_2.pdf

1-2 kms, presence, functioning and disposal point regarding common environmental infrastructure (like common effluent treatment plant and common hazardous waste treatment and disposal facility), number of public complaints received, issues and severity etc.

The Professor continued as we took a taxi. He asked the taxi driver to take us to the Neeti Ayog – *new avatar* of the earlier planning commission. "Hope you will join me" he said. The Primate Minister has asked me to develop an Environmental Performance Index (EPI) for each State. The EPI, as usual, will range from 0-10 and the higher the value, the State will be considered as better performing on environmental matters. EPI will be used to allocate State budgets. Today's meeting is to finalize the parameters that will be used to arrive at the EPI apart from the mathematical function (e.g. Linear, weighted linear, maximum operator etc.) and the weights. It's a high level meeting as it has 'money at stake'. This approach will however transform India from an 'unsustainable nation' towards the path of sustainability. I have arrived at a fuzzy formulation of EPI to account for the foggy, manipulated and incomplete data. And I feel that this kind of formulation will make EPI look "state of the art" or contemporary and impressive.

I was overwhelmed. I realized the importance of environmental indicators in the progress of India, in environmental management (like using CEPI), in environmental communication (like the AQI) and in influencing our lifestyles through mechanisms like the Green Card.

Professor paid the taxi bill, looked at me intensely for a while and then said with his characteristic serious tone "Prasad, it's finally a game. The Minister wants me to develop that structure of EPI which will somehow provide least central allocation to the States ruled by the Opposition – I am identifying therefore those parameters that are representative and defensible and yet help me achieve this *differential objective*"

At that point I wasn't envious of Professor's job.

I also realized how and why such indicators were developed – essentially to fudge the real data and project the outcome what we want…. Clever.

57

I met my Professor friend at the EXIT of an international exhibition on air quality monitoring instruments in Mumbai. This exhibition had stalls of some of the leading suppliers of automated air quality monitoring instrument suppliers from all over the world. It was a great display of sophisticated instruments across some 50 stalls and a series of seminars running concurrently. There must have been at least 1000 footfalls a day. Most visitors were industries who were forced to install automatic air quality monitoring stations by the Government.

I asked the Professor how was his experience.

He seemed quite happy but not very excited. "It's a good expo but I have some other views". He said with a pause. "We need to chat one of these days". I knew that given my friends hectic work schedule, this chat was never going to happen. Chatting with the Professor had always been interesting and stimulating. So I suggested that we sit at one of the restaurants outside the EXIT gate for some coffee. "They have a verandah behind and they let you smoke there" I told him as additional information – as if it mattered.

We chose a table with a round top and cane chairs and ordered some Ethiopian coffee that was served in large cups along with some bitter cookies. When the waiter brought an ashtray for the Professor, the 'stage was all set' for our conversations.

He took a deep puff from his cigar and said "Monitoring with sophisticated instruments is fine. We do need to have good quality, high frequency air quality data on key parameters but what I don't like is the absence of the involvement of people. We need to involve people in environmental monitoring if we want to see action. Most of the time, monitoring remains a 'bilateral' activity between the 'polluter' and the 'regulator'. People or the key stakeholders learn about the outcomes of this bilateral transaction only when there are serious violations leading to punitive actions or legal consequences.

"People watch on TV or read occasionally in the newspapers, graphs and statistics on ambient air quality, especially about how it is much higher than the standard. Firstly, they don't understand the terms (parameters and units) and secondly, they don't know what should be done, or what the Government is doing about it. **It is often a passive receipt of information**"

I said you need something sensational to happen if you want to make people understand how bad our ambient air quality is. As you know United States may curb President Barack Obama's

early morning schedule during his visit to Delhi this month. Air pollution monitoring agencies have found that the levels of $PM_{2.5}$ (the term used to describe fine, respirable particles) that get lodged in the lungs are likely to be in the range of moderate to high, during Obama's stay in Delhi. So Obama may find it difficult to be the chief guest at the Republic Day parade which is held in the open and in the morning when air pollution levels are usually high. He will probably have to wear an oxygen mask on the stage and look like Darth Vader of Star Wars. This should wake up citizens of Delhi and force the Government to take some concrete action to reduce the levels of $PM_{2.5}$ or not invite people like Obama again who have poor pollution resilience.

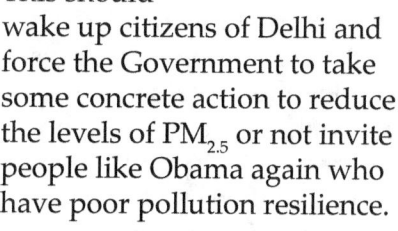

The Professor smiled. "You cannot ask the US President however, to visit all the polluted cities in India just to raise awareness of Indian citizens – and his travel will cost more than the Ministry of Environment's budget. We have to find ways ourselves". He rested his cigar on the ash tray.

Many years ago, in Mumbai, at Shivaji Park I did an experiment on how to involve citizens in air quality monitoring. Here some 200 odd citizens participated. We don't need to make use of sophisticated instruments many times. Even basics like dust jars work. So I used dust jars that were sponsored by one of the major polluting industries of Mumbai. (They wanted to feel 'good'). A call was given through the newspaper (that was kind enough to publicize at no cost) asking interested citizens to assemble at the Shivaji Park Gymkhana if they were interested in learning about the air quality in Mumbai.

On a Sunday morning, some 200 citizens from different corners of Mumbai walked in. They represented all ages, gender and professions. I gave a 10 minute presentation on the basics of air pollution in cities and then spoke about the dust jar. The idea was to give every attendee a dust jar that they would place in the balcony or terrace where there was as much free air flow as possible. The jar was to be kept for one week and all

were expected to meet again at the Gymkhana, get the dust jar weighed and compare the results. Some students then showed the participants how the dust jar works. Names and addresses of the citizens were recorded (and later mapped).

I think the idea of comparing dust fall levels really motivated the citizens to come back on the next Sunday. My students did some random visits to some 20 houses across the city to check if the dust jar was placed alright – and this also helped as some sort of a reminder.

On the next Sunday we got more than 200 citizens as they had brought along their neighbors and friends. All were curious. We weighed each dust jar and a couple of my students did a quick mapping of the dust levels on the map of Mumbai to project on a screen.

I had organized for the display of lungs of industrial workers that were preserved in jars with formalin. This was courtesy KEM hospital's Air Pollution & Heath Unit. These jars showed the amount of particles lodged in the lungs of the industrial workers cause due to exposure to dust in the work space. While my students were doing dust fall mapping, the citizens crowded around the tables to see the 'display of consequences'. This was certainly scary. I could hear first whispers and later, raised voices.

When Mumbai's dust fall level map was projected, it led to an intense debate. Why are the dust fall levels high here and why so low in another place? What dust fall levels are permissible? And what can we do about it? One participant said that particle size should also matter and not just the weight. Another one said that local release of dust e.g. due to construction activities makes a difference. All were excited about learning more and came up with suggestions for city-wide as well as local actions. They wanted me to repeat this exercise on the terraces of schools and involve school children and teachers.

"Let the students get involved as an assignment where they will record dust jar levels in various seasons – see the variability and whether the trends were decreasing or rising. At the end of the year, all school principals should get together, compile data and publish a report for the citizens and the Government"

Wow – I exclaimed. "That's real participatory air pollution monitoring. Much better than just making use of automated instruments. Your experiment is unique as it builds citizen awareness, and imparts education. Importantly it promotes ownership, opens collaborations and leads to collective actions."

So did you repeat the 'experiment', I asked.

The Professor extinguished his cigar and I asked for the bill.

I did this experiment in 1985 in Mumbai. Always wanted to repeat, escalate and replicate but couldn't do so for various reasons. Would love to action again. May be through Ekonnect. If anyone is interested to emulate this experiment, do let me know. I will be most happy to guide/help. These dust jars were used heavily in China in 1990s for ambient air quality monitoring. There have been interesting Chinese publications on the dust fall technique and results. Of course the method has its own limitations. There are however several extensions possible. Even more recently, dust jars are used for air quality monitoring[90].

Applying science to society is key. A lot happens when done well.

---

90 See "Evaluation of Dust fall in the Air of Yazd" by K. Naddafi, R. Nabizadeh, Z. Soltanianzadeh, M. H. Ehrampoosh in Iran (http://diglib.tums.ac.ir/pub/magmng/pdf/3344.pdf).

58
SMART CITIES V/S DUMB CITIES

I was about to leave my office for the day and my good friend Professor knocked on the door. *Are you free to join me tonight for dinner at the Taj with mayors of the Smart Cities? Prime Minister may be attending – but we are not sure about that. But certainly the Minister for Urban affairs will be there. Why don't you join?*

I did not have any dinner engagements that day and my wife was away at a party with her friends so I had no reason to refuse. But still I protested asking how I would fit in with the mela of smart mayors. Professor said that the organizers wanted some independent experts to be around as 'knowledge nodes' mingling around in the crowd for the purpose of 'illumination' and 'inspiration'. I could perhaps fit in that schema he said. In order to be able to play such a role, I needed to understand what a smart city is. When asked, my Professor friend as usual gave a mysterious smile

and said – oh, you will learn as you will talk to the mayors. Just relax!

We reached the Taj by 8 pm. After the preliminaries of security checks, the lady at the registration desk handed over tiny smart cards that looked real impressive. *Put the card in the pocket of your shirt and then everything will be taken care off.* She said this in a voice that resembled a machine.

The lounge was packed. There were mayors moving around the lounge with Modi style bundees (a bundee is like a jacket and is now India's current national attire) sporting various shades of green. All looked smart, confident and intelligent. There were however some who were wearing grey colored bundees with faces meek. Professor whispered "those with dark green bundees are the mayors of smartest cities and those with pale green bundees are mayors of smart but not so smart cities". And what about those with grey colored bundees?, I asked and Professor replied, *oh these are the mayors of dumb cities. Only when their cities become smart, will they be allowed to wear green bundees.*

Typical Smart City Mayor

Typical Dumb City Mayor

I joined the first round table that was occupied by four smart city mayors. One of the smart city mayors was telling the others how smart his city was. *We are focusing on solar street lamps. All street lamps in my city are solar powered cutting down thereby, major emissions of greenhouse gases.* Another mayor said that well, this was no big deal. *We already have solar street lamps in place, we now have intelligent traffic signal systems that optimize the signal timing based on real time traffic data, this reduces the queue length and the idling emissions from vehicles –this leads to reduced exposure of air pollutants to pedestrians.* The third mayor said that his smart city was doing even better. Most of the vehicles are either electric powered or based on bio-gas.

Hydrogen cars are expected in a year. This is expected to lead to a major reduction in fossil fuel consumption and of course in air emissions. The fourth mayor said that his city has done all this already and is now moving on to promoting telecommuting to avoid or minimize travelling to the offices. *Most offices are now providing this option to the employees – he said – thanks to the IT infrastructure provided by the city administration in the buildings.* About half a million people will work from home. I liked this idea as I always wanted to watch some of the afternoon TV shows that I often missed.

I thought that all this conversation was getting so positive and interesting. I took down names of the four cities so that I could plan to visit them to experience such smartness of transport planning and infrastructure.

At the next table I saw that more serious discussions were happening. The smart city mayors on this table were accompanied by some of country's top robotics experts. One of the experts was wearing thick spectacles and was talking about cars that would be driven by robots. This will be the latest in the future smart cities. Here you will be able to order a robot driven taxi with instructions on where to come and where to go. You will be able to indicate whether you want to take the fastest route or the cheapest route or the most scenic route and the robot will help you reach your destination accordingly. I said that using a robot driven car would help reduce cases of assaults on women and perhaps reduce accidents as robots wouldn't drink. This comment was not well appreciated by the Expert – that's beside the point he said.

I realized that the smartness of

the city was getting even more escalated. For sure, it was going to be another world!

The Professor appeared suddenly, *Oh I have been looking for you. Where were you my friend? I want you to meet the Chairman in charge of the National Program on Smart Cities.* He introduced me to the Chairman with a lot of good words about me and how involved I was in sustainability. *A city when smart becomes sustainable automatically,* the Chairman said this in a dense voice while sipping white wine.

I was not sure whether smartness meant sustainability. A sustainable city was an effort on a participatory basis I thought, involving stakeholders and not an ad-hoc fitment of "smart projects" decided by someone in the administration as a *show off* or by someone at the political helm of affairs deciding what's good for the city on an autocratic basis. But I decided to keep quiet as I sensed that the Chairman was not in a mood to listen to terms such as participatory or stakeholder driven process.

The Chairman had convincing arguments however. A smart city will have the least water, energy and waste related footprints, and it will provide infrastructure and deliver services to its citizens at highest point of the efficiency curve. Everything will be wired, data managed and optimal decisions will be taken on this basis.

When I narrated to the Chairman the great initiatives I learnt from the mayors of the smart cities in the first two roundtables, he smiled and said that that was just tip of the iceberg and there were several more startling innovations happening. Cars in smart cities will have a fitment of online medical and psycho diagnostic tools placed on the steering wheel. By the time you reach your office, your blood pressure, sugar levels, eye ball movements (apparently an indicator of anxiety) and the ECG will be monitored without you knowing anything. You will get a full medical report that will tell you how fit you are for the day. All this data will be pooled to city's central server as 'big data' to come up with city health analytics so that we can understand the root cause of the problem and come up with solutions.

I thought that this was getting much too personal – almost violating privacy. I was uncomfortable. I envied the lives of people living in dumb cities in this perspective

and thought of going to the tables where the mayors with grey bundees were sitting. These tables had relatively poor illumination and had normal bottle of water (not the ultra-pure Himalayan water that others tables had). The waiters were serving them cheaper wine on someone's instructions.

One of mayors of the dumb cities was saying "We are trying to become a smart city – but people simply don't want to. They still want to live unregulated, not be monitored and enjoy the *chaos*. Life in our type of cities creates something unexpected every day. People feel that this surprise is the essence of vibrance and something that makes their lives interesting – essentially a pinch of *pain and pleasure*." I thought that he had a good point to make and so I decided to write down the names of the dumb cities for my retirement life but as I was about to do so, the Chairman raised a toast and announced that dinner was ready.

So I went to the buffet counter to sample some food. The buffet counter had some of my favourite dishes like chicken dum aloo, punjabee shira and prawn curry. As I was working on taking a large helping of the dum aloo, the smart card from my pocket spoke *"Dear Dr Modak, we just completed full analyses of your body health using our smart body scanner. The results show that your levels of cholesterol and sugar are not within the limits as they should be. We strongly discourage you therefore from taking dum aloo, punjabee shira and prawn curry. Please therefore move to the table with salads and low salt soup."*

I was really shocked with this mechanized voice emanating from the smart card. The voice resembled the voice of the lady at the reception. *This is too much I say* – I told my Professor friend. *For God' sake, let us not get that smart!!* And the Professor smiled.

You may like to read newspaper articles on smart cities in India[91]

91 http://timesofindia.indiatimes.com/india/Narendra-Modi-Cities-must-compete-with-each-other-for-smartcity-tag/articleshow/45683012.cms

59

BUSINESS CASE OF CLIMATE CHANGE

[This post is a fictitious story and not real! No offences meant to the names cited. All said or written here is to be taken in the spirit of humor]

My Professor friend called me on Sunday morning. "Would you like to come to Mr. Ambani's house for a breakfast meeting? The topic of discussion is Climate Change and Mr. Ambani wants me to facilitate the discussions. I want you to join as my assistant and take down notes. And sorry for this short notice"

"Of course count me in – Who else is joining?" I asked with all excitement.

Well Professor said "The invitations have been sent to select top honchos of India Inc. This includes biggies like Kiran Shaw Mazumdar, Naina Kidwai, N. Narayan Murthy, Anand Mahindra, Ratan Tata, Rana Kapoor and Kumarmangalam Birla just to name a few. Some politicians are also invited like Sharad Pawar as these leaders are more like business men and actually part of the industry.

The leaders are unhappy with Government of India (GoI) the way climate negotiations are handled. They feel that the industry is practically neglected and advice is taken mainly from Economists who are from Delhi and live close to JNU campus and from retired Indian bureaucrats who are sour as they could not get foreign postings. There is no business perspective"

"Meet me at the entrance of Mr. Ambani's residence. The code word is 247. You will need to punch in this number correctly and only then the door will open"

"Why 247?" I asked

Don't you know? Professor said. 247 corresponds to three scenarios of 2°, 4° and 7° rise in the global mean temperatures.

The Professor then educated me on the significance of 2, 4 and 7.

Two degrees: The United Nations framework convention on climate change aims to avoid potentially dangerous climate change and has adopted a long-term goal of keeping global average warming below 2°C above pre-industrial levels. (2° rise will be crossed at 60% probability by year 2040 in the worst case)

Four degrees: The recent IPCC report concluded that, global climate change risks are high to very high with global mean temperature increase of 4°C or more above preindustrial levels. The impacts could include substantial species extinction, large risks to global and regional food security, and the combination of high temperature and humidity compromising normal human activities, including growing food or working outdoors in some areas for parts of the year (4° rise will be crossed at 60% probability by year 2080 as the worst case)

Seven degrees: There has been much less research focusing on the impacts at higher temperatures but limited studies suggest the possibility of even greater impacts, with a rise in temperature of around 7°C potentially giving rise to extreme heat events in excess of human physiological tolerance in some regions. (7° rise will be crossed at 60% probability by year 2200).

Professor added "Recognizing the importance of 2, 4 and 7, I told Mr. Ambani to choose 247 as the secret entry code as it would remind him of the climate change and its implications every day. Not only just him, but the 600 staff who work in his house will think of climate change whenever they punch this secret code. I was told that the staff has now installed the same secret code at the door locks in their houses. Number 247 is in fact spreading in the town as the climate sensitive secret code. My only worry is that it won't remain a secret code anymore if it spreads too much. I am now thinking of another number"

I was always curious about Mr. Ambani's residence on Pedar Road. Antilia as it is called is a name given of a mythical island in the Atlantic. (Apparently this name was chosen by Mr. Ambani as he wanted to remember the threat to the islands of the Atlantic from submergence due to sea level rise). Antilia is believed to be worth $1 billion USD today and is deemed to be the world's second most expensive

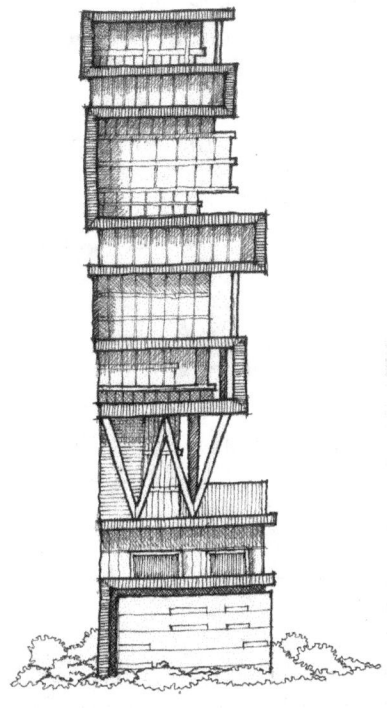

residential property- after Buckingham Palace.

The structure of Antlia was designed to survive an 8-Richter scale earthquake. But to Mr. Ambani, making a building resilient to earthquake was something rather trivial. Few know that Antilia incorporates features that withstand risks due to climate change. The risks addressed include extreme events that could happen in Mumbai such as floods (remember 2006?), cyclones, tsunamis and the like. For Antilia, these risks were considered both in isolation as well as in combination. This feature was implemented by my Professor friend – something not even thought of by President Obama for his White House in the United States. What a pity!

When Professor explained, I realized why the building profile and architecture of Antilia was ugly and an eye sore as the science of climate risk adaptation and mitigation required weird shapes of architecture and absurd floor heights. For instance, Antilia has 27 floors with extra-high ceilings (other buildings of equivalent height could have had as many as 60 floors). The critics however do not understand the secret i.e. a unique risk insulation of Antilia from climate change.

The breakfast meeting began with a few opening remarks by Mr. Ambani stressing the need to discuss business implications due to climate change. We need to change he said. (Later I realized that what he actually meant was we need the change. This must be a typo made by his personal assistant in preparing the breakfast speech)

Professor then gave a summary presentation largely drawn from the report

"Climate Change – A Risk Assessment" written by David King, Daniel Schrag, Zou Dady, Qi Ye and Arunabha Ghosh[92]"

The report indicated that the temperatures in North India are going to be on the rise causing severe heat stress. In the 4oC rise scenario, there would be 80% probability that a north Indian would encounter heat that would prevent core body temperature from falling down to normal (i.e. 37° C) during eight hours of rest at night. This would lead to affecting person's sleepability. Such heat stress would also mean a reduction of around 40% in workability. Further, there is about a 40% chance that individuals in northern India will not be able to participate in competitive outdoor activities in summertime when global average temperatures would have risen on average by 1° C compared to the present. With 4° C of warming, this probability will be around 80-90% in northern India.

Mr. Sharad Pawar said that this would mean that the business of ICL and the likes of BCCI would be affected in the States of Punjab, Rajasthan, Haryana and Union Territory of Delhi. The Sports Stadiums constructed there would remain deserted for over four to six months in the year. Further, due to heat stress, the cricket players may not be able to meet the secret expectations of the bookies. This will lead to a loss of revenue to the Film industry.

No worries, Mr. Ambani said, we will convert these sports stadiums into Solar Parks taking advantage of the existing structures and the rising temperatures. These gigantic solar parks will help close the national energy deficit.

All appreciated the idea and Mr. Pawar offered help in this transaction. I thought that was a pretty friendly gesture.

As people in north India will have a disturbed sleep at night, they will need to kill time somehow. People with disturbed sleep will probably watch TV and look for late night TV shows. Arnab Goswami of Times Now said that his channel will launch a special breaking news bulletin and a SuperPrime News-hour debate between 1 am to 5 am. This night channel will be called 'Times Then' instead of

92 See: http://ceew.in/pdf/DK-DS-ZD-QY-AG%20-%20Climate-%20Change-A%20-Risk-%20 Assessment-6Jul15%20.pdf

'Times Now'

Indeed, Times will make money in this process but as a principle, Arnab said that it will allow advertisements of only low carbon goods and services. Or the advertising rates of high carbon goods and services will be kept 4 times high. This principle was really laudable I thought only challenge was how to define what was low carbon. In Arnab's words, India would need to know.

I was also not sure whether the disturbed sleep at night would happen solely due to climate change or due to listening to Arnab Goswami late at night in addition to listening to him over the day!

Mr. Rana Kapoor expanded on the point of low carbon goods and services. He said that his Bank would lend money only to those enterprises who make climate friendly goods. 'Yes Bank' would be recognized as 'Yes and (sometimes) No Bank' when financing business that is not climate friendly. Premium accounts would be offered to citizens with higher interest who demonstrate lower carbon footprints. There would be an online carbon foot print calculator to be filled when accounts are to be opened. These strategies would distinguish the Bank from conventional ones like ICICI Bank and HDFC and accumulate more deposits.

There was a group of industry leaders representing the refrigeration and HVAC sector. They had smiles on their faces. They heartily welcomed global warming and climate change. Mr. Bon-Joon Koo, Vice Chairman and CEO of LG Electronics, who flew specially from Seoul said that air-conditioning would become a defacto standard for buildings in India for the future – and even the slum dwellers would afford air-conditioned housing. For them the air-conditioners installed would be second hand imported from China as China believes and practices in 'circular economy'. For the rich, he said that LG will come up with personal aircon costumes similar to what astronauts wear. At a flick of a button on your special wrist watch like device, you can cool your body to a preset temperature. This will greatly reduce heat stress to people and maintain work efficiency even outdoors.

There were more happy industrialists like Kiran Shaw Mazumdar who were launching in advance a range of preventive medicines that would help combat new disease vectors arising due to rise in the temperatures. Naina Kidwai of HSBC spoke about the business of climate insurance that they would promote and Shilpa Divekar Nirula CEO of Monsanto India region talked about the opportunities to the GMO market as climate change would bring threat to food security. Anand Mahindra said that his company would produce electric vehicles 10 times the number of the previous year to commit to the mitigation measure for climate change and lead the automobile sector business.

We want the climate to change in our favor – all of them said.

When the breakfast ended and all the industry doyens left, Mr. Ambani closed the door and looked at the Professor in a deep gaze. "Have you got Jitong Wang here?" Yes Mr Ambani I have. Professor said. Should I get him?

Please, said Mr Ambani. I want to discuss with him the polymer he has developed to suck CO2 from air. We would be interested in manufacturing this polymer on a global basis, capturing CO2 to reverse climate change. We will need to ensure that we position carbon capture in the climate negotiations to our advantage. Once pushed, we will surprise everyone. And it will be a new business game that only Ambani's can play! I want us to perfect the technology as soon as possible"

I then realized the complexity of the business of climate change. I took the elevator to the ground floor and punched 247 to exit. My Professor friend stayed.

For those who don't know about sucking of CO2 and the polymer polyethylenimine (PEI), here is an interesting article[93]

93 See http://www.jesc.ac.cn/jesc_cn/ch/reader/download_new_edit_content.aspx?file_no=201203270000009&journal_id=jesc_cn

60

Transforming India in Just 21 Days (with Harun Al-Rashid)

On a Sunday, the doorbell of my apartment rang. I opened the door expecting my maid but instead found a stranger, dressed in the clothes of a King. The stranger gave me a warm smile, extended greetings and shook my hand. "Good morning Dr. Modak, I am Harun Al-Rashid. The Caliph of the Arabian Nights"

I couldn't understand what was going on. Was I dreaming? Or was it a joke or a prank from one of my friends?

"Well Dr. Modak, I am here to bring in a change in the behavior of the Indian citizen, Indian businessman, Indian Administrator, Indian Politician and all the Indians of all kinds. I have been charged with a task to make them responsible towards the environment and become ethical. A renowned Professor, who claims to be your friend, has highly recommended you. I need your help and you will be suitably rewarded"

"You know that for a long time the Government of India has been doing its best to enforce good behavior across citizens in India. You will see hoardings like "do not spit, do not urinate, do not litter" and exactly next to these warnings you will see a mess… You have anticorruption bureau, income tax departments, excise officers, enforcement directorate whose job is to ensure that all pay taxes and don't ask for bribes – but despite the presence of these law enforcing bodies only a meager percentage of population pays taxes. And "black money" or illegal wealth is expected to be several times that of the National GDP. Worst of all, those who are supposed to be the

guardians of the environment, i.e. the pollution control boards and departments of environment are hand in glove with the industrialists, real estate builders and politicians. In this nexus, India's environmental resources are simply butchered. And the poor and vulnerable sections of the society are the worst affected.

If all citizens of India decide to abide by the law, show responsibility towards nature and follow ethical practices, then India will shine"

I ushered Harun Al-Rashid into my drawing room and brought him some black coffee. I asked "How can I help?"

"Oh just accompany me and take me to places. And I will also need a number of your students to tag along. You will also keep a record of our trail"

"I cannot stay up whole night although my students may" I said this because I remembered that Harun Al-Rashid used to roam at night in Bagdad, hence the stories, Arabian Nights.

"Don't worry. We will go out in the day time and may be stroll at night only on a few occasions" Harun Al-Rashid assured.

And we will start from tomorrow.

For those who do not know about Harun Al-Rashid.

Harun Al-Rashid became the fifth caliph (religious and political leader of an Islamic state) of the Abbasid dynasty (ruling family) in September 786 at the age of twenty. During his reign, power and prosperity of the dynasty was at its height, though it has also been argued that its decline began at that time.

Harun Al-Rashid was very anxious that his people be treated justly by the officers of the government; and he was determined to find out whether any had reason to complain. So he sometimes disguised himself and went out at night through the streets and bazaars, listening to the talk of those whom he met, asking them many questions. In this way he learned whether the people were contented and happy, or not. Harun is the hero of several of the stories of 'Arabian Nights,' a famous book. Al-Rashid was essentially a people's person.

I was wondering how Harun Al-Rashid would transform the people of India who are stubborn and resistant to change.

Harun Al-Rashid explained his theory and plan to me.

It seems that a person adopts any habit if it was practiced over 21 days. Say, if you want to go for a morning walk to lose weight, then you must ensure that you go for a walk every day for at least 21 days. Having done so, taking a walk in the morning becomes a habit. You now don't need your doctor or your wife to remind you or nudge you.

No one is entirely sure where the 21-day rule originates, but it seems to have first been set forth in a book called "Psycho-Cybernetics." It's a self-help book first published in the 1970s, and in it, you find out how to create or break a habit in just 21 days. Take a look at the video clip at http://science.howstuffworks.com/life/inside-the-mind/human-brain/ form-a-habit.htm or even better – then visit http://www.21habit.com/

Now apply this theory of 21 days to bad habits, irresponsible and unethical behavior.

Let us assume that you tend to spit on the side of the street. Just imagine that if you don't spit for 21 days, then you won't spit again on the street ever!

I asked Harun Al-Rashid, but why should someone change to be good.

"Easy, I will offer, depending on the case, a tempting reward. Reward plays an important role in making or breaking a habit. I will give this reward only when I observe that such a change has happened after 21 consecutive days"

The next day morning my doorbell rang and I saw a Social Worker with a jholi (shoulder bag), standing outside the door. He looked like Arvind Kejriwal. I was shocked. The man said "It's me, Harun al-Rashid and not Arvind Kejriwal. You know I always go disguised".

I thought this was a very clever and perhaps an appropriate choice. Besides, Kejriwal is known only in Delhi and not in Mumbai.

We started walking on the street. Six students from IIT Bombay joined us.

We saw a guy who came outside his house and threw kachara (waste) on the streets. He did it shamelessly and casually.

Harun Al-Rashid caught hold of the guy and confronted him.

"Why are you doing this?" He asked

The Man said, because everybody does this. There is a lot of litter on the street anyway. What difference will it make if I segregated waste as per the rules and put in the right bins? The municipal staff that comes to collect the waste mixes all the waste from the bins and dumps it all into the pick-up truck.

Al-Rashid said "I understand your point of view. But why don't you attempt proper segregation of waste and place the waste in the separate bins as per the color code?? I will reward you with 10,000 Rs if you do this every day for the next 21 days"

The Man was shocked. "Will it be in cash?" he asked. Al-Rashid said "Yes, the cash will be delivered to you at your residence on the 22nd day" He then turned to me and said "Dr Modak, please put

two of your students to track this gentleman over the next 3 weeks and report".

The Man promised that he will behave accordingly. He thought that a reward of Rs 10,000 for such a simple thing was worth it.

As we continued ahead, Al-Rashid said, the poor guy does not realize that he is now in a trap. Once he behaves alright for 21 days, his whole life he will keep segregating waste, storing in the right bins and stop littering. This is going to become a habit.

I was impressed. What a strategic approach!

We went further ahead and reached the office of the Pollution Control Board. Amongst other things, the Pollution Control Board's job is to enforce regulations to achieve environmental compliance.

There was a discussion going on between the Officer and a Man from the industry. The Officer was asking for a bribe. The Man from the industry was negotiating an amount to a figure that was more reasonable.

Al-Rashid asked the officer "Why are you doing this?"

The Officer said "Everybody in my office is doing this

– not just me. I told this Man to pay me a small fee of Rs 50,000. In return, I told him that I would let him pollute and not invest in building an effluent treatment plant. This plant would cost him at least 5 million INR But he does not understand and is proposing to pay only Rs. 25,000. Please help me convince him"

"How much money do you need?" Al-Rashid asked.

The Officer said, INR 100,000 a day. It's not just for me.

"No problem" said Al-Rashid. Don't take any bribes from any industry for the next 21 days. I will pay you 21 lakhs or 2.1 million INR in cash on the 22nd day.

The Officer was astounded! Are you sure? He looked at Al-Rashid closely – Are you Arvind Kejriwal by any chance? I am not sure you will keep this promise.

Al-Rashid reassured him and said don't worry. I will personally come to deliver the cash. The money will be packed in an imported leather bag with your name (initials) engraved on the side as a bonus.

He then turned to me and said "Please put two of your students at the office of the Board and check whether our friend asks for any bribe over the next 21 days"

The Officer said he will not take or ask for any bribe.

As we started walking ahead, he smiled "Poor guy, he does not know that after 21 days, he will not be asking for a bribe from anyone anymore. Not asking for a bribe will become his habit!"

We continued the journey and met with a corrupt technical committee member who made money on sanctioning speedy environmental clearances by manipulating or sometimes flouting the rules. Al-Rashid fixed him by offering a hefty sum of 20 million INR after 22nd day. Two more students of IIT were planted to monitor him.

We also made a visit at night and caught the Production manager of an industry who was habituated to bye-pass and discharge untreated effluent into the water body at night. He was offered a reward of INR 1 million for not doing so for 21 days.

My job was to supply students as watchdogs. I had to poach students from other institutions as I was fast running out my stock. Al-Rashid suggested that I speak to Communist Party Leaders like Sitaram Yechuri as he felt that the CPM party workers don't have much work to do and could take up this task.

I was maintaining a record of the promises Al-Rashid was making. On the very first two days and one night, the total money committed to be paid crossed 10 crores or 100 million INR This amount was staggering.

I asked al-Rashid "How are you going to settle? Do you have a Swiss bank account as most rich Indians do?"

Oh, no worries. The entire project is sponsored by Mr. Azim Premji of Wipro. Premji is too rich a person, equally very generous and already has a problem of not knowing how to spend his money. He has earmarked INR 532,840 million for his foundation with the objective of helping society – mainly supporting education. And he is the one who has asked me to implement the 21 day strategy of transforming India breaking the bad habits of Indian citizens. This effort is in fact equivalent to educating people. I love him.

I was impressed. I now understood how we could potentially reach a new regime of a self-transformed India– something that is reward driven while abandoning the traditional and ruled out techniques of enforcements and punishments.

But I still wanted to put in a word of caution and so I asked Al-Rashid. By now he had shed the face of Arvind Kejriwal and was back in his caliph dress – He was looking majestic.

"Don't you think we should appeal to other rich corporate leaders in India to pledge their CSR funds for such a noble and innovative initiative? They could follow Premji's wisdom and generosity. The Government could facilitate"

Al-Rashid smiled and said softly "Do you think the Government and Corporate India are interested in such a transformation? Probably they would like to see that the present conditions continue to prevail…."

I could not disagree. Al-Rashid was perhaps right.

He then said "Well, see you tomorrow morning – we have a lot of work to do"

He then gave me a box of dates coated with a thin film of Gold as the reward for my two days work.

And he disappeared.

GREEN FROM THE OTHER SIDE

Hard Hitting – makes one sit up and take notice

Prof Modak is known to be an accomplished environmental expert. However, this blog also brings out the accomplished writer in him. Normally, scientists and engineers tend to be very dry and matter of fact while writing on technical issues. However, Prof Modak's blog posts are full of humor and satire which make them such pleasant reading. "How to get Speedy Environmental Clearances" was one such piece which I enjoyed. His elephantine memory and penchant for details are amazing. Some of the blogs like "Supreme Pollution Control Boards" on the regulators were hard hitting and made everyone sit up and take notice. He has a vast national and international experience on environmental regulatory issues and pollution control. 'Consent to Close' is a thought which needs to be incorporated in environmental laws after due deliberations. Prof. Modak's blogs address every one whether you are a domain expert or a commoner. "Wear Oxygen masks When Indoors" or "Waste Segregation" are highly informative and educative to every citizen. I only wish Prof. Modak tries his hand in writing pure fiction. Keep writing sir!

Dr Vijay Singhal
Chief Engineer, Rajasthan Pollution Control Board, India

. . . .

Informative, Educational, Entertaining

Prasad is like a Pied Piper marching into the sixties with the 60 posts following him. I have been an avid reader of all blog. Technology has made life easier. As a result, most of the blog posts were read within a few hours of getting posted on either the net or Facebook. I found all his blog posts informative as he has a lot to share due to his wide experience and exposure. And he is happily doing so. The blogs are educational and here I notice his academic instincts, flair and achievements come into the play with a professional presentation of the material at hand. He is a born teacher. I also see the blog posts entertaining with a sniff of a Shivaji Park, Balmohan, Busybee (Behram Contractor) and Marathi Manoos humor. Of course the blog is packaged with international finesse and the Queen's English.

For the above selfish reasons, I wish Prasad a long innings in writing more. Sixty is only a number, so more the merrier.

Nayan Khambati
Partner at Econ Pollution Control Consultants

. . . .

Compelling Sustainability Stories!

Compared to writing a newspaper article a blogger has much greater freedom of expression and Prasad shows this well in his blog. All the blog posts are compelling sustainability stories, always "witty" (like the state of the art eye clinic at COP 21!), informative with useful websites and never boring. And we keep wondering who his friend the "Professor" is?

I always tell my students that to pass a message we should never ever preach but try to tell sustainability stories through events or people. And Prasad shows how this blog can be a powerful platform in reaching the public.

We admire people because we recognize something in them that we see in ourselves — a quality we recognize, a quality we someday hope to possess, or a dream we share. And this is why we like his blog. As a Professor in a University, I could relate easily to many of the stories he himself has experienced in his journey as an academic.

Looking forward to the next blog post and to learn from it and feel inspired!

Dr Toolseeram Ramjeawon
Professor of Environmental Engineering,
University of Mauritius

• • • • • • • • • • • • • • • • • • •

Think Differently

Prasad Modak's blog posts have always reminded me of a famous book by Sharu Ranganekar "In the wonderland of Indian Managers". Ever since the first post on July 30, 2014 on Environmental Impact Assessment these posts have provoked and expected the reader to look and think differently at tools and objectives of environmental management. I never felt that these posts were for earning appreciation and praise. Prasad never looked for it in his life. Through his blogs, I was amazed to know of the persons Prasad has met, the interactions he had and his process of continuous learning.

Many a times, experts are not aware of objectives and scope of the EIA process and inclined to raise issues just to exhibit their domain expertise. I am not aware if in any country appraisal bodies are expected to review 30 to 40 proposals in single sitting. We need to have a re-look at our implementation mechanism and augment the same, to start with, in terms of number of persons in organizations like MOEF&CC, PCBs, etc. This blog raises such fundamental issues.

Books that Matter! made me realize what I missed in life. I graduated from Sangli. We used to follow books by Indian authors. Even for the college library, budget and space were constraints. I had excellent opportunities and access to quality publications, somehow, I failed to make best use of it. I am accepting my mistakes, hoping students who read this blog do not repeat the same.

'The National Anthem, Me and Cleaner Production' really pinched me. Perhaps I found the answer to why 'We' had

263

limited success. For over three decades, we environmental professionals, have convinced ourselves that we can change industry by showing them how concepts like CP, SD, EIA, CC are good for them. We have achieved some success. But then the driver always remained 'making profits'. As I am approaching the end of my professional career, I feel that we must inform all in business, that it is their moral responsibility to make best use of the available technologies for making 'more from less'. Profit may be a spin off benefit but it cannot be the sole motive. I wish that reading this blog is made compulsory reading for all post graduate courses in environmental management.

Vijay Kulkarni
CSO and Sr. VP ESH-CSR, Shapoorji Pallonji Infrastructure

. . . .

Tagged as part of 'must read' list, fresh and inspiring!

Modak's blog posts are interesting to read, as they contain simple yet effective story telling of inspiring ideas on environmental technology, management and policy issues. His posts are as inspiring as he is in person- a man full of energy and enthusiasm, and passionate about environmental issues. For the past one year, reading his posts has become a ritual for me during the week-end, and often on my travel. His posts reflect good story telling skills that he has, and also his enriching knowledge and experience to explain complex issues in a simple manner, hence catching the readers' attention.

As a regular reader of his blog, I have read and enjoyed almost all his posts. Nevertheless, there are a few that remain in my mind as fresh as when I read them first. One; "Why the Fuss." Here he takes us back to the early 1980s when we had limited laboratory and professional guidance in the Environmental Engineering field of study. He shares his dilemma in choosing his research topic, and yet how motivated he was by his Professors and advisors. This post came at the right time, just when my students were about to begin their theses. I shared with the post with them; they found it motivational and helpful in choosing their research topics. "Travelling Professor" is another blog that I not only enjoyed reading, but also was inspired on planning my own retirement life as an academician. Through "Never Jump the Queue", he takes us through his dramatic experience at the Egyptian Immigration in 1992. It is indeed a reminder to people like us who travel a lot for our work, to follow immigration rules sincerely. This blog is the best way to share your experience and learning with the younger generation.

I sincerely hope to read more of his posts in 2016, and tag them as part of my regular weekend 'must read' list. I do hope he balances his future posts targeting all sectors, as in: academia, environmental consultants, environmental business/private sector and government, and talks about new and happening topics in the environment field.

Dr. C. Visvanathan,
Professor, School of Environment, Resources and Development, Asian Institute of Technology, Bangkok, Thailand

• • • • • • • • • • • • • • • • • •

Awareness without preaching

Each one of Prasad's blog posts are unique. Both Sathya and I enjoyed reading all of them. These blog posts convey excellent messages on sustainability, still an abstract theme for most of us, in a simple and humorous manner so that everyone can enjoy and appreciate the concept. Prasad has an art of delivering complex messages on controversial topics in a simple and humorous way that is simply awesome and brilliant! What struck us the most was that he is able to bring awareness without preaching. We are certain that this book will make lots of people happy and bring out lots of humor becoming a stress reliever in this modern world!!

I am sure that these blog posts have created lots of converts —it has made several of us look at our day-to-day actions through the sustainability angle. We convey our appreciation and thanks to the 'Professor' for being there to listen Prasad's ideas, as he seems to have lots of influence on politicians and bureaucrats.

Our list of favorite blog posts is long ... though these three posts seem to have stuck in our minds forever ... Creative Fusion, New Year Resolution, and Washing Machine... The one on creative fusion is an outstanding, brilliant piece. We really enjoyed every bit of it, and were amazed at how good a professor Prasad is and how he has and will mold young and old minds alike. He is the kind who can bring a change and not the politicians...the change may look like a drop in the ocean but we should remember that droplets make the ocean. Sathya could relate more to the article, as her passion is art, nature and children. The Montessori Method of teaching also believes in this principle. We think that there is a deep connection in all this though we never realized it until we read your blog post on Creative Fusion. We love the idea of creative fusion and do hope and pray it will become mainstream one day.

Panneerselvam Lakshminarayan
Ex-Lead Environmental Specialist, The World Bank

• • • • • • • • • • • • • • • • • • •

What's True and what's fiction?

Dr Modak's blogs serve to bring him into the reader's company. As his friend, I have to wait to get an opportunity to be in his company. So, I relish the blog more for this reason than for the literary value of the writing. He writes in an autobiographical style and names many characters which keeps one guessing what is true and what is fiction. I have a strong belief that his Professor friend is none other than himself.

His blog posts have all the traits of a good short story of which I enjoy the humor most of all and appreciate, in particular, his visualization of the state of elite society. The impact of his blogs is not only pleasure but also much enlightenment.

Paritosh Tyagi,
Consultant and Ex-Chairman, Central Pollution Control Board, India

• • • • • • • • • • • • • • • • • • •

A split personality in the blogs

Prasad Modak's blog reveals his split personality-the committed Environmentalist, in sync with the World's pressing ecological issues, and a Connoisseur of a spectrum of sensual delights encountered in his everyday life! The blog posts are written in an engaging style, which educates the readers while maintaining their interest, with nuggets of key information embedded within the whole 'khichdi'!

His good friend, the Professor, is roped in at the concluding part of the posts and Professor delivers the closing punch every time (he is really Bolshoi the Boxer in disguise, from another endearing Blogger of the 70s /80s). Prasad (No! Not Dr.) has thrived in his chosen sphere of specialization and the blog posts delightfully disseminate his vast knowledge in the domain of Sustainability and Environment! I am glad that the collection is being published, and be warned....when making a Busy B line to the nearest bookshop, take your 'Datun' and green mobile with you, but PLEASE DO NOT JUMP THE QUEUE!

Jayesh Antani
Consultant at Enbridge, Houston

. . . .

Informative, succinct compilation of current developments.

I wanted to compliment you on "Sixty Shades of Green". I found the book very informative. I do get snippets about the recent developments in Indian environmental sector via the internet, but it can be tricky to wade through vast amounts of data to get to the relevant portions. Your book provided me a succinct compilation of current developments. The style of writing was engaging and avoided a mere "reporting" of facts. More importantly, I appreciate your conversations with your "Professor" friend. These provided a mature and balanced view emphasizing the need to think holistically and to maintain a balance between the costs and benefits of a proposed environmental action. The occasional appearance of mythological characters, such as Yama or Chitragupta, was amusing. I hope to get continually enlightened and entertained by your writing. More power to you!

Omkar Aphale
Lecturer (Stony Brook University, NY)

Anil Paranjpe : *Can you get anymore tongue-in-cheek and still have so much to say? I hope those who matter are tapping into your knowledge and capabilities to really address that which needs addressing.*

M C Badarinarayana : *Knew your excellence in teaching, communication, consultation in the field of environment, sustainability; this blog amazes me to know that your expertise is far, far more extensive. Hats off!*

Pravina Parikh : *Wonderful simplicity and flow in the language exhibits an excellent teacher! So many things said without saying anything!! Congratulations!!!*

Shailesh Singh : *Your articles are like a lens which zooms into erupting 'FAULT-LINES'.*

Akhilendra Bhushan Gupta : *The humor, as usual, is subtle – keeping a thin boundary between satire and criticism.*

Vijay : *It is fictitious but really fabulous … what a blog … all my college friends turned colleagues started laughing and continued for a few minutes during recitation of the blog by one colleague … Relevant, because we are also inter-related to this business!!!*

Debashish Manna : *This is the only blog I follow and eagerly wait for every article that you post. I think this is for people who know and admire you. I guess many professionals like me are grateful to you for sharing your thoughts, your take on various issues and experiences with an element of*

humor, which unfortunately is difficult to find these days.

Swaminathan Krishnamurthy : *Excellent. It has been a great pleasure and I have always enjoyed reading your articles. These articles give a sense of identification and realism through several practical first-hand experiences rather than a one dimensional technical aspect.*

Chetan Shah : *Prasad, Great write-up. Interesting read for everyone. Did you graduate in engineering or humanities – I wonder! Keep writing and doing good work. You make all IIT-B 78 proud!!!*

Aniruddha Agnihotri : *Brilliant article Sir!! Been reading your blogs regularly. Didn't know you were a great writer as well!!*

Kanika Mehra : *I have been following your blogs for some time, and I must say, I am a real fan of how you engage the readers in clever story-telling and put across some really pertinent observations in an extremely subtle manner.*

Shridhar Karandikar : *This simplicity of Dr Modak is amazing, somehow his word smithy is pragmatic, and at the same time, inspiring – making us feel, 'Achhe Din Ayenge' in Sustainability Space.*

Amruta : *You are one inspiration not just to students but to everyone. I enjoyed your post and I am glad I am a part of your memory lane. It has been a pleasure to be a part of your on-going effort to be the change the world needs.*

Ananth S Kodavasal : *As they say, inscrutable are the ways of*

Chinese. Your story is so evocative I can visualize the gentle smile on Prof. Fude's face as he shares his knowledge of the subject and of life in general. Wonderful stories and all with a memorable message. Modern day Aesop's fables, only these are from real life.

Paresh Thakar : *While we didn't get the chance to have local or imported beer in your class but you are in the same category as Professor Fude who inspires many students and professionals. I used to eagerly wait for your session. You are role model for many professionals in this field including me.*

Vijay Kulkarni : *Sometimes I feel you are less ambitious and hence an under-achiever. Not just for praising you, I firmly believe that you are a gifted and fortunate person. India as a country has not made full use of your potential and expertise. Perhaps, industries/organizations/people outside India understood you better and availed your expertise. I just wish that we in India realize importance of your decision of staying back in India.*

Sunil Herat : *Enjoyed reading every bit of it. One of those rare readings where you can't wait to read what happens next ...*

Shripad Nimbhorkar : *I feel you could write more and contribute to literature. I have not heard Asimov in Environment. Science fiction based on Environmental problems from you will be a gift to Environment.*

Jillian Bhambhani : *Excellent Doctor. Will share this with friends. I have started reading my book it has*

turned out very well. Look forward to the next 40.

Environmental Management Centre (EMC) LLP

Environmental Management Centre (EMC) LLP was established in 1996. EMC's consulting services are essentially strategic, knowledge driven and supported through research and training. In all consulting assignments, EMC's expertise lies in harmonizing economic, environmental and social considerations (often called triple bottom line) in business logic, development plans and policy frameworks.

Since inception, EMC has built together a team of environmental professionals trained in engineering, science, economics and planning. This core team is supported by Associates that work from India as well as from abroad on a part or full time basis. Associates bring in skills and experience in specialized areas. EMC operates a unique environmental internship programme that is sought after by top students from reputed universities in India as well as overseas.

Over the past 20 years, EMC has conceived, developed and executed a number of national, regional and international assignments that have set several "firsts". Many of these assignments have stimulated action leading to policy reforms, sustainable investments and led to long term capacity building. EMC is perhaps one of the very few Indian companies that operates from India and offers services globally.

Visit www.emcentre.com

Ekonnect Knowledge Foundation (Ekonnect)

Ekonnect is a nonprofit section 8 company set up with the aim of increasing understanding and imparting education to address challenges and offer solutions in arena of Environmental Management and Sustainablity. Ekonnect is an initiative of Dr.Prasad Modak who is Founder and Director of this company.

All programs at Ekonnect are designed for action: each ensures that participants apply solutions to real world problems and leverage on opportunities. Ekonnect invests time and thought in custom designing learning programs for the intended audience making the best of resources available. The pedagogy, armed with an E-learning platform, is unique providing flexibility and practical applications.

Ekonnect believes in collaboration; pooling in resources, people, associates and organizations as and when required in the best interest of the program/project at hand. Examples of Ekonnects programs are Disha - a career counselling program, Finishing School, Anvaya - a short film contest, Not Just Walk in the Park - targeting children and Tree Revival campaign in cities.

Ekonnect hosts Green Purchasing Network of India and works closely with the International Green Purchasing Network to promote Sustainable Consumption and Production (SCP). An Ekocalendar is brought out each year to raise awareness and promote positive action *every day.*

Visit www.ekonnect.net